Australian Cinema

Australian Cinema

by

Brian McFarlane

Columbia University Press
New York
1988

Printed in Great Britain

Library of Congress Cataloging-in-Publication Data

McFarlane, Brian, 1934–
   Australian cinema
   Bibliography: p.
   Includes index.
   1. Moving-pictures—Australia—History.   I. Title.
PN1993.5.A8M35   1988   791.43′0994   87–23890
ISBN 0–231–06728–3

For my wife Geraldine
and my parents Campbell and Jean McFarlane

We would like to acknowledge the assistance of the Australian Film Commission in the publication of this book.

Contents

Introduction

The chief purpose of this book is to examine the kinds of film which have been produced by the new Australian cinema in the 1970s and 1980s. It is essentially concerned with the feature film revival, and the central chapters of this book (Chapters 4 to 9) consider the ways those features have explored various themes related to the society in which they were produced. The reasons for such an approach, and the rejection of others, are explained in Chapter 3. The decision to concentrate on feature films was based partly on my personal interest, partly on the fact that it is the feature film industry which has been largely responsible for the renewal of interest, both here and overseas, in Australian cinema. This is not intended to undervalue the achievement of documentary and independent film-making, which some people would certainly value more highly than the mainstream feature films.

Though the book's emphasis is as described above, it seemed to me important to give some sense of the early history of film-making in Australia as a background for the revival of the 1970s. I have also tried to sketch some of the main factors which contributed to the re-emergence of Australian films in the present period. More detailed treatments of these factors and of the pre-1970 history of the Australian cinema are now available elsewhere. Like all others interested in these matters I am indebted to two major pieces of research: Andrew Pike and Ross Cooper's *Australian Film 1900–1977*, a film-by-film account of every feature made in this country during the first eight decades of the century; and Graham Shirley and Brian Adams' *Australian Cinema: The First Eighty Years*, an exhaustive account of industrial ups and downs, of government intervention and non-intervention. Among the books listed in my Bibliography, these two offer the most valuable factual information.

Given the kind of organization I have adopted, certain films are referred to in several chapters. Nowhere have I sought to give a comprehensive account of a particular film, but have discussed any given film in as many contexts as it seemed useful to do so. As a convenience to the reader, I have given the year of release and the director's name at the first reference to a film in each chapter in which it occurs. This makes for some repetition of information but is probably preferable to flicking through other chapters to find it.

I have previously written on Australian films in, for example, the journal *Cinema Papers* and my earlier book *Words and Images: Australian Novels into Film* (1983). I should like to make general acknowledgment of such sources in relation to the present book and, where appropriate, I have referred to them directly.

I am grateful to many people for their help in the preparation of this book and I should particularly like to acknowledge the contributions of Scott Murray, Helen Greenwood, Tom Ryan, and John Fox who all read slabs of the manuscript and offered valuable advice on it. Thanks are due to the following who gave time to discussing various aspects of the industry with me: Penny Chapman, Director, Project Development Branch of the Australian Film Commission; Alan Finney, National Director, Marketing and Distribution, for Village Roadshow; Mary Gibson, Projects Officer, New South Wales Film Corporation; Bill Macartney, Chief Executive, Hoyts Edgley Productions Ltd.; Terence McMahon, then Chief Executive, Film Victoria; Greg Tepper, Projects Officer, Film Victoria; Michael Thornhill, Producer and Director, Edgecliff Films and former Board member of the New South Wales Film Corporation; and David Williams, Managing Director, Greator Union Organization. I should also like to thank Ian Kerr and the video library staff of Village Roadshow, Melbourne; the Malvern Video Library; Jenny Whitelaw of Palace Home Video Library; Lisa English and Communications and Entertainment Ltd.; Adrian Brown, Publicity Co-ordinator, Film Victoria; and Mal Bryning who all helped me by lending video-tapes of films I had not previously seen or needed to see again. I am grateful to Greater Union Organisation, The Hoyts Corporation Pty Limited, Twentieth Century Fox (for one still from *Walkabout*) and Village Roadshow Corporation Limited for permission to publish stills from films which they have distributed; to Nick Roddick, the Editor of *Cinema Papers*, Melbourne, for allowing me to borrow stills from the journal's collection; to Brian Kavanagh and Ray Marshall for the loan of stills; and to Jennifer Trigger and Val Grinblat, of the Chisholm Institute of Technology, who typed most of the manuscript. John Kerr, formerly of Heinemann Publishers, Melbourne, offered ready assistance and advice; I thank him, Jill Taylor of Heinemann for editorial assistance, and Laura Morris, of Martin Secker and Warburg, London, who was enthusiastic about this project from the outset and has been a sympathetic and helpful editor throughout.

Melbourne, Australia, August 1985

Part One: ON THE BRINK

1 Background

The last sentence of a book written fifteen years ago reads:

> How typical that, at a time when the concept of 'national' cinema has become *passé*, Australia should be on the brink of its first true film industry.[1]

Just how prescient the author, John Baxter, has proved to be is one of the tasks which the present volume will seek to address. What is revealing about histories of earlier Australian cinema, and there are now several, is the sense of precariousness that has hovered about film-making in this country. The remarkable efflorescence of the 1970s and 1980s — although producing a body of work which may well justify the badge of a 'national cinema' — has still not been able to shake off the uncertainties of those earlier decades, sometimes for the same reasons. The prevailing dominance of American cinema, even in its comparatively straitened days; the inadequacy of the local market to support an indigenous industry; the need for continuing government support; the vexed issue of whether to make *Australian* films or films with an eye on the international market, or whether both these demands could be met concurrently: these are matters that film-makers have had to juggle with in this country. There is, as well, a surprising thematic continuity from the early years of the century to the present day. A book about the new Australian cinema ought, then, to pay some introductory attention to its sources, in terms both of earlier attempts to establish a thriving industry and of the recurring cultural motifs which, allowing for variations in how they are presented, have informed film-making here over eight decades.

For overseas filmgoers (and possibly for some local ones), whose notion of the Australian film industry is that it began in the mid-1970s with *Picnic at Hanging Rock* and *Sunday Too Far Away*, it may be surprising to know that in 1911 no fewer than fifty-one Australian films were released here. Before the American product had established its powerful hold on world cinemas, Australia was already producing feature-length films on themes of particular appeal to local audiences. As the film historians Andrew Pike and Ross Cooper have noted:

> In those early years it was essentially an indigenous cinema, reflecting the producers' direct responses to the Australian audience, without reliance on established models from overseas.[2]

At this stage, in fact, the history of Australian feature films pre-dates that of either America or Britain. Running more than an hour (approximately 4,000 feet), *The Story of the Kelly Gang* (1906) may well be the world's first feature film; and, as Pike and Cooper point out, the longest film made in Britain in 1911 was 2,500 feet, compared with the twenty Australian films of more than 3,000 feet (and nearly half of those of more than 4,000 feet) released in 1911.

The first film screening in Australia took place at the Melbourne Opera House on 22 August 1896, as the audience watched scenes from London life, screened by one Carl Hertz who was billed as the 'premier prestidigitateur and illusionist of the world'. Later in the same year, the oldest surviving Australian film, a record of the 1896 Melbourne Cup, the work of Frenchman Marius Sestier, was screened at the Criterion Theatre Sydney to great audience excitement. The kind of enthusiasm that greeted such screenings was of course that of novelty and particularly, in the Melbourne Cup film, that of seeing in flickering two-dimensional representation an event that has long since been part of Australian folklore. A more ambitious venture was *Soldiers of the Cross* (1911), produced by the Salvation Army, which had set up a Limelight Department in Melbourne in 1892 under Joseph Perry. The aim of the Department was the propagation of Christian teaching which it carried out through lectures illustrated by lantern slides. *Soldiers of the Cross* was not the first Australian feature film as it was long thought to be but, rather, a multi-media presentation of slides, lecture, music, exhortations to prayer, and thirteen short film sections depicting scenes from the life of Christ and the early Christian martyrs. Its importance in Australian cinema history is in its use of film as propaganda and as a medium for narrative.

During the First World War, the government would come to see the value of film as propaganda; in the meantime, narrative was established as the key function of mainstream cinema in Australia as elsewhere. Christian Metz, more than sixty years later, writes: 'The basic formula, which has never changed, is the one that consists in making a large continuous unit that tells a story and calling it a "movie". "Going to the movies" is going to see this type of story.'[3] The Australian cinema's first contribution to this 'formula' is *The Story of the Kelly Gang*, directed by Charles Tait, which was screened at the Athenaeum Hall, Melbourne, on 26 December, 1906. The film, which now exists only in incomplete form, used no inter-titles to tell its story of Australia's most famous bushranger but relied on a lecturer and actors providing voices behind the screen to clarify its narrative. Apart from its status as a 'first', *The Story of the Kelly Gang* was also important for what would prove to be a rare example of the assistance of government authorities (the Victorian Railways Commission) in film production, for the entrepreneurial zeal of Tait and two of his brothers in marketing the film, and for establishing a popular 'genre' in Australian film-making: that is, the bushranging film.

As for the latter, the film adopted a romantic attitude to the Kellys, heroicizing the outlaw image, in a spirit that still informs some Australian films in which authority is treated with scant respect. Between 1907 and 1911, there were fourteen bushranging films, with titles such as *Robbery Under Arms* (1907), the first of several versions of Rolf Boldrewood's classic novel, *The Life and Adventures of John Vane, the Notorious Australian Bushranger* (1910), *Thunderbolt* (1910), *Moonlite* (1910), *Ben Hall and his Gang* (1911), and *Captain Midnight, the Bush King* (1911). The other films of this period, which reached a peak in 1911, were very often on similarly Australian themes. There were tales of the country's convict beginnings: the first version of *For The Term of his Natural Life* (1908), from Marcus Clarke's novel of the escape from Van Diemen's Land (Tasmania) of a wrongfully arrested convict, much more lavishly remade in 1927, by the American director Norman Dawn; *It is Never Too Late to Mend* (1911); and *The Romantic Story of Margaret Catchpole* (1911), the second feature directed by Raymond Longford, perhaps the greatest director of the Australian silent film. These films were invariably sympathetic in their treatment of convicts and critical of the harshness of the criminal code that transported them to Australia.

There were other films which exploited Australian rural scenery and a climate suitable for filming, as well as aspects of the country's history. *The Golden West* (1911), 'a romance of the West Australian goldfields'; *Eureka Stockade* (1907), 'throbbing with the Pulse and Memories of the "Roaring Fifties"'; and *All for Gold, or Jumping the Claim* (1911), first feature of another notable pioneer, Franklyn Barrett, drew on the gold rushes of the mid-nineteenth century. And there were films which dramatized the hardihood of Australian bush life: *The Squatter's Daughter* (1910), directed by Bert Bailey from his own play (and remade by Ken G. Hall in 1933), *The Squatter's Son* (1911), *The Drover's Sweetheart* (1911), and *Mates of the Murrumbidgee* (1911). There were, as well, adaptations of a number of stage melodramas, less obviously Australian in theme and setting. However, in these years of vigorous film-making activity, of which distressingly little survives, the emphasis seems to have been on films geared to local audiences and drawing on that mixture of local myth and history which has been an element of the new Australian cinema of the 1970s and 1980s, even though displayed in more sophisticated narrative forms.

Decline and War

From the fifty-odd films, produced by more than ten companies, in 1911, the number dropped to thirty, then seventeen, then four in the next three years.

This decline may be partly attributed to the increasing competition of overseas (especially American) productions; partly to the banning by the New South Wales Police Department in 1912 of the popular bushranging genre which was held to be unhealthily influential on young viewers because of its unflattering depiction of the police; but most importantly to the rise of the notorious 'combine'. The 'combine' was formed by the merging of certain key Australian exhibition, distribution and production companies. The result was a two-armed monopoly which comprised Australasian Films for distribution and Union Theatres for exhibition. The 'combine' showed little interest in Australian production and independent production companies began to disappear as they could find no reliable outlet for their films. As Pike and Cooper claim, the Australian film industry was 'the victim of a struggle for power within the distribution and exhibition trades'.[4] This occurred several years before Hollywood's ascendancy in world cinema, and, although the monopoly was broken by the establishment of American film exchanges in Australia during the First World War, this did little to encourage local production, outlets for which remained elusive, and the companies of the 'combine' remained a power in the land for six decades.

Australia Responds to England's Call is the title of a documentary released in Sydney in August 1914, and it suggests the pro-Empire spirit which informed the feature films of the early years of the First World War. The historic defeat of Gallipoli, at which Australia fought for the first time as an independent nation, added a further powerful element to the image of the Australian man as a lean, bronzed outdoorsman: that of the loyal, courageous fighter in a good cause.

In 1915, Alfred Rolfe's *A Hero of the Dardanelles* (the story of 'The "Imperishable Glory" won by the Gallant Australians at Gallipoli', as it was advertised) captured a widespread spirit of patriotic fervour and received official support from the Department of Defence. There was military assistance for Frank Harvey's *Within Our Gates, or Deeds that Won Gallipoli* later in the same year, and other wartime titles included *How We Beat the Emden* (1915, directed by Rolfe), a narrative film using documentary footage shot around the defeated Emden and made with the co-operation of the Australian Navy; *The Martyrdom of Nurse Cavell* (1916), directed by John Gavin and C. Post Mason and starring Vera Pearce, later a star of British stage and screen; *If the Huns Came to Melbourne* (1916), directed by George Coates); and Franklyn Barrett's *Australia's Peril* (1917), exploiting the fear of German spy activities in Australia.

If the authorities saw in the cinema a means of promoting the war effort, such films as those named above were not the major productions of the war years. Longford's *The Silence of Dean Maitland* (1914), re-made in 1933, was a popular melodramatic brew of sex and religion; and his *Mutiny on the*

Bounty (1916), shot mainly in New Zealand; and *The Woman Suffers* (1918), a tale of seduction and revenge, starring Lottie Lyell who became Longford's regular collaborator and the first Australian film star; also found audiences, although Longford's great creative period lay in the decade ahead. As the war dragged on, the public lost interest in simple patriotic stories, and sought escapism rather than the realities of war. Beaumont Smith's series of bucolic comedies, based on the exploits of the 'Hayseed' family and drawing on a tradition of outback comedy, interspersed with the rigours of rural life, was a popular example. Titles such as *The Hayseeds Come to Town* and *The Hayseeds' Back-Blocks Show* (both 1917) do not suggest works of intellectual distinction but Smith's films enjoyed regular box-office success.

The Post-war Years

Between the end of the First World War and the coming of sound in the late 1920s, the Australian silent film reached a creative peak not attained again until the revival of the 1970s. Longford made fifteen films during this period although he, like Franklyn Barrett, suffered much frustration from the workings of the 'combine', and even though this was the decade which saw the entrenchment of Hollywood's domination of Australian screens. The setting up of branch offices in Australia of most of the major American studios may have challenged the autocracy of the 'combine' but it did little to encourage local production. An exception was Hercules McIntyre, who, as managing director of Universal Pictures in Australia (1920–1960), distributed many Australian films and supported several productions in the 1940s.

Longford's *The Sentimental Bloke* (1919), based on C.J. Dennis's popular and populist verses, was an enormous success with the Australian public and with the British, although its casual colloquial humour did not 'translate' successfully into American slang. The film is notable for its naturalism, both in its use of Sydney settings and in the performances of Arthur Tauchert as Bill, the Bloke; and Lottie Lyell, as his 'ideal tart', Doreen, who tames the 'larrikin' in him, not by unmanning him but by gently redirecting his energies. Widely accepted as Longford's best film and, indeed, as the best Australian film to date, it enshrined such Australian values as a distrust of formality and culture and a nose-thumbing attitude to authority, and, notably, not in an idealized bush setting but with a regard for the actualities of the country's urban life. *Ginger Mick* (1920), a sequel to *The Sentimental Bloke*, was made by the same team and, in charting Bill's married life with Doreen and the vicissitudes of his friend Mick who is killed in the war, it enjoyed similar popularity.

Following the death of Lottie Lyell in 1925 and his anger at the importation of the American, Norman Dawn, to direct the large-scale remake of

For the Term of His Natural Life (1927), Longford resigned from his position as Director of Production for Australasian Films. His career never recovered, and he lobbied vigorously to help bring about a governmental inquiry into overseas domination of Australian cinema. Franklyn Barrett, after *The Breaking of the Drought* (1920), which ran into censorship problems because of its graphic depiction of actual drought conditions; *A Girl of the Bush* (1921), stronger in its location footage of station life than in its melodramatic plot; and two further films, also fell foul of the 'combine' and was forced out of production and into distribution. While both Longford and Barrett drew on bush themes, in the interests of both comedy and melodrama, they were both distinguished by a greater concern for realism than their predecessors had been. Both, too, provided impressively strong depictions of women — whether of urban Doreen gradually domesticating her Bloke or Vera James as the eponymous Girl of the Bush managing a sheep station — even if the resolution of their plots scarcely threatened a male hegemony.

The two silent films directed by Paulette McDonagh, *The Far Paradise* (1928) and *The Cheaters* (1930, shot as a silent, released as a part-talkie), which were produced by her sister, Phyllis, and starred another, Isobel, who acted under the name of Marie Lorraine, each offered plots which revolve around the efforts of a woman whose resourcefulness and fortitude are more striking than those of the men around her. Although both exist only in fragments now, Pike and Cooper quote flattering reviews of the former ('decision in every detail') and claim that the surviving talkie sections of the latter 'stand up well as a vivid crime melodrama'.[5] They enjoyed apparently unanimous support from the trade and from reviewers. In his account of the period, John Tulloch claims that: 'The McDonaghs' films were genuinely respected. But the respect was based on a meeting of opinion between the film-makers' formal and thematic preoccupations and the exhibitors' ideological and market ambitions.'[6] They were, that is, more clearly in line with the Hollywood narrative traditions exhibitors and audiences knew and trusted.

Although Barrett, Longford (especially in his association with Lottie Lyell) and McDonagh are perhaps the key directors of this comparatively flourishing period, there are several other names which should be noted. Beaumont Smith continued his commercially successful run of 'Hayseed' comedies until 1923 and made two comedies, *Hullo Marmaduke* (1924) and *The Adventures of Algy* (1925), starring British stage and music hall comedian Claude Dampier in 'silly ass' roles; Arthur Shirley starred in and directed a popular version of Fergus Hume's melodrama, *The Mystery of the Hansom Cab* (1925, previously filmed in 1911); Charles Chauvel, whose main career was in the sound era, made two silent films: *The Moth of Moonbi* (1926), the story of a girl who is lured by city lights but who finally returns, chastened, to the rural life, and *Greenhide* (also 1926), about a city girl who finds true love in the outback; documentary film-maker Frank Hurley made two feature films in 1926, *The Jungle Woman* and *The Hound of the Deep*, although his reputation really rests on the records he made of, for example, Mawson's Antarctic expeditions and Australia's Second World War role in the Middle East; Tal Ordell, in his humorous and charming adaptation of the 'Fatty Finn' comic strip, *The Kid Stakes* (1927), made one of the major Australian silent films. Although set in inner-city Sydney and ostensibly a tale of rival children's gangs and a runaway goat, it draws on various themes (mateship, competitiveness) that figure largely in many Australian films; and, in John Tulloch's words, 'a dream of authentic urban living is fused with the mythical structures of the bush'.[7] Largely dismissed as a children's film at the time, its reputation now stands deservedly high.

In spite of the activity suggested above and in spite of the real achievements of the period, the 1920s was also the time in which American domination of the Australian market became a fact of life. The 'combine's' exhibition arm, Union Theatres, had a local rival, Hoyts Theatres, later American-controlled, as well as competition for its distribution arm, Australasian Films, from the American production and distribution companies which had set up branches in Australia. The growing dissatisfaction and, increasingly, despair of Australian producers, faced with difficulties of production, distribution and exhibition, led some of them, including Longford and Barrett, to press for government intervention. The Royal Commission of 1927–28 was the result of such pressures. The 'combine', no doubt prompted by the imminence of the Commission and by increased competition for overseas films, showed a rare interest in Australian production. It need not have worried that the Commission would actually achieve anything.

Some of its main recommendations are summarized as follows by Graham Shirley and Brian Adams:

> ... the establishment of a Board of Censors and Censorship Board of Appeal; the re-classification of censorship categories; the limitation of distribution–exhibition contracts to twelve months; a five per cent rejection clause in all such contracts to make way for Australian productions; a three-year Empire quota; annual awards of merit for the best Australian production and best scenario; increased customs duty on foreign films; and an upgrading of the Commonwealth produced series *Know Your Own Country* ...[8]

Of these recommendations, which seemed to answer anti-American agitation from various points of view, none of the main ones (especially those to do with quotas) came to anything. The awards lasted for five years, from 1930 to 1935, but by that time cinema, not only in Australia but wherever

10

films were made and screened, had entered a new phase with the arrival of sound.

The Sound Era

If the advent of talking pictures created problems everywhere — problems of production and exhibition — it happened in Australia at a time when the industry was at a low ebb in the wake of the Commission's failure. Only one Australian film was released in 1929, Gerald M. Hayle's *Tiger Island*, which quickly sank without a trace as talkies began their irresistible takeover of the cinema. Paulette McDonagh's *The Cheaters* (1930) was adapted into part-talkie form, and several others experimented with sound; but F.W. Thring's *Diggers* (1931) was the first full sound film, made with imported American equipment. Thring and Ken G. Hall are the two names which dominate the first decade of talkies in Australian film production, both setting up their own companies for the purpose: Efftee (a name derived from Thring's initials) and Cinesound. Efftee's most ambitious feature was a remake of *The Sentimental Bloke* (1932) which lacked the warmth and naturalism of Longford's version. However, Thring had three popular collaborations with the vaudeville comic, George Wallace, in *His Royal Highness* (1932), *Harmony Row* (1933), and *A Ticket in Tatts* (1934), and completed two further films, *Clara Gibbings* (1934) and *The Streets of London* (1934), both based on stage melodramas, before his death in 1936 when Efftee Productions stopped.

Wallace also appeared in two films for Hall at Cinesound, *Let George Do It* (1938) and *Gone to the Dogs* (1939), but Hall's range proved wider than Thring's. He made fifteen features in the 1930s and his feature film career reached a peak with his final feature production, *Smithy* (1946), based on the life of the famous Australian aviator, Sir Charles Kingsford Smith. In the 1930s, he remade two silent successes — *On Our Selection* (1932) and *The Silence of Dean Maitland* (1934) — as well as two further films based on Steele Rudd's characters, *Grandad Rudd* (1935) and *Dad and Dave Come to Town* (1938). Neither of these, nor *On Our Selection*, bore much resemblance to Rudd's tales of outback life and the first two were in fact based on the coarsened stage adaptations by Bert Bailey who starred as Dad Rudd. Crude as it is, especially in its bucolic comedy, *On Our Selection* is still interesting for its celebration of rural virtues and the statement of faith in the land which Dad makes; it is also visually sophisticated in ways that are sometimes at odds with its naive narrative.

Hall's period as head of Cinesound from 1932–56 saw Australia's nearest approach to a production company on American lines, until 1940 at least. Cinesound had three studios (two in Sydney, one in Melbourne) which produced a steady stream of profitable films throughout the 1930s, provided a training ground for skilled technicians, and developed a mini-star system of its own. Two of his actresses Jocelyn Howarth and Shirley Ann Richards went on to Hollywood careers (as Constance Worth and Ann Richards) as did the South African-born Cecil Kellaway, and Hall imported the Hollywood star Helen Twelvetrees for *Thoroughbred* (1936) and the British actor John Longden who appeared in *The Silence of Dean Maitland, Thoroughbred,* and *It isn't Done* (1937) in which he co-starred with Richards and Kellaway. As well as the films he made with George Wallace, he also starred the stage and radio comic Roy Rene in his only film *Strike Me Lucky* (1934) although the latter was Cinesound's least commercial venture. However, Hall showed a thorough appreciation of the viability of the studio and star systems in a manner that is unique in Australian film history. The success of Cinesound in the 1930s belongs largely to him and to Stuart Doyle, who, as Managing Director of the 'combine' in the 1920s and 1930s, provided much of the initiative for its production, first in its Master Picture series until 1929, and then in Cinesound, its wholly-owned subsidiary.

Charles Chauvel's first talkie was *In the Wake of the Bounty* (1933), a retelling of the mutiny led by Fletcher Christian (played by Errol Flynn in his first feature film) against Captain Bligh, and using a good deal of documentary material. In similar historical vein, his next films, *Heritage* (1935), a chronicle of colonial life, and *Uncivilised* (1936), starring the British actor Dennis Hoey, both made much of location shooting, though their grasp of narrative and dramatic elements was less sure. Chauvel occupies an honoured place in the history of Australian film production, but, in truth, his films all reveal a debilitating stiffness in his handling of human drama compared with his flair for a certain epic sweep in relation to setting and thematic aspiration. He is now best-known for *Forty Thousand Horsemen* (1940), his tribute to the exploits of the Australian Light Horse in the Middle East in the First World War; *The Rats of Tobruk* (1944), starring Grant Taylor, Peter Finch, and Chips Rafferty as three infantrymen engaged in the Second World War North African campaign against Rommel; *The Sons of Matthew* (1949), which starred Michael Pate in a three-generational saga of pioneering hardihood; and *Jedda* (1955), which traces the career of an Aboriginal girl who is brought up in a white family but is drawn back to tribal life and a tragic death. These are all ambitious films; they all touch on themes of consequence in Australian cinema and have some natural heirs, thematically, in the revival of the 1970s; they are virtually the last important batch of wholly Australian films before the late '60s stirrings of this revival.

War and After

During the Second World War, only ten Australian features were released. Apart from Chauvel's films, there was another Rudd family entry, Ken

Hall's *Dad Rudd, M.P.* (1940), by now owing little to Steele Rudd's stories and a good deal to Bert Bailey's well-known and popular interpretation of Dad; Noel Monkman's *The Power and the Glory* (1941), about a Czech refugee scientist in Australia, characterized by a strong anti-Nazi stance; and several other now-forgotten titles. Grant Taylor, featured in *Dad Rudd, M.P.*, became a leading Australian star in *Forty Thousand Horsemen* and *The Rats of Tobruk*, and appeared in seven more feature films in the next two decades.

Feature films were at a low ebb in Australia during the war for several reasons. For one, the country's production resources were channelled into newsreels and propaganda made with government support. Further, the war drained the manpower which might have been available for feature production, and there was an acute stortage of raw film stock, partly because of government import controls, partly because of an international shortage. In this context, directors such as Chauvel and Hall threw themselves into the making of propaganda films of which little evidence remains today. The most famous wartime name is probably that of the legendary cameraman, Damien Parer, whose film coverage of the war in New Guinea, *Kokoda Front Line* (1942), won Australia's first Oscar, as the best documentary of the year. Parer was killed in 1944 while filming American action on Peleliu Island. It had really been little more than Parer's work and the international success of *Forty Thousand Horsemen* that kept the idea of an Australian cinema alive during the war years.

It is scarcely an exaggeration to say that there was no indigenous Australian cinema in the twenty years after the war. Australian film-makers made newsreels and documentaries while American and, to a lesser extent, British films occupied cinema screens, American and British production companies being responsible for most of the major films made here in the 1950s and 1960s, although there were barely forty films of any kind made in the twenty years following the Second World War. Further, the introduction of television to coincide with the Olympic Games in Melbourne in 1956 dealt another blow to the prospects of local production.

Chauvel's two post-war films, *The Sons of Matthew* and *Jedda*, commanded healthy local followings, but, despite cuts and re-titling (*The Rugged O'Riordons* and *Jedda the Uncivilized* respectively), they met with little success overseas. They do attempt to come to terms with important aspects of Australian life and history — pioneering hazards in a hostile country, the difficulties faced by one civilization in understanding another — and this is more than can be said for the feature films made by the Southern International Company. This latter, the result of a collaboration between actor Chips Rafferty (icon of lean, laconic Australian-ness) and director-writer Lee Robinson, and superseding their 1952-formed Platypus Productions, made a series of unambitious formula films which exploited genre elements in Australasian settings. These films are: *The Phantom*

Stockman (1953), released in America as *The Return of the Plainsman*; *King of the Coral Sea* (1954), a tale of pearling and skulduggery in the Torres Strait; *Walk into Paradise* (1956), shot in the New Guinea highlands and released in America as *Walk into Hell* (!); *The Stowaway* (1957), a French co-production set in Tahiti with a cast including Martine Carol, Roger Livesey and Arletty; and *Dust in the Sun* (1958), shot on locations near Alice Springs and in the old Cinesound studio at Bondi, based on a Jon Cleary novel about an Aboriginal brought to trial for a tribal killing. Most of these films did satisfactory business but, although receiving praise for their use of unusual settings, none of them was dramatically or thematically complex or exciting. They were essentially double-bill fare, of a kind one finds still being made in Australia when, of course, there are no double bills for them to fill. There is no sense about the films from this company of a commitment to a distinctively Australian ethos or industry. Made with an eye on overseas markets, they did not hesitate to import stars although they did also give opportunities to local players such as Charles Tingwell, Rod Taylor, and Reg Lye, who went on to busy careers at home and abroad.

More in line with an egalitarian Australian tradition were the two 1950s feature films of the New Zealand-born documentary maker Cecil Holmes. His bushranging melodrama, *Captain Thunderbolt* (1953), and the portmanteau film *Three in One* (1957), were both strongly marked by his left-wing sympathies and his admiration for the great Soviet director, Sergei Eisenstein. The former film, scarcely seen in Australia, doubled its production costs in overseas sales. *Three in One* was never fully released in Australia, although it did receive some enthusiastic overseas reviews. It consists of three studies in mateship, that recurring theme of Australian cinema and folklore. The first, 'Joe Wilson's Mates', is based on a Henry Lawson story of Union solidarity in the bush; 'A Load of Wood', from a story by socialist author Frank Hardy, is set in the Depression and concerns two unemployed workers in a small country town who distribute stolen wood to the town's needy; and 'The City', a modern romance of a factory worker and a shop assistant. As John Baxter has said, 'Uneven, episodic, sometimes poorly acted, *Three in One* is still a major work',[9] and its failure to find release in Australia is an indictment of the pusillanimous commercial orientation of local distributors.

Visitors

Distributors were, of course, far more interested in the American and British films shot in Australia in these decades during which local production ground to a halt. The American films essentially used Australia as an exotic backdrop for the sorts of films which, with minor adjustments, might have been shot anywhere. *The Kangaroo Kid* (1950) was the first of the post-war films with American participants. An undistinguished 'Western', with

14

shots of Australian wild-life as if to prove it was not shot in Republic Studios, it was directed by Lesley Selander, director of innumerable bottom-of-the-bill (and -barrel) genre movies, and starred Jock O'Mahoney and Veda Ann Borg (scarcely stars of the first magnitude). It caused hardly a ripple; neither, despite a much bigger budget, massive publicity, and well-known names, did *Kangaroo* (1952), directed by Lewis Milestone for Twentieth Century Fox and starring Maureen O'Hara, Peter Lawford and Richard Boone. In spite of its location shooting in South Australia and Sydney and of that hardy perennial narrative-resolver — the breaking of a drought — *Kangaroo* resisted Milestone's attempts to give the film any authentically Australian flavour. This was true of the remaining American-made films of the 1950s, with the exception of Fred Zinnemann's *The Sundowners*, completed in 1960. *The Sundowners*, adapted from Jon Cleary's novel about itinerant labourers in outback Australia, was made with real affection for its people (even if most of them were played by English and American stars, led by Deborah Kerr and Robert Mitchum) and for the conditions of their lives. It proved a popular entertainment locally and overseas, and was well-received by the critics. *On the Beach* (1959), directed by Stanley Kramer from Nevil Shute's novel about the aftermath of nuclear war as it affected, chiefly, Gregory Peck, Ava Gardner and Fred Astaire, might have been made anywhere. The importance it might have had as a document of the times is vitiated by its concentration on the stars' romantic problems rather than on its larger implications. The American Hecht-Hill-Lancaster production of *Summer of the Seventeenth Doll* (1959), directed by Leslie Norman, all but emasculated Ray Lawler's play which had been one of the milestones in Australian theatre. Lawler's unillusioned approach to the myth of the sun-bronzed Australian male and the onset of middle-age is transformed into a much more conventional romance, set against Sydney backgrounds which remain no more than backgrounds.

The British-backed films of the post-war years were at least concerned with presenting more distinctively *Australian* versions of the life of the country. The most substantial British contribution was that of Ealing Studios which was the first British company to set up production here and which made five features in the years from 1945 to 1959. Three of these were directed by Harry Watt who had a background in documentary as well as in feature film-making. His first film in Australia was *The Overlanders* (1946), the basis of which was a real-life cattle drive from Western Australia to the Queensland coast when Japanese invasion seemed imminent in 1942. His documentary skills stood him in good stead for depicting the hardships and hazards of the drive, into which was woven a slender fictional romance. The central character, however, was that of the stockman Dan McAlpine, played by Chips Rafferty in a role which established the *persona* he projected in films over the next twenty years. He starred again in Watt's second Australian-Ealing film, *Eureka Stockade* (1949), in which he played Peter

Lalor, leader of the Ballarat gold-miners in their rebellion against the injustice of the government-imposed miner's licence. However, the film is less impressive as a study of democracy in the making than as an action melodrama, and it is generally conceded that Rafferty was miscast. 'The portrayal, although earnest, robbed the film of much of its ideological depth':[10] this is a widely shared opinion. But Rafferty was now a star, perhaps the archetypal Australian star of this period, and not until Ted Kotcheff's *Wake in Fright* (1971), his last role, is there any serious questioning of his characteristic *persona*. In Ealing's *Bitter Springs* (1950), directed by Ralph Smart, he begins as an intolerant white invader in Aboriginal territory, but ends by shearing sheep side by side with the Aboriginal chief.

It was seven years before Ealing filmed again in Australia, the government having refused to extend its lease on Sydney's Pagewood Studios. In 1957, it co-produced, with the British branch of MGM, an attractive, episodic version of D'Arcy Niland's novel *The Shiralee*, directed by Leslie Norman and starring Peter Finch, by now internationally known. In *The Shiralee* he played Macauley, a romantic drifter who seizes his five-year-old daughter from his unfaithful wife and heads for the roads with her, gradually coming to respond to the affection this burden or 'shiralee' so tenaciously offers him. The film was generally well-liked, if less tough-minded than its source novel, and its central character revealed a strong streak of that independence which has so often characterized the protagonists of Australian films. And, as in so many later Australian films, the women — the wife and the faithful old flame — have essentially subsidiary roles. Ealing's last Australian film, and indeed the last film to bear the Ealing trademark, was Harry Watt's *The Siege of Pinchgut* (1959), a thriller set on a fortified island in Sydney Harbour. From this island, known as Pinchgut, an escaped convict (played by American star Aldo Ray) makes his bid for re-trial so as to prove his innocence. It bore the stamp of Ealing's sympathy with the individual seeking his rights from an impersonal officialdom, an attitude not uncommon in Australian films of the decades ahead.

The Ealing films were typically more serious-minded than the other British ventures of the post-war years. These included Ralph Smart's good-natured children's adventure, *Bush Christmas* (1947), recently re-made, about children tracking down a bunch of comically inept horse thieves; Anthony Kimmins' *Smiley* (1956), and its sequel, *Smiley Gets a Gun* (1958), both chronicling the adventures of a likeable small-town boy who craves a bicycle (in the first film) and a rifle (in the second); and Jack Lee's *Robbery Under Arms* (1957), with Peter Finch following his *Shiralee* success in the leading role of Captain Starlight. This sporadic British intervention straggled to an end in the latter 1960s with two engaging films from Michael Powell — *They're a Weird Mob* (1966), about an Italian migrant coming to terms with Australia, and *The Age of Consent* (1969), based on

Norman Lindsay's novel about an artist (played by James Mason) who falls in love with his model (Helen Mirren) in the picturesque setting of the Great Barrier Reef — and with Tony Richardson's Woodfall production of *Ned Kelly* (1970). The latter, with a budget of $2,500,000, and Mick Jagger in the title role, attracted a great deal of publicity, but Richardson signally failed to repeat his 1963 British success with another freewheeling hero, *Tom Jones.* Neither critics nor public cared much for his stylized representation of a legendary Australian-Irish folk hero.

The central part of this book comprises a thematic examination of the new Australian cinema and, from this point of view, it is instructive to note how much continuity there is between its motifs and concerns with those of the earlier decades. For the revival of the 1970s and 1980s has produced, for all its real achievements, an essentially conservative cinema. As late as 1985, for example, the most expensive film yet made in Australia is another remake of *Robbery Under Arms*,[11] offering new star Sam Neill in another romantic incarnation of Captain Starlight but no new insight into the bushranging hero stereotype so popular in the first decade of Australian feature films. The heroes of Australian films are still very often the bronzed, anti-posh, anti-authority types, casually gallant in war, at home on horseback, often in silhouette against what is still seen as a wide open country. Such stereotypes are challenged from time to time and there have been perceptive accounts of Australian urban life, but a deeply romantic notion of the Australian man as one of the world's last pioneers is upheld far more than it is criticized. The Gallipoli spirit, reinforcing the bush-nurtured mythology of mateship, that laconic give-and-take of male camaraderie, is still alive in the world of the Australian cinema. I find it hard to agree with Andrew Pike's claim that: 'Thematic continuity between the past industry and the present is not strikingly evident . . . in general, the present industry seems divorced from the one that existed in earlier decades'.[12] The bush may no longer be represented unequivocally as a repository of all the manly virtues but the idea still surfaces in films such as Don Crombie's *The Irishman* (1978) and George Miller's enormously popular *The Man from Snowy River* (1982). As a corollary to this ideological slant, there is still only a limited interest in the exploration of male-female relationships, and in the role of women in Australian society; in fact, too, those strong-minded young squatter's daughters of earlier decades seem at least as much in command of their own destinies as most of the women in the new Australian films. The images of Australia presented by the latter are still overwhelmingly those of a man's world.

None of the foregoing is meant to imply that the new Australian cinema is merely more of the same, that it has not sought any new directions, or that it has not been an occasion for genuine excitement. It *has* taken notice of Australia's urban life; it *has*, at the cost of a certain literariness, aspired to a deliberate 'anti-ockerism'; and, since 1975 at least, it *has* made a real impression on the outside world. It is not, however, a phenomenon without roots, either specifically cinematic or more broadly cultural. If it were, it might be more iconoclastic than it customarily is.

1   John Baxter, *The Australian Cinema*, Sydney: Angus & Robertson, 1970 p.110.

2   Andrew Pike and Ross Cooper, *Australian Film 1900–1977*, Melbourne: Oxford University Press and The Australian Film Institute, 1981, p.3.

3   Christian Metz, *Film Language: A Semiotics of the Cinema* (trans: Michael Taylor), New York: Oxford University Press, 1974, p.45.

4   Pike and Cooper, *op. cit.*, p.4.

5   *Ibid.* pp.190 and 202.

6   John Tulloch, *Legends on the Screen: The Australian Narrative Cinema 1919–1929*, Sydney: Currency Press, The Australian Film Institute, 1981; p.305.

7   *Ibid.* p.415.

8   Graham Shirley and Brian Adams, *Australian Cinema: The First Eighty Years*, Sydney: Angus & Robertson and Currency Press, 1983, p.98.

9   Baxter, *op. cit.*, p.82.

10   Shirley and Adams, *op. cit.*, p.181.

11   Since I wrote this, *Mad Max: Beyond Thunderdome*, with a budget of $13m, has been released.

12   Andrew Pike, 'The Past: boom and bust', in Scott Murray (ed.), *The New Australian Cinema*, Melbourne: Thomas Nelson, 1980, p.25.

2 A New Start

It is simple enough to make a list of key dates in the recent history of the cinema in Australia; it is less so to try accounting for the shift in cultural climate which enabled Australian film-makers to get their projects off the ground and encouraged the growth of audiences interested in seeing the results of their efforts. By general consensus, the late 1960s witnessed a stirring of new life in Australia after the long, comfortably affluent sleep of the Menzies-led Liberal Government (1949–66), during which, at least as far as cinema was concerned, Australia was prepared to rely almost entirely on the USA and Britain for its source of supply. This dependence was only a minor symptom of broader cultural dependence in the light of which many older Australians still thought of England as 'home' (Menzies' own Anglo-philia was legendary) and still doubted Australia's capacity to produce art works of world stature. Politically, Australia had been ready to shelter under the American wing, and to follow its lead in the Vietnam conflict. However, by the end of the 1960s, the atmosphere was changing palpably: there were huge demonstrations in Sydney and Melbourne protesting Australia's involvement in Vietnam; there was a distinct lessening of deference for the 'old country'; and there was a growing agitation for re-establishment of an indigenous film industry.

Stirrings

If, in 1985, the significant discussion about the future of Australian film is more likely to be located in the financial pages of the newspapers and weekly journals, in the mid-1960s the main voices raised were concerned to create a climate that *wanted* an Australian film industry. By an Australian film industry they meant a feature film industry because that, in the words of film-maker and former reviewer, Michael Thornhill, is 'the locomotive that drives everything else'.[1] Thornhill claims that the three seminal figures in creating this all-important climate of opinion, 'the key proponents of that agitation, the people who argued from different perspectives for the right of a film culture to exist here', were Colin Bennett, Sylvia Lawson, and Cecil Holmes. The first two were writers on film; Holmes, who also wrote articles on film in various journals, was the director of the intelligent, ill-fated *Three in One* (1957). Throughout the 1960s, Bennett, regular film reviewer for the Melbourne newspaper *The Age*, kept up a steady insistence on the need for a local industry, as distinct from the use of Australia as a back-lot for overseas companies; and Thornhill himself, writing in the national daily, *The Australian*, added his voice to the demand. Lawson, who wrote in a number of journals and newspapers, made an impassioned — and important — plea for an Australian industry in the literary periodical, *Quadrant*, claiming 'that cinema is always, inextricably, bound up with its point of origin'.[2] This being so, she argued, casual overseas visitors could not hope to capture that 'sense of identity which a community's own film-making confers upon it as nothing else can'.[3]

As early as October 1963 there was a Senate Select Committee set up to enquire into Australian television production. This committee, chaired by Senator V.S. Vincent, lamented the decline of the film industry, believing that television and film production in this country should not be developed in isolation from each other. Although the Vincent Report echoed the protectionist arguments of the 1927 Royal Commission, as Graham Shirley and Brian Adams have noted: 'What had altered was not so much a concern for defending Australian culture as one for developing it'.[4] The Vincent Report recommended that £1m be made available annually as government aid to film-making, that there should be a system of tax relief for investors, tax concessions for producers, and that the Department of Trade should provide knowledgeable assistance with overseas markets. Sadly, the Report received scant public attention and the Menzies Government showed even less interest in debating it. Despite its intelligent and far-sighted recommendations, it was not until the end of the decade that governmental intervention would make itself felt.

Other arts in Australia — literature, music, drama, painting — had taken on a new lease of life; and throughout the 1960s, in the Vincent Report and elsewhere, there was a growing belief in the need for a national film culture: that is, primarily for a *feature* film industry. And such a need was not answered by Australian–overseas co-production. It could only be answered by an industry rooted in this country: the work of 'craftsmen who master the language of film, not only for the purpose of advertising-copy and plain journalism, but towards its own sorts of poetry and fiction',[5] in the concluding words of Sylvia Lawson's influential essay.

The Vincent Report, although its recommendations were never put into practice, played its role in fostering the growing determination of Australian film-makers and their supporters that there should once again be an active film industry in this country.

Political Steps

Throughout the 1960s, the agitation led by people such as Bennett, Lawson, Holmes and Thornhill insisted that a film culture could not exist in a country with a domestic market too small to sustain an industry without government stepping in. The retirement of Menzies as Prime Minister in January 1966 did not bring an immediate gust of fresh air into the national life. His successor, Harold Holt, with his famous catchcry of 'All the way with LBJ', announced an increase in Australia's commitment to American foreign policy in Vietnam. However, a month before his death in December 1967, Holt had set up the Australian Council for the Arts (ACA), a federally-funded body, and the arts now included film. In June of the following year, John Gorton, the new Prime Minister, appointed members to the Council from the various states and one of the Victorian members was Barry Jones. Jones, a former television quiz star, university lecturer, and a member of the Victorian branch of the Labor Party, and the Melbourne-based journalist Phillip Adams played a crucial role at this stage in the resuscitation of the Australian film industry. There is now a suggestion that their contribution has been overstressed, perhaps at the expense of the climate-changers earlier in the decade; what is certain, however, is that they had Gorton's ear and that Gorton was sympathetic to their urgings. Perhaps they 'were able to persuade [him] that to establish a film industry would be a great monument to him',[6] as David Stratton somewhat unkindly claims; it is a fact, however, as Stratton notes, that he sent them, together with Peter Coleman, Liberal politician and chairman of the Film and Television committee of the ACA, on a world trip to study government-funded film and television industries abroad.

Growing out of the report these three prepared for Gorton were three main developments set in motion by his government; the setting up of the Australian Film Development Corporation (AFDC), the Experimental Film and Television Fund, and a national Film and Television School. The AFDC received the support of both the government and opposition parties in both houses of the Federal Parliament in 1970. Its function was to assist the financing of feature films and television programmes; it was given a budget of $1m, and its objective was the establishment of a commercially viable industry. *The Adventures of Barry McKenzie* (1972), directed by Bruce Beresford, was the AFDC's first major investment, the corporation providing the whole of its $250,000 budget. In 1975, it was re-constituted as the Australian Film Commission and given wider powers: by this time the AFDC had become the target for criticism from film-makers — and for its 'random and unsatisfactory' decisions, in director Tim Burstall's words,[7] and from the trade — for its criticism of Australian distribution and exhibition practices. However, its importance at the outset of government intervention in the industry should not be discounted.

The Experimental Film and Television Fund (EFTF) was the first of the three recommendations of the report to come into being, with money from the Film, Radio, and Television Board of the Australian Council for the Arts, and administered by the Australian Film Institute. The first allocations from the EFTF were made in July 1970, chiefly for short films and to encourage

Edna Everage (Barry Humphries) and Barry McKenzie (Barry
Crocker) in Bruce Beresford's *The Adventures of Barry McKenzie*
(1972).

new film-makers. As well, it also helped to fund several low-budget feature
films, including Burstall's *Stork* (1971) and Esben Storm's *27A* (1973),
which cost $70,000 and $40,000 respectively. The EFTF, cynically
regarded by the film trade, was subsumed in 1975 by the Australian Film
Commission, as part of its Creative Development Branch. Apart from *Stork*,
the first box-office success of the Australian film revival, the films funded by
the EFTF usually relied on alternative cinema outlets such as the Sydney
Film-makers' Co-op and film societies. It is a curious irony that 'under-
ground' film-making should, in the early 1970s, have become largely reliant
on government funding.

The third recommendation — the setting up of the Australian Film and
Television School (AFTS) — was announced in 1970 but did not become an
actuality until 1973, when Jerzy Toeplitz was appointed its foundation director. By this time, not only Gorton but his successor, William McMahon, and
the Liberal Government were out of office and replaced by the first Labor
Government in twenty-five years, led by Gough Whitlam. Whitlam himself
headed an Arts Ministry which was to be responsible for the Australian
Council for the Arts and for the AFTS. The school was to provide a training
ground for film-makers, a function previously exercised sporadically by the
Commonwealth Film Unit which, during the 1960s, had employed film-

makers chiefly engaged in producing television commercials. In 1974, a student from the first intake, John Papadopoulos, made the critically-praised *Matchless*, the story of an alcoholic, an epileptic, and a schizophrenic who live together for mutual stability; and in 1975, several of the school's students worked on and appeared in Tom Cowan's *Promised Woman*. To date, the two most successful graduates of the AFTS are Gillian Armstrong and Phil Noyce (from its first intake), who went on to direct such notable films as, respectively, *My Brilliant Career* (1979) and *Newsfront* (1977).

For those outside the industry trying to sort out the lines of political intervention in the Australian cinema's re-birth in the early 1970s, it is possible to become bogged down in a series of administrative moves which led to the establishment of bodies with somewhat confusingly similar names. The Shirley–Adams book, *Australian Cinema: The First Eighty Years*, is the most comprehensive account to date, and, according to Anthony Buckley,[8] one of the most significant producers of the revival, providing an accurate survey. The present account aims only to draw attention to some of the major steps in the setting up of the new industry in this country, and the Gorton initiatives, whatever criticisms they subsequently attracted, are important in this respect. So, too, is the Tariff Board inquiry of late 1972 because, among other matters, it addressed itself to problems of distribution and exhibition as well as of production.

Over one hundred witnesses appeared before the Tariff Board's inquiry. There were attacks from the Film Producers' Association of Australia on the way the AFDC selected the projects it assisted, but the chief thrust of the hearings was as it had been at the time of the 1927 Royal Commission: hostility against the film trade which was interested, as ever, in the profits to be had from ditribution and exhibition, rather than in assisting local production by enabling its end results to be widely seen.

In 1970, John B. Murray made the light-hearted sex documentary, *The Naked Bunyip*, and decided to exhibit the film himself, rather than to work through a regular distributor. The success of this direct approach to exhibition encouraged Tim Burstall to follow suit in releasing *Stork* (1971) himself, with similarly encouraging results. Following its initial success, *Stork* was widely released throughout Australia by Roadshow Distributors which, like the Greater Union Organization, another local theatre chain, shortly after became involved in production. The success of some early 1970s films at the box office, especially *Stork, Alvin Purple* (1973), made by Hexagon Productions for Roadshow distribution, and *The Adventures of Barry McKenzie*, for which distribution was handled personally by producer Phillip Adams, led to some freeing up on the part of local exhibition and distribution organizations in the showing of Australian films. It is also likely, as historians Pike and Cooper suggest, that 'the fear of government intervention in exhibition practices'[9] prompted some change of attitude.

At the time of the Tariff Board inquiry, producers on the one hand spoke bitterly of their frustrations at the hands of distributors and exhibitors and of how they had sought to circumvent the costs and obstacles involved by exhibiting their own films. On the other hand, the distributors, while not assuming any responsibility for the industry, wanted to have a say in which features would attract government money. The managing director of Greater Union accused the AFDC of 'having mounted a smear campaign against distributors and exhibitors',[10] while others such as Dr H. C. Coombs, chairman of the Australian Council for the Arts, and Michael Thornhill believed that the 'reported restrictive trade practices' of the large distributors and exhibitors should be investigated. By the end of the hearing in November 1972, the battle lines between the producers on the one hand and the distributors and exhibitors on the other were drawn in much the same way as they had been in 1927. However, as Shirley and Adams note, there was now 'an increased awareness of film and the potential for an Australian film culture which had simply not existed before . . . and the trade discovered it would have to do considerably more than file the report away'.[11]

The rest of the decade saw a gathering momentum in production here, despite various crises (for example, the economic cutbacks of the Fraser Government which replaced the Whitlam régime in 1975), and there was perceptible erosion of the unsympathetic attitude of distributors and exhibitors to local product. At one point in 1977, for instance, no fewer than eight Australian features were being screened in Melbourne cinemas: it had been proved that Australian films could draw substantial audiences. Furthermore, Greater Union and Roadshow both became substantial investors in local films: Roadshow, through its association with Hexagon Productions (*Alvin Purple, Petersen,* 1974, *Eliza Fraser,* 1976) and Greater Union, through investment in films such as *Break of Day* (1976), *Summerfield* (1977) and *My Brilliant Career.* The third major chain, Hoyts, like the other two, opened its doors to Australian films when they appeared commercially viable (for example, *End Play, Eliza Fraser,* both 1976). However, although it invested in *The Chant of Jimmie Blacksmith,* it did not take an active role in production until the early 1980s. David Williams, general manager of Greater Union, claims that his organization is 'a little old-fashioned, preferring to go for an Australian theme, rather than one geared to the international market place',[12] but agrees with most commentators on the industry in the belief that Australian films cannot generally survive on local markets alone. The changing attitude of distributors and exhibitors towards Australian films in the 1970s, along with their role as investors in production, has clearly been an important factor in the industry's revival. To this extent the Tariff Board inquiry of 1972 achieved a good deal more than the Royal Commisson of 1927; however, despite a more sympathetic response from distributors and exhibitors, the revival could scarcely have happened without the intervention of the federal and state governments.

The Government Bodies

The Australian Film Commission (AFC), the federal body, grew out of the Tariff Board's proposal for an Australian Film Authority to replace the Australian Film Development Corporation, and was set up in 1975. The AFC, while intending to encourage production, was also expected to use its powers to facilitate the exhibition and distribution of Australian films, and, significantly, it was to be a statutory body under the Prime Minister's Department. It took over the AFDC's role in offering financial aid to production (the AFDC had contributed to such crucial films as *Sunday Too Far Away* and *Picnic at Hanging Rock* in 1975) and the AFC's involvement appears on the credits of many of the most notable films of the 1970s. These include *The Devil's Playground* (1976), *Don's Party* (1976), *Love Letters from Teralba Road* (1977), *The Getting of Wisdom* (1977), and *The Last Wave* (1977). Finance for these, and many others, was usually raised in conjunction with one of the distribution chains and with one of the state film corporations. The contribution of the AFC is summed up by Sue Mathews as follows: 'Over the first ten years of the new industry, an average of 50 to 60 per cent of film's production costs, 75 to 80 per cent of marketing expenses, and 95 per cent of the vital script development funding came from the AFC'.[13] Consequently, there was much influence exercised by government money over what films were made.

In the 1970s, virtually no film could be made without government money. The South Australian Film Corporation, set up in 1972 by Don Dunstan's Labor Government, was the first of the state government production bodies established during the 1970s, and its high profile was secured by its substantial involvement in *Sunday Too Far Away* and *Picnic at Hanging Rock,* two films widely viewed as heralding the new Australian industry. The Dunstan Government had acquired an enviable reputation for its interest in and support for the arts. The SAFC also produced the highly successful *Storm Boy* (1976) and was a major investor in Peter Weir's *The Last Wave.* The Victorian Film Corporation (now Film Victoria) began in 1977, its first project being *The Getting of Wisdom*, a film somewhat at odds with that 'certain cheeky larrikan quality'[14] that had characterized those earlier examples of popular Victorian film-making, such as *Stork* and *Alvin Purple.* An interim film commission was set up in New South Wales in 1977 and was incorporated the following year to invest in, and to develop production and marketing of, Australian feature films. Among the first films in which it invested were *Newsfront* and *My Brilliant Career,* the films which 'gave the corporation its reputation in the early years',[15] according to its present

Projects Officer. The Tasmanian Film Corporation (1977), the Queensland Film Corporation (1977) and the Western Australian Film Council (1978) were all founded with similar aims: that is, the investing in, and developing of, films in or about the state involved.

The key role of government bodies in the revival of the Australian film industry in the 1970s has been characterized by certain trends. For one, the film corporations tended to favour nationalist themes and projects which bespoke 'quality' in theme and treatment (for example, adaptations of classic Australian novels), as distinct from the cheerful money-makers of earlier in the decade. Since they were so influential in determining what films got made, it is tempting to attribute a certain decorousness about 1970s Australian films to their involvement. Second, since the industry has not developed a regular studio system (in the manner of Hollywood or even of Cinesound in the 1930s), the system of financial support has involved an allocation of funds to individual producers for particular films, encouraging at the same time the search for private investment. The federal body, particularly, encouraged distributors to become investors as well, so as to give them a greater interest in screening the local products. One way or another, it is scarcely possible to overestimate the importance of the government bodies in shaping the 1970s revival.

Inroads Abroad

Securing distribution was as crucial to the emergent industry as production, but as the decade wore on it became increasingly clear that overseas — especially American — sales would be a rule of life for Australian feature film-makers. In concluding this chapter's sketch of 'how it happened here' in the 1970s and 1980s, it is therefore important to give some idea of how the local product came to make its presence felt overseas. For, despite its essentially local orientation, at least at levels of story and setting, the new Australian cinema has sought — and sometimes found — enthusiastic audiences abroad. And it has needed to, for as director Bruce Beresford has said:

> A population of fifteen million people back home [he was working in the US at the time] is a ludicrously small audience for a movie. America is somewhere between 60 and 70 per cent of the world market for films, because it's such a wealthy society and there are so many outlets for movies, with television and the huge number of cinemas.[16]

As well as raising Australia's cultural standing abroad and the film-makers' natural urge to be internationally recognized, it is also increasingly a matter of economic necessity for Australian films to achieve overseas distribution. In the process of gradual recognition abroad for the new Australian cinema, it is impossible to overstress the importance of the Cannes Film Festival.

Positive exposure at any international film festival — whether New York, London, or Moscow — is no doubt always valuable to a film's commercial prospects but Cannes is still regarded as the major showcase for new cinema, as much a place, too, for making deals as for showing films. The history of Australian films at Cannes from 1974 to 1980 is one of steady infiltration, from the screening of Peter Weir's *The Cars That Ate Paris* in the Marketplace (1974) to Jack Thompson's receiving the best supporting actor award for *Breaker Morant* (1980), the film having been invited into the Competition. There are three key terms to be understood in assessing Australian progress at Cannes: the Marketplace *(Le Marché)* refers to the unofficial screenings held at every cinema in central Cannes from morning to night, the Directors' Fortnight *(La Quinzaine des Réalisateurs),* and the Competition. The latter two carry the prestige of invitation, of the invited films' being there in an official capacity and with a certainty of being seen, whereas films shown in the Marketplace must scrabble for attention from critics and buyers. David White discriminates between the other two events in these terms:

> The Competition is open to new films which have not previously been exhibited outside their countries of origin. The Directors' Fortnight concentrates on works by new film-makers or by those who have not achieved the recognition they are judged to deserve.[17]

The Volkswagen dressed up with plastic spikes, used for publicity for Peter Weir's *The Cars That Ate Paris* in Cannes, 1974.

The Competition has 'significantly more status and is more likely to provide a commercial springboard for a film', White adds.

When *The Cars That Ate Paris* was taken by Weir and his producers Hal and Jim McElroy to Cannes in 1974, they dressed up a Volkswagen with plastic spikes and drove it round the streets of Cannes. In the fiercely competitive Marketplace, a gimmick of some kind was needed to lure people to see the film; however, *Cars* did not succeed commercially at home or abroad, the American distributor pulling out after 18 months of negotiation. Weir's next film, *Picnic at Hanging Rock*, was screened in the Marketplace in 1976, and subsequently scored considerable success in Europe and South America. Between the two Weir films, there was a real breakthrough at Cannes when *Sunday Too Far Away* was shown in the Directors' Fortnight in 1975. Its success in Cannes was largely the work of Pierre Rissient, the skilful and sympathetic French publicist hired by the South Australian Film Corporation to promote its film. *Sunday Too Far Away* initiated a new responsiveness to Australian Films,[18] and in 1976 Fred Schepisi's *The Devil's Playground* was invited to the Directors' Fortnight. Not a notably commercial director, Schepisi was nevertheless noticed as one of the most talented of the new film-makers. Meanwhile in the Marketplace in 1979, *Mad Max* created a new respect for Australian technical achievement, especially for its photography. Australian cameramen were offering (and have continued to offer) stunningly beautiful images of Australia.

Shearer Foley (Jack Thompson) in Ken Hannam's *Sunday Too Far Away*, breakthrough film at Cannes, 1975.

Another major breakthrough occurred in 1978 when Schepisi's *The Chant of Jimmie Blacksmith* was invited into the official Competition and, in the same year, in the Marketplace, Phil Noyce's *Newsfront* secured critical success[19] and Richard Franklin's underrated *Patrick* acquired international sales. There were in fact twenty Australian films at Cannes in 1978: the Cannes Festival had become news in Australia where its value to film-makers was now appreciated, and both film-makers and press from Australia began to see the wisdom of being there. Gill Armstrong's *My Brilliant Career* was invited to the Competition in 1979, post-production on it having finished just a few days before the Cannes screening. It was an immediate success at Cannes and, perhaps reflecting this glory, all but scooped the pool at the Australian Film Institute awards for the year. To crown the 1970s onslaught on Cannes, in 1980 Bruce Beresford's *Breaker Morant* was the third Australian film in three years to be invited to the Competition and this time Jack Thompson received the jury's award for Best Supporting Actor. By 1980, Australian films had 'arrived' in Europe: in that year, the Incontri Internazionali del Cinema showed a thirty-film retrospective of Australian cinema to enthusiastic Italian press reports; however, success in Europe, encouraging as it was, was only a forerunner to the major challenge of securing necessary American distribution.

It was not until the 1980s that the two George Millers (no art-house types, they) finally launched Australian movies into the mainstream of US distribution. There had been a *succès d'estime* in the 1970s: Donald Crombie's *Caddie* opened the 1976 San Francisco Film Festival; John Power's *The Picture Show Man* appeared at the Telluride (Colorado) Film Festival in 1977 and secured a minor US distribution; *Newsfront*, in 1978, was the first Australian film invited to the New York Film Festival; and in the same year there was critical enthusiasm for an Australian Film Festival in New York, organized by the New South Wales Film Corporation. *Picnic at Hanging Rock*, one of the most successful Australian films at home, did not find an American distributor until after the new Weir film, *The Last Wave*, was bought by Northal Films for distribution in the US and Canada. *The Last Wave* did modestly good business on the art-house circuit but *Picnic at Hanging Rock* never did well in the US.

The successful penetration of the American market may be traced through observing what happened to three pairs of films during the years 1979–81. *My Brilliant Career* in 1979 and *Breaker Morant* in 1981 both achieved American distribution and were both well-received; however, both were limited to the art-house circuit, rather than to the mainstream cinemas, and were later sold to television and cable. They had established the Australian film's advantage, among 'foreign' films in the US, of being in English but there was still some residual concern about their being too Australian in theme for widespread acceptance. However, *Breaker Morant* was second in popularity in its year to *The French Lieutenant's Woman* among foreign films — and that had Meryl Streep as a box-office attraction. The next pair were *Gallipoli* and *Mad Max* which both achieved mainstream North American distribution. *Gallipoli* was distributed by Paramount in the US and though it did reasonably well it did not rival its Australian success; *Mad Max* was sold to American International Pictures for North American distribution while Warner Brothers International handled it elsewhere. Its box-office potential was recognized but not fully realized because of a management reshuffle in AIP which saw Sam Arkoff, the film's enthusiastic champion, removed from power. It was immensely successful elsewhere (in Japan particularly) and, when it was later re-released in the US in the wake of its sequel, fared much better.

It was the third pair, *Mad Max 2* and *The Man from Snowy River*, which really broke the ice as far as mainstream American distribution was concerned. The former, released in North America by Warner Brothers under the title of *The Road Warrior* (on the grounds that the original *Mad Max* was not sufficiently well known in the US), was not promoted on the basis of its Australian-ness; nor, however, did Warners try to suppress its origins. Its myth-making vision of a stranger in an alarming wasteland was effected with an extraordinary technical skill that won it high praise as well as vast, appreciative audiences. With the other, George Miller had achieved a huge success in Australia, outdoing *Star Wars* as box-office leader, despite widespread critical indifference. That *The Man from Snowy River* took off in the US with such *éclat* may be due to a combination of factors: its slotting into an easily recognizable genre (that is, the Western); its simple — some would say simpleminded — morality; the casting of Kirk Douglas, an ageing star presence, in a dual role; the sheer beauty of its Australian landscapes. For whatever reasons, its American distribution has set a new standard for Australian films abroad.

One hopes that it will pave the way for better films to do well in the US — better certainly than Ken Annakin's unspeakable *The Pirate Movie* (released in the US in 1983) which has become the third highest-grossing Australian film in the US. Others which have had limited release with satisfying results are John Duigan's *Winter of Our Dreams* (1981), Bruce Beresford's *Puberty Blues* (1981), Carl Schultz's *Careful, He Might Hear You* (1983), and Paul Cox's pleasing small-scale romance, *Lonely Hearts* (1982). Peter Weir's *The Year of Living Dangerously* (1982) was distributed by M-G-M but, owing to what was later seen as a miscalculated release pattern, fared disappointingly. More recently, *Phar Lap* (1983), its origins carefully suppressed in the advertising, has failed completely to repeat its Australian success with American customers. Despite the impressive successes of *Mad Max 2* and *Snowy River*, it is clear that the American market will not automatically respond to Australian films. A cold comfort may be that it no longer responds automatically to *American* films. Increasingly, however, it is clear that, for reasons of survival, an Australian

George Miller's *Mad Max 2* (1981) the first Australian film to win mainstream American distribution.

Kirk Douglas as Spur, one of his two roles in George Miller's *The Man from Snowy River* (1982), widely distributed in the US.

film industry must take this vast market into account. As production costs rise (and though they are still much below those for American films), most Australian films cannot succeed financially without doing so.

By the end of the 1970s, it is clear that a great deal of ground had been traversed: from the days of Murray arranging his own release of *The Naked Bunyip* in 1970, to the prestige of international festivals, to the securing of *Mad Max's* US release in 1979. And, to look even further ahead, to 1984 when the enormously successful Kennedy-Miller organization was able to raise the money for *Mad Max Beyond Thunderdome* from American investment and the film itself was released simultaneously in theatres from coast to coast in the US. The quest for overseas recognition — not so much a matter of Australia's 'cultural cringe', to use A. A. Phillips' famous term, as of economic viability — leads one to consider how far this has influenced the output of the country's film industry. There are several half-answers, although attempts to equate overseas market predictions with production determinants must remain speculative. Certainly there have been signs of trans-Pacific yearnings. American stars have been imported presumably to improve the chances of distribution in the US, although Geoff Burrowes, producer of *Snowy River*, somewhat high-mindedly refutes such a motivation, claiming that Kirk Douglas was 'the best actor among those available to play the very difficult role that we had scripted. So he was chosen for being the best, not to sell it'.[20]

The luring of overseas talent to this country, as noted in Chapter 1, is not merely a phenomenon of the 1970s revival. From the 1920s on, there was a steady trickle of British and American stars and directors working here. It is hard, however, to assess the importance of American stars in the setting up and selling of Australian films in the 1970s and 1980s. Presumably Richard Chamberlain's name helped to sell *The Last Wave* in the US but, despite Geraldine Fitzgerald's fine performance in Kevin Dobson's *The Mango Tree* (1977) the latter has not achieved much success overseas. The imported stars of the last decade have been scarcely major box-office draws: for example, David Hemmings, Broderick Crawford, Joseph Cotten, Rachel Roberts, Stacy Keach and Sigourney Weaver. In general, their talents are not in question but if their presence is largely intended to provide draw-cards for the US and European distributors and markets, they seem scarcely potent enough names for the purpose.

Whatever one's views on local industrial action by Actors' Equity which has recently all but blocked such importations, it could perhaps be argued that their exclusion is necessarily damaging to the Australian film industry's chances overseas. Increasingly, the building up of Australian stars such as Judy Davis, Jack Thompson, Bryan Brown, and Mel Gibson may be seen as a more influential response to the pressures exerted by the need to capture international markets. The *idea* of a star system is perhaps an inevitable and healthy sign of the international influence on the Australian industry and,

Geraldine Fitzgerald as Grandma Carr, Hollywood import for Kevin Dobson's *The Mango Tree* (1977).

especially in view of the absence of a studio system with its star-making machinery, the number of stars to emerge from the revival is impressive.

Attempts to develop films with an international appeal by playing down their Australian origins have not generally been significant. For example, Simon Wincer's absurd *Harlequin* (1980) talks of 'governors' and 'senators' with a view to familiarizing, no doubt, the scene for American audiences. Richard Franklin's *Patrick*, on the other hand, successfully recalls Hollywood thrillers while playing down the Australian-ness of the setting. Its use of Melbourne cityscapes is no more emphatic than the use of Sydney in Henri Safran's charming comedy, *Norman Loves Rose* (1982, with Warren Mitchell and Carol Kane as — surely modest — guarantees of overseas distribution). The pleasures of both these genre pieces have little to do with their being Australian but a good deal to do with their re-working of genre conventions. They do not go out of their way to suppress their origins, nor do they flaunt them. Cinema audiences everywhere have for decades allowed Hollywood to represent the rest of the world in its films, whether in the use of location shooting or in calling on great studio back-lots to represent the North-West Frontier or Lourdes. Indeed, one writer has spoken of that 'corner of M-G-M that is forever England'.[21]

The Australian film-maker does not in general have at his disposal the resources for either expensive location shooting or the elaborate re-creation of exotic settings. Even the highest Australian budgets are still low compared with American. This may mean that Australian films need to exploit the local or settle for the sort of intimate, small-scale film in which elaborate sets are unnecessary. Paul Cox's lovingly filmed 'romances' have conducted a gentle affair with Melbourne suburban lead-lighting: to those who know Melbourne, there is the sharp pleasure of recognition; to those who do not, it is presumably pretty but irrelevant to the drama in hand. The Cox trilogy offers a good example of films which have been modestly popular overseas without flogging their origins. In the end it will be quality and talent, not origin, that determine the success at home and abroad of Australian films. It is no longer necessary for them to inscribe the action with shots of indigenous fauna; equally, there is no reason for them to suppress the fact that Australia is in the Southern Hemisphere, and cannot, therefore, be the US.

[1]   In interview with the author, June 1985.

[2]   Sylvia Lawson, 'Not for the Likes of Us' *Quadrant*, 1965, p.31.

[3]   *Ibid.*, p.29.

[4]   Graham Shirley and Brian Adams, *Australian Cinema: The First Eighty Years*, Sydney: Angus & Robertson and Currency Press, 1983, p.210.

[5]   Lawson, *op. cit.*, p.31.

[6]   David Stratton, *The Last New Wave*, Sydney: Angus & Robertson, 1980, p.13.

[7]   Quoted in Shirley and Adams, *op. cit.*, p.248.

[8]   In a conversation with the author.

[9]   Andrew Pike and Ross Cooper, *Australian Film 1900-1977*, Melbourne: OUP and the Australian Film Institute, 1980, p.305.

[10]   Shirley and Adams, *op. cit.*, p.248.

[11]   *Ibid.*, p.249.

[12]   In interview with the author.

[13]   Sue Mathews, *35mm Dreams*, Melbourne: Penguin, 1984, p.13.

[14]   Terence McMahon, managing director of Film Victoria, in an interview with the author.

[15]   Mary Gibson, Projects Officer, in an interview with the author.

[16]   Quoted in Mathews, *op. cit.*, p.15.

[17]   David White, *Australian Movies to the World*, Melbourne: Fontana Australia and *Cinema Papers*, 1984, p.11.

[18]   Alexander Walker of London's *Evening Standard* thought it 'stole the show' at Cannes. Quoted in White, p.52.

[19]   Robyn Campbell-Jones of Roadshow Distributors opted for Cannes over the Sydney Film Festival to launch *Newsfront* on the grounds that 'a bad review at the Cannes Film Festival could be buried on the grounds that the standards at the competition were high'. Michael Harvey 'Selling *Newsfront*', *Cinema Papers*, July–August, 1979, p.437.

[20]   Quoted in White, *op. cit.*, p.103.

[21]   Jeffrey Richards, *Visions of Yesterday*, Routledge and Kegan Paul, 1973, p.110.

Part Two: SIX THEMES

3 The Boom: Four Hundred Films

In the years 1970 to 1985, nearly four hundred feature films were made in Australia; that is to say, about twenty more than were made in the preceding seventy years. Even allowing for a full quota of duds, many of which — mercifully — will never have been seen beyond these shores, in the context of the preceding decades of drought such a figure probably justifies the term 'boom'. No doubt that is not how it would always appear to those actively engaged in the industry, involved as they are in scrabbling for money, in setting up deals with distributors, in wondering what successive governments will do to help or hinder their progress. However, to one engaged in writing about the Australian cinema, the sheer bulk of films produced here in the last fifteen years is both exhilarating and perplexing: exhilarating in the sense of there being enough that is worth writing about, and perplexing as to how best to organize one's perceptions of such a period.

In settling for an exploration of the ways in which these films have offered interpretations of Australia, to itself and the world, the present volume has rejected three other approaches to the period's films: the chronological, the genre-based, and that of the director-as-*auteur*. A year-by-year account may be amenable to recording the growth of the film industry in economic and political terms but emerging patterns in the films themselves tend to get lost in such an approach. This is not to say that a comparative study, of, for example, 1974 and 1984 in terms of output, would not be revealing, but, in considering a decade's films, it is more instructive to try to place particular emerging trends in a broader context.

Perhaps because the new Australian cinema — unlike the American cinema is its heyday — has failed to produce a studio system, its films do not slot easily into genre patterns. The genre films — Westerns, musicals, thrillers, screwball comedies, and others — were essentially the products of, and sustained by, the great Hollywood studios and their tapping of vast mass audiences. They required the resources and personnel of the film factories for exploiting and rapidly repeating proven formulas. Ironically, the two most commercially popular Australian films to date — *Mad Max* (1979) and *The Man from Snowy River* (1982) (both directed, improbably, by men called George Miller) — come closer to satisfying genre conventions than most. *Mad Max*, whatever else it is up to, is clearly a 'thriller', *Snowy River* a species of (wallaby?) Western. However, if their success outside Australia, notably in the US, implies a message about the profitability of genre film-making, it is not one that has been much heeded. Besides these, one could point to a couple of musicals (Gill Armstrong's *Starstruck* and Ken Annakin's *The Pirate Movie*, both 1982), a few flings at horror (Terry Bourke's *Inn of the Damned*, 1975) and fantasy (David Hemmings' *The Survivor*, 1981), but in general the new Australian cinema is not one very fruitfully open to genre study. Those films which fall easily into one or other genre are inconsequential generally, compared with the major films which are difficult to classify. Not least, this is often because they tend to cut across genres, sometimes producing a genuine work *sui generis*, such as Peter Weir's *Picnic at Hanging Rock* (1975) (part thriller, part horror, part fantasy, part 'school' film) or George Miller's *Mad Max 2* (1981) (part fantasy, part thriller, part road movie). It is not that one fails to detect the presence of certain genre conventions in recent Australian films; it is rather a matter of not having applied them with the structuring force-fulness that characterizes the prime examples of classic Hollywood genre film.

Perhaps a studio system — at any rate, a much more securely established industry than Australia's — is necessary also for the emergence of the director-as-*auteur*. David Stratton's book, *The Last New Wave*,[1] is organized primarily on the basis of directorial proclivities, and one finds chapters headed 'Mystery and Imagination: Peter Weir' or 'Chronicler of the Under-dogs: Donald Crombie'. Although Stratton has obtained some lively and

Jackie (Jo Kennedy) and the Wombats on stage at the Sydney Opera House in Gillian Armstrong's *Starstruck* (1982).

useful information from the dozen or so directors he has interviewed, and valuable insight into how each made their way into feature film-making, his book does not provide a strong case for considering the decade's cinema from the auteurist stance of *Cahiers du cinema*. Weir is perhaps the only one who might reasonably have been saddled with such a label, in 1980 at least: there was a recurrence of thematic and stylistic concerns in his first four features, although *Gallipoli* (1981), *The Year of Living Dangerously* (1982), and the American-made *Witness* (1985) have notably extended his range: in fact, he himself considers 'the word *auteur* has become devalued and we probably have to put it aside'.[2] A more recent book, *35 mm Dreams*, is a record of 'Conversations with Five Directors about the Australian film revival'[3]; the directors ('among the most widely known, and among the most successful'[4]) are Weir, Fred Schepisi, Gillian Armstrong, John Duigan, and George (*Mad Max*) Miller. The book's title seems to point to an auteurist orientation, as if the process of film-making were primarily concerned with the realization of a director's dreams. None of the five interviewed, however, takes such a lofty, romantic view of their role, and George Miller's comment — that 'film-making is essentially an organic process in which all the elements are interactive'[5] — is a fair summary of the views of the other four.

If auteurism seemed in the 1960s a valuable approach to the anatomization of a national cinema, especially of American cinema, this was perhaps because it was addressing itself to a massive, uncharted body of work for which no parallel exists in Australia. Unlike the studio contract directors of Hollywood in the 1930s and 1940s who left their imprint (along with other imprints such as those of genre or studio house style) on the movies they made, Australian directors have never worked in this kind of flourishing mass production system, and have missed both its constraints and its opportunities. Even Australia's busiest directors have scarcely produced a body of work large enough or, in terms of personal imprint, coherent enough to warrant organizing a history around key directorial figures. Further, some of the most prolific, such as Bruce Beresford (nine films in ten years), have shown themselves gifted in a number of sharply dissimilar modes, or, like Brian Trenchard-Smith (also nine films in the decade), have shown little flair for anything but keeping the action on the move.

On the whole, it seems most profitable to consider the body of films produced in the context of the period's films as a whole, insofar as they offer certain discernible tendencies which recur from director to director and from year to year, and which do not fit easily into genre categorization. The literary adaptation, for instance, has been a common feature of the cinema of the last decade or so, but it has elicited such a variety of treatments (faithful reconstruction, interpretive commentary, etc.) that it is more useful to consider it as it intersects with the preoccupations of the period as a whole than as a separate element. In the 1970s particularly, the reliance on novels and plays threatened to encourage a somewhat decorous cinema, drawing on a respectability established in other media. Further, it drew attention to what is still perhaps the Australian cinema's chief weakness: a meagre supply of original scriptwriters. Its undeniable strengths have been the product of the collaborative efforts of directors and producers willing to take an imaginative risk, of gifted directors of photography and production designers, and of a growing stable of world-class actors. Directors who have worked in other countries, Britain or the US, have commented on the egalitarian spirit that pervades Australian film sets and locations; it may be appropriate, in this light, to consider the films in ways which reflect a multiple contribution rather than, romantically, as the product of a single dominant sensibility. To this end, the following chapters will consider some of the chief ideas and images which have dominated the much-publicized 'renaissance'.

Projecting Australia and Australians

Whether it means to do so or not, any country with an even half-way thriving film industry will inevitably reveal a good deal about itself to the rest of the world. The vogue for *film noir* in the American cinema of the post-Second World War period or the popularity of the Hammer horror cycle from the late 1950s are revealing of, respectively, a widespread malaise and a freeing up of certain repressed elements in the national life of the countries that produced them. The renascent Australian cinema of the 1970s and 1980s is no exception: what is perhaps more striking is the highly conscious preoccupation with manufacturing fictions that will present the Australian-ness of Australian experience. If it is true that all films are ideologically charged in ways their makers may or may not be aware of, it is equally true that such diverse films as *Gallipoli*, Bruce Beresford's *The Club* (1980), *Picnic at Hanging Rock*, Ken Hannam's *Sunday Too Far Away* (1975), *The Man from Snowy River*, Simon Wincer's *Phar Lap* (1983), Phil Noyce's *Newsfront* (1978) and Michael Thornhill's *The FJ Holden* (1977) are overtly concerned to present and examine the myths and realities of Australian life. It is as though there were some kind of tacit understanding that, if a new film industry were to emanate from Australia, it would be largely the result of exploiting the balance between what would be locally and instantly recognizable and what would be seen internationally as new and exotic.

In considering some of the ways in which these films 'present and examine the myths and realities of Australian life', it is possible to identify a number of thematic preoccupations which recur often enough to form some useful categories. The six which have been chosen as a focus for exploring the films can be listed roughly as follows: those concerned with examining recognizable national images; those which particularly address the rural landscape; films of city life; films of the sexual and emotional life; the 'rites of passage' films which focus on the problems of growing up; and those which can be loosely grouped as 'historical'. It is obvious that many films will be relevant to several of these categories and their relevance to any particular category will govern their treatment in the following chapters.

1   The 'ocker' image of Australia which characterized the highly success-ful, critically savaged comedies of the early 1970s — Bruce Beresford's 'Barry McKenzie' films (1972, 1974), and Tim Burstall's *Alvin Purple* (1973) — did not persist once the revival got into its stride. Or, rather, where it did appear it was more likely to be subjected to the sort of critical scrutiny it received in Burstall's *Petersen* (1974) and Beresford's *Don's Party* (1976). 'Ockerism', the depiction of Australian men as boorish but good humoured, sexually and nationally chauvinistic, may well have been an essential element in overseas perceptions of Australia, but, as if in reaction to such a label, many of the films of the past ten years have sought to establish different kinds of national images. They have been explicitly con-cerned with exploring and articulating a national identity and certain recur-ring characteristics and motifs call for attention. First, these films tend to be set in the past as if in conscious search for the roots of national mythology. Not that they reach back very far: if the nationalism of the 1890s were taken as the remotest starting point of such explorations, this would exclude very little of value: Philippe Mora's *Mad Dog Morgan* (1976), and Tim Burstall's

Don (John Hargreaves) and his wife Kath (Jeanie Drynan) welcome a guest in (and to) Bruce Beresford's *Don's Party* (1976).

Eliza Fraser (1976), both evocations of a remoter nineteenth century. The 'Nineties', with the enshrinement of a distinctively Australian ethos in the writings of Henry Lawson, A. B. Paterson and *The Bulletin,* may be seen as having laid down some crucial guidelines for ways in which Australians wanted to see themselves and to present themselves to the world. Second, some of the aspects of the national identity held up to and for inspection in recent films can trace their provenance to that period. There is, for example, a recurring — even *pervasive* — anti-authoritarian, anti-boss attitude running through films as varied as Bruce Beresford's *The Getting of Wisdom* (1977), *Sunday Too Far Away* and *Phar Lap,* not to mention the films which depict Australians at war: Beresford's *Breaker Morant* (1980), *Gallipoli,* and Tom Jeffrey's *The Odd Angry Shot* (1979). In these latter, anti-imperialism becomes a further subversive element. The mateship motif, a powerfully suggestive and for the most part unexplored element in the national identity, is cruelly tested and found largely wanting in Ted Kotcheff's *Wake in Fright* (1970), is romanticized and 'heroicized' in *Gallipoli,* viewed with affectionate irony in *Newsfront,* and made (unintentionally no doubt) to look like empty boorishness in Igor Auzins' *High Rolling* (1977).

Some of the contradictory elements in the national identity have also found their way into the films. Australians love a hero, whether a horse (*Phar Lap*); a passionate taker of the law into his own hands, like George Miller's *Mad Max*; an athlete, like Ken Hannam's *Dawn!* (1979) or Don Bradman in the television serial *Bodyline* (1984). Equally, however there is affection for the underdog, the battler, whether on the individual level as in Donald Crombie's *Caddie* (1976), the life and hard times of a Sydney barmaid; *The Irishman* (1978) and *Cathy's Child* (1979); or institutionalized in the striking miners' union in Richard Lowenstein's *Strikebound* (1984), in which the anti-boss ethic reasserts itself. Not that the categories are exclusive: Phar Lap, for instance, is as much battler as hero.

2   Australia is still sufficiently unknown in the northern hemisphere for there to be a major interest in the way places represented in its films *look.* Even in small-scale films focusing on intimate personal relationships, there is a degree of fascination in the use of cities like Melbourne and Sydney as backdrops: for example, in Paul Cox's loving recreation of Melbourne suburbia in *Lonely Hearts* (1982), *Man of Flowers* (1983) and *My First Wife* (1984) or in the use of Sydney in *Caddie* and John Duigan's *Winter of Our Dreams* (1981). In a sense, this kind of interest in place is a bonus in these films, but there is a whole range of films which draws significantly on the unusualness of the landscape. Two 1971 films, both made by overseas directors, began the decade's response to the threat and beauty of the landscape. They were Nicolas Roeg's *Walkabout* (1971), based on a children's novel by Englishman James Vance Marshall (1959), and *Wake in*

Fright, two films good enough to set the whole 1970s revival going several years before it in fact took off. Widely different in theme and style, they had in common a visually stunning evocation of the landscape and a powerful sense of its being a component in the drama of the films. *Picnic at Hanging Rock*, one of the crucial films of the revival, made much of the surface beauty of the Australian scene, with its lurking horror, a physical representation of director Peter Weir's fascination with the way the extraordinary and irrational lurk threateningly at the edges of the ordinary and the rational; Colin Eggleston's ecological thriller, *Long Weekend* (1978), makes drama from suburban man's maladaptation to the natural world, as the sophistication of a young couple proves inadequate to the threat of the landscape when they set up their camp on a remote beach; and films as diverse in feeling as *The Man from Snowy River* and Fred Schepisi's *The Chant of Jimmie Blacksmith* (1978) are full of images of man presented against a vast and dwarfing background.

No account of Australian films of the past fifteen years could fail to consider how landscape has been used in fiction films. Just as Australian poetry came to terms with a strange and often hostile landscape before addressing itself to the issue of man in society (that is to say, largely, man in urban life), so there seems to have been a need felt on the part of many of the major directors of the new Australian cinema to respond to the physical facts of the country. Sometimes, of course, the landscape has seemed no more than a picturesque backdrop to the film's central preoccupation (for example, John Power's 1977 film *The Picture Show Man*), but at their best, in films such as *Wake in Fright*, *Picnic at Hanging Rock*, *The Chant of Jimmie Blacksmith*, or Richard Franklin's black comedy thriller, *Roadgames* (1981), they have created a powerful sense of the interaction of person and place. And they have gone past the simple celebration of Dorothea Mackellar's 'sunburnt country' image, with its sentimental tribute to the nation's resilience in the face of 'flood and fire and famine', to visual exploration of the inherent contradictoriness of the place.

3   If the Australian landscape offers vistas as majestic and challenges as daunting as John Ford found in the American West, there has also been a heartening move towards examining on film the pressures of urban living in Australia. Since the vast majority of the continent's population is concentrated in the towns and cities which fringe it and since Australia is one of the most urbanized nations in the world, a film industry which ignores the cinematic possibilities of this populous fringe would be shutting itself off from centrally important aspects of the nation's life. As David White has pointed out, 'the era of British production [including the Ealing ventures of the 1940s and 1950s] . . . projected a single image of Australia: the bush,[6] and the sporadic American forays — for example, Lewis Milestone's *Kangaroo* (1952), Fred Zinnemann's *The Sundowners* (1960) — reflected 'a common

American perception of Australia as the last new frontier, almost an extension of the old West'.[7] Part of the excitement of the 1970s and 1980s in Australian cinema has lain in its representation of the urban life that most of the population lives.

This is not to suggest that a national cinema acquires maturity simply by addressing itself to significant social issues: the significance cannot be imported from the society on which it draws for its themes: the measure of the films will be the effectiveness of their representation in cinematic terms. From this point of view the Australian films which have been set in the cities have been marked by a very perceptive attention to *mise-en-scène* and by narrative structures which have related breakdowns in relationships and social dislocations to the peculiar stresses of urban life at various levels of class and education. These films have sometimes been cast in the form of genre thrillers (for example, Phil Noyce's 1982 *Heatwave* or Bruce Beresford's 1979 *Money Movers*); some have made romantic drama out of the cities' ethnic mix (for example, Paul Cox's *Kostas,* 1979 or Sophia Turkiewicz's *Silver City,* 1984); Peter Weir's *The Last Wave* (1977) explored the city's way of alienating man from his deepest instincts; others, like *The FJ Holden,* John Duigan's *Mouth to Mouth* (1978) and *Winter of our Dreams,* and Ken Cameron's *Monkey Grip* (1982) examine the sterilities of inner city living, beset by intersecting social and personal problems.

4   At their best, the films of the most recent period, unlike those of earlier boom times (1910–20, the 1930s), have gone beyond 'the use of local stereotypes to establish immediate rapport with audiences' so as to develop 'a sense of knowing complicity between the audience and the film-maker'.[8] The films already referred to — those consciously anatomizing national myths or the influence of landscape or city sprawl — may sometimes elicit the pleasures of recognition by local audiences, but they have moved some distance from the Barry McKenzie films which *depend* on doing so for their comedy. There is now a growing range of films whose concerns are essentially with personal relationships and in which specific geography is incidental. Paul Cox's three major films are each structured around sexual relationships in ways that are both serious and somewhat off-beat, and in each case the structure is fleshed out with an unusually fluent visual style and an interest in details of behaviour. Carl Schultz's touching *Careful, He Might Hear You* (1983), while firmly set in Sydney in the Great Depression, organizes the conflicting demands of two life-styles on a small boy, and there are two very perceptive small-budget films, *Love Letters from Teralba Road* (Stephen Wallace, 1977) and *A Most Attractive Man* (Rivka Hartman, 1982), which dramatize some of the ways relationships work — or fail. If there has been little evidence of the full-blown romantic melodrama, of the kind made famous by classic Hollywood, at least two films have achieved some success in this genre through judicious star-casting, Peter Weir's *The*

Estranged husband and wife (Bryan Brown and Kris McQuade) in
Stewart Wallace's *Love Letters from Teralba Road* (1977).

Year of Living Dangerously and John Duigan's *Far East* (1982). They
exhibit a Hollywoodian confidence (of the kind that, in the circumstances,
inevitably recalls *Casablanca*) in structuring the central romance against
the exotic background of a country in turmoil. Relations between men and
women, surprisingly often revealing the man as the weaker, more vulnerable partner, have, *not* surprisingly, been the most prevalent, but relationships between men and between women have lain as sub-texts in films like
Gallipoli and *The Getting of Wisdom*, *Sunday Too Far Away* and *Caddie*.

5　In the 1980s, film-makers' attentions have been prominently directed
towards the representation of teenage life, particularly in Australian cities.
Films such as Michael Pattinson's *Moving Out* (1982), and *Street Hero*
(1984), Michael Caulfield's *Fighting Back* (1983), and Ken Cameron's *Fast
Talking* (1984) may be seen as antipodean responses to, say, Francis Cop-
pola's *Rumble Fish* and *The Outsiders* or Ken Loach's *Looks and Smiles*.
Equally, however, they represent a concentration of interest that has been
fitfully evident in the new Australian cinema since *The FJ Holden*, *Mouth to
Mouth*, Don McLennan's *Hard Knocks* (1980), and Bruce Beresford's
Puberty Blues (1981), in which unemployment, brushes with the law, and
sexual fumblings provided, respectively, different shades of emphasis.
These were welcomed for their tuning in to contemporary teenage life.
They were, that is, direct confrontations of the shaky structures on which
urban teenagers built their lives, without the distancing glow of nostalgia
that engulfed Kevin Dobson's *The Mango Tree* (1977), or *The Getting of
Wisdom* and *The Irishman*, and without the self-conscious lyricism of
Henri Safran's *Storm Boy* (1976). They evinced a tough-mindedness and
realism that made them more attractive *to* teenagers than the visually ele-

Vinnie (Vince Colosimo) and Gloria (Sigrid Thornton) in Michael Pattinson's *Street Hero* (1984), a film of teenage urban life.

gant evocations of the past. Not that a 'period' film needs to be soft-centred, as Gillian Armstrong's *My Brilliant Career* (1979), with its feminist response to teenage aspirations in 1900, attests; and Michael Blakemore's eulogy to a happy boyhood in *A Personal History of the Australian Surf* (1982) makes equally clear that gritty realism is not the only honest approach to filming teenage ambitions and frustrations.

6 The last of the six categories of thematic preoccupations which this book will deal with in some detail contains a group of films which might loosely be described as 'historical' or 'of the past'. Naturally none of these categories is more than a useful way of marshalling films which exhibit certain common traits and many of the films can be usefully considered in several other contexts. This is certainly true of those films set firmly in a more or less distant past; what links them here is their varying approach to the past. Some, like *Gallipoli*, Graeme Clifford's *Burke and Wills* (due for release in late 1985), and Tom Haydon's documentary *The Last Tasmanian* (1978) deal with actual historical events: however, Peter Weir places fictional figures in 'actual' events; the title of Clifford's film indicates that its reconstruction of the past includes the representation of famous figures who were prominent shapers of that past; the documentary makes extensive use of research to get at the facts about a shameful episode in our history. No less important in the way the new Australian cinema has sought to present and interpret the country's history are such wholly fictional films as Michael Thornhill's *Between Wars* (1974), or *Careful, He Might Hear You*, or *Picnic at Hanging Rock* with its perception of European influences incongruously at work in an Australian girls' school at the turn of the century, or *Newsfront's* cunning welding of fictional narrative with newsreel footage of the 1940s and 1950s. Igor Auzins in *We of the Never Never* (1982) and Tim Burstall in *Eliza Fraser* both make historical 'fictions' — the former reverential, the latter semi-parodic — from the documented lives of two women famous in Australian history. The questions of what makes an historical film so, of what happens to our view of history when reconstructed fictionally, could well embrace a study of most of the films referred to so far. The chapter on filming the past will in fact restrict itself to those clearly set at a remove from the present, films in which a question of perspective on the past becomes a major issue for their makers and audiences.

The foregoing outline of some of the major themes and preoccupations discernible in Australian films of the past decade is not to suggest that a film's 'subject', manifested either overtly or obliquely, is in any sense the determining criterion for judging its quality. It is used as the most convenient way of considering the output of recent Australian cinema because there has been an unusual degree of thematic convergence. In their preoccupations they offer some important evidence of how Australia was thinking about itself during the 1970s and 1980s, and are more significantly in tune with the national life they both reflect upon and help to create than, say, literature or music. At the same time the successes they have enjoyed, both in Australia and, in a more limited way, abroad, point to more than their offering merely the pleasures of recognition — of daily experience being defamiliarized into film narratives — or of the exotic. The examination of how certain controlling ideas have been worked out in cinematic terms will suggest that the most interesting films of the revival tend to be those which work from a particular time and place to set up narrative structures whose significance goes beyond those limits.

[1]   David Stratton, *The Last New Wave*, Sydney: Angus & Robertson, 1980.

[2]   'Peter Weir: Towards the Centre', Interview with Brian McFarlane and Tom Ryan, Melbourne: *Cinema Papers*, September–October 1981, p.325.

[3]   Sue Mathews, *35 mm Dreams*, Ringwood: Penguin Books, 1984.

[4]   Ibid. p.20.

[5]   Ibid. p.255.

[6]   David White, *Australian Movies to the World*, Melbourne: Fontana and Cinema Papers, 1984, p.21.

[7]   Ibid. p.22.

[8]   Andrew Pike, 'The Past: boom and bust' in Scott Murray (ed.), *The New Australian Cinema*, Melbourne: Thomas Nelson, 1980, p.20.

4 Mates and Others in a Wide Brown Land: Images of Australia

The images of a nation, as it manufactures them for itself and presents them to the world, will inevitably make themselves felt to a greater or lesser degree, overtly or covertly, in all its cultural artifacts. The most potent of such images through recurrence will gradually accrete the resonance and achieve the quintessence of myth, until eventually the line between myth and reality will be blurred in the national consciousness. All films necessarily present images of their countries of origin, whether setting out deliberately to do so or not. With varying degrees of obliqueness, aspects of the ideology of a film-making country seep through the *mise-en-scène*, through the prevailing narrative paradigms, through the kinds of film made, and the kinds of stars they produce. Because of their high level of iconicity and their widespread dispersion, films, more powerfully and endemically than, say, novels, are remarkably influential in shaping and rendering the images which encapsulate the national life. It is one thing to read Henry Lawson's moving stories of bush mateship or Dorothea Mackellar's well-loved doggerel about a 'wide brown land': it is another — and more tenacious in the mind's eye afterwards — to see two young men solitary in a vast empty salt-lake bed. Everyone who sees Peter Weir's *Gallipoli* (1981) will receive *exactly* the same visual image even if everyone may *perceive* it differently: the mediation of director, writer, actors, and cameraman has had its way with the image before the viewer sees it, whereas the purely verbal image relies for its collective reception on the uncertain visualization of every individual reader. The film's image, that is, through the relative directness of its representation of the actual, stands a better chance of being received intact and by numbers large enough to confer on it more or less instantly the status of myth distilled.

Among the most commonly recurring images projected by Australian films of the last dozen or so years are those denoting (a) a man's country, (b) mateship, (c) anti-authoritarianism, (d) a wide, open land, (e) the Aussie battler, and (f) the competitive instinct. All of these imagistic categories have some basis in reality (for good and ill); all at various times have been promoted in idealized forms as inflections of a comprehensive image of rugged individualism embodying an energy and innocence that distinguish its exponents from more effete civilizations Over There. The ideology that shaped Raymond Longford's *The Sentimental Bloke* (1919) or Tal Ordell's

The Kid Stakes (1927) has undergone some sophisticating transmutations, but the films of the 1970s and 1980s throw up images that reflect some points of continuity with those earlier films. In some ways, the recent films, at their less adventurous, look indeed a little old-fashioned, a little nostalgic in the images they evoke. The categories listed above were all represented in the earlier periods of film-making in this country: the actual physical paraphernalia of the representations — their iconic elements — may have changed but very often their symbolic aspects resonate as they might have in earlier decades. In discussing the image of mateship, Sylvia Lawson compares a key shot of the 1915 recruitment–propaganda feature, Alfred Rolfe's *The Hero of the Dardanelles*, with a scene from *Gallipoli* (both silhouetting soldiers against the Pyramids at sunset). She writes: 'There are sixty-six years of history between these two intensely mythic shots; there is almost no ideological space between them at all.'[1] This is perhaps an extreme example but the prevailing images of the new Australian cinema are essentially conservative.

A Man's Country

It is no accident that the two most commercially successful Australian films to date announce in their titles the sex of their protagonists — George Miller's *Mad Max* (1979) and the other George Miller's *The Man from Snowy River* (1982). The images by which Australia is instantly recognizable in the world at large are of men, of *white* men, and the establishment and promotion of these images has had certain corollaries, both in cultural products and in the life of the country. Among these corollaries have been the suppression of the role of women, relegated to the sidelines in most recent Australian films, neglect — in fact and fiction — of the country's Aboriginal population and its history, and a playing up of the Australian male's engagement with a demanding natural environment.

Those films which depict Australian men engaged in rugged occupations (work or leisure) adopt generally a myth-espousing approach as in *Gallipoli*, *The Man from Snowy River*, and Donald Crombie's *The Irishman* (1978). In fairness, though, it must also be noted that there are some intelligent attempts to debunk or at least to understand the nature of such images of Aussie manhood. Ken Hannam's *Sunday Too Far Away* (1975), Tim Burstall's *The Last of the Knucklemen* (1979), and, most trenchant of all, Ted Kotcheff's *Wake in Fright* (1970) are concerned less with perpetuating images than with testing them. *Mad Max*, with its central figure of the family man who takes the law into his own hands to execute justice in a society on the brink of chaos is, in terms of Australian folklore, nearer to myth-*making* than the films in the other two categories. This has not been a recurring figure in the country's history: his motives have less in common with Ned Kelly's or Mad Dog Morgan's than with, say, Charles Bronson's or

Mel Gibson in the title role of George Miller's *Mad Max* (1979).

Clint Eastwood's urban vigilantes. Mel Gibson's undoubted charisma has made the image of Max, leather-clad dispenser of rough justice, as powerful as any in recent Australian cinema and has brought a new, curiously discordant element into the image of the Australian male.

The figure of Mad Max assorts ill with the heroic images of these young men, Archy (Mark Lee) and Frank (Mel Gibson again), in *Gallipoli*, with Tom Burlinson's incarnation of the man from Snowy River, or with the teamster's son, Michael Doolan (Simon Burke), in *The Irishman*. These are characteristically presented in visual compositions that stress youthful vigour and innocence against romantically conceived backgrounds, whether of the Australian (or Egyptian) desert, of the awesome grandeur of the Australian alps (throwing the banalities of the human story into sharp relief), or of Queensland's outback respectively. None of these protagonists or the values they embody — manly venturesomeness, courage in dealing with the vicissitudes of landscape or the challenges of war or those rites of passage which separate the men from the boys — would have been out of place in the film scene of the 1920s as described by John Tulloch in *Legends on the Screen*. In fact, Tulloch claims, 'The Anzacs refurbished the bush legend powerfully, at just the time that the Australian film industry was trying, most self-consciously, to get off the ground'.[2] Tulloch is writing of the 1920s but what he says could apply as well to the 1970s and 1980s, and finds an echo in Sylvia Lawson's tetchy question in her review of *Gallipoli*: 'For how much longer must it be assumed that we should identify "Australia" with images of innocent youth, opposed by repressive Authority and doomed by forces beyond any visible source of control?'[3]

'Innocent youth', of the kind represented in the roles played by Gibson, Lee, Burlinson, and Burke, has been an important element of the 'man's country' image offered by Australian films. These young men are all associated with the challenges of the outback: Lee and town-wise Gibson are most memorably seen against the emptiness of the Western Australian desert (foreshadowing those later tableaux in Egypt and Gallipoli itself); Burlinson on horseback stops to survey the vastness of the mountain country ('You've got to treat the mountains like a high-spirited horse', he says, before the camera cuts to a Marlboro Country shot of him in silhouette against sky and mountain ridge); and Burke is finally seen riding on the last of the great draught-horses that belonged to his father (Michael Craig). These images combine, then, youthful innocence with incipient heroic achievement. These young men are all on the brink of manhood, a status they can achieve only by grappling with heroic challenges. In this way, they are presented as analogous to Australia's national status: it is as though (as Sylvia Lawson has suggested) there is a perennial immaturity in the national images Australian films promote as long as such characters, locked in the past, are uncritically displayed in narratives that never question the validity of their conflicts or the way these are resolved. Australia is forever being called ' a young country' but such a mindless designation can hardly justify the jejuneness of these handsome young hero figures. *The Man from Snowy River* is a foolish film, full of visual posturings, but it has clearly struck a responsive chord at home and abroad. The images of men taming the outdoors and of a boy (a country?) becoming a man (a nation?) are, one is forced to accept, what many people want to believe about Australia. There is more to be said about *Gallipoli*, one of the key image-making Australian films, and about *The Irishman* which, flawed as it is, has moments of romantic power in its evocation of historical change, but their excellences derive from sources other than their youthful heroes.

There are more interesting examinations of men in rugged circumstances in the less heroic images of *Wake in Fright, Sunday Too Far Away*, and *The Last of the Knucklemen*. The other side of the sun-bronzed Anzac coin is mercilessly revealed in the first-named in which outback schoolteacher John Grant (Gary Bond) falls in with some of the locals in a hideous mining town, Bundunyabba, when he gambles away his fare to Sydney. These locals include an alcoholic ex-doctor, Tydon (Donald Pleasence), the too-friendly Hynes (Al Thomas), and two miners Dick and Joe (Jack Thompson and Peter Whittle), who insist on Grant's joining them on a disgusting kangaroo-shooting expedition. The Grant figure, vaguely middle-class-cultivated, has no resources to withstand the cheerful brutalities of Dick and

Joe or the more sinister ploys of Tydon and Hynes. Aussie hospitality and mateship are scrutinized and found to be mindless and potentially threatening; the heroic figure of the great outdoorsman is tarnished by the loud, boring, crude witlessness of Dick and Joe and the appalling cruelty of their sport. The film realizes certain ugly aspects of Australian outback life with a vigour and exactness rare to the point of uniqueness in Australian films. This may be partly due to the fact that the film is being seen through the eyes of a 'foreigner', director Ted Kotcheff being a Canadian. It offers an important corrective to the idealized and idealizing images of *Gallipoli* or *The Man from Snowy River*, but it cannot be said that it has much influenced the films of the decade-and-a-half that followed it.

Sunday Too Far Away and *The Last of the Knucklemen* are less concerned with myth-debunking than with understanding the pressures on tough men doing demanding work in an isolated setting. The men are shearers in *Sunday Too Far Away*, and 'Shearers' was the title of scriptwriter John Dingwall's first treatment for the film, drawing attention to one of those occupations associated with the near-mythic status of the outback Australian male. Dingwall and director Ken Hannam have preserved some of the traditional elements of the shearer image — the competitive, anti-boss feeling, the rough camaraderie of the shearing shed and the shearers' quarters — but they have also sensed the loneliness of the life. Among the cross-section of types who fetch up at the remote South Australian property, the central figure is Foley (Jack Thompson again), brash, likeable but emotionally vulnerable. Foley, who ends by leading his mates against the strike-breakers led by his old rival Davis (Ken Shorter), in many ways offers a typical image of the Australian male, physically tough, capable of arduous work, quick to respond to perceived injustice. However, the film blurs the image somewhat by an ill-motivated scene in which Foley breaks down and cries, a scene which really belonged to a sub-plot which had been scrapped. The cliché of the tough outback man is further undermined by the character of Beresford (Sean Scully), the quiet non-drinker who incurs suspicion by writing letters to his wife and generally refusing to conform to the expected pattern. The kind of life led by these men is not idealized; it is seen to make demands on them which some are ill-equipped to meet.

Perhaps surprisingly, this rather gentle, reflective treatment of what might have seemed a 'typically, Australian' subject enjoyed a notable local box office success, and in retrospect it and Peter Weir's *Picnic at Hanging Rock* (1975) may be seen as having launched the film revival. *The Last of the Knucklemen*, set in a mining camp in South Australia and based on the play by John Powers, is a more tightly organized but less subtle account of the build-up of tensions among men isolated by their work from ordinary relationships and pursuits. There are outdoor shots of the men at work but the film's essentially claustrophobic drama is shaped by a clash between Pansy (Mike Preston), one of the miners, and their leader, Tarzan (Gerard

Kennedy), whose prowess at bare-fist fighting Pansy challenges. The film presents an unattractive image of the tough outback worker, and the little community the miners create is precarious. Although it contains some of Tim Burstall's best work and there is fine ensemble acting from the small cast, *The Last of the Knucklemen* failed with the public. Perhaps its critique of Australian male stereotypes was simply too uncongenial for local audiences: the underlying ruthlessness of both Pansy and Tarzan discourages empathy and none of the others is strong enough to invite it.

In all the films discussed here, as well as in Bruce Beresford's *The Club* (1980), dealing with rivalries in the power structure of a football club, or Ian Pringle's *The Plains of Heaven* (1982), full of skilfully composed images of man in the natural world contrasted with man at the controls of modern technology, women are wholly peripheral. This is in itself a comment on the national image in which few women (for example, Henry Lawson's 'The Drover's Wife' or Mrs Aeneas Gunn, of *We of the Never Never*) have acquired anything like mythic quality. In Australian popular culture and indeed in serious literature, Australian women are most usually standing and waiting, serving their myth-making masters. Those films which emphasize the idea of Australia as a man's country (whether or not they merely present or seek to criticize such a concept) inevitably make the women's roles seen marginal. Again, it is *Wake in Fright* which is most sharply *aware* of this. Grant's Sydney girl-friend appears only in his day dream, as a man's view of allowable, respectable female appeal. The 'Yabba girl, Janette Tydon (Sylvia Kay), who readily unbuttons her dress for him, is the subject for crude jokes. Kay endows her brief scene with a touch of poignancy: after Grant has thrown up just as he was about to mount her (and the metaphor is apt), she turns away sadly, does up her dress and then wipes her face. The film invests this gesture with honesty and compassion before an ugly experience that causes the viewer to re-appraise Janette's apparent sexual readiness, acknowledging in her some sense of generous life which is characteristically misunderstood even as it is exploited.

Elsewhere, the films simply give women nothing significant to do. Sheila (Lisa Peers), the boss's daughter, in *Sunday Too Far Away*, is present at Foley's breakdown but one might well ask why. The women in *The Man from Snowy River* are hoary stereotypes overlaid with a spurious gloss of the new feminism; those in *The Last of the Knucklemen* are prostitutes in a touring brothel; no woman distracts attention from the centre-stage heroes of *Gallipoli*; Mad Max's wife (Joanne Samuel) has to die to become significant, in providing Max with a motive for action; and Robyn Nevin as Jenny, wife and mother in *The Irishman* (as she is again in Igor Auzins' *The Coolangatta Gold*, 1984), worries convincingly at the film's edges. The point is that women have to be in some way remarkable, like Sybylla Melvin (Judy Davis) in *My Brilliant Career* (1979) or Mrs Gunn (Angela Punch-McGregor) in *We of the Never Never* (1982), to command the narrative centre, and they do so rarely enough not to disturb the 'man's country' image.

If the prevailing image is of a man's world, it is also that of a *white* man's world. Representations of the country's Aboriginal population have been few in number and their *absence* testifies to white neglect — and worse — of Aboriginals. There are barely more than half-a-dozen films in which they are allowed a place in the foreground — Nicholas Roeg's *Walkabout* (1971), Henri Safran's *Storm Boy* (1976), Peter Weir's *The Last Wave* (1977), Fred Schepisi's *The Chant of Jimmie Blacksmith* (1978), John Honey's *Manganinnie* (1980), Ned Lander's *Wrong Side of the Road* (1981), *We of the Never Never*, and Donald Crombie and Ken Hannam's *Robbery Under Arms* (1985). Of these only *The Chant of Jimmie Blacksmith* and *Manganinnie* are centrally concerned with dramatizing the plight of Aboriginals in this country: that is, their exploitation and the brutal extirpation of their culture. The former film is passionately (sometimes didactically) bent on making this point; the latter, set in the wake of Tasmania's notorious 'black drive' of the 1930s, is primarily an account of the journey together of a lost white child and an Aboriginal woman separated from her tribe. The appearances of David Gulpilil, Australia's best-known Aboriginal actor, in *Walkabout* and *Storm Boy* have a touch of the noble savage about them, intelligently located in the narrative of the former, pictorially exploited in

Ronnie Ansell, bass player of the Aboriginal rock band 'Us Mob', encounters highway cop (Chris Haywood) in Ned Lander's *Wrong Side of the Road* (1981).

the latter. This may well be the most 'acceptable' representation of the Aboriginal in Australian films, from the point of view of offering a romantic image which provides no threat to white self-esteem. The sympathy may lie with Roeg's Aboriginal in *Walkabout* but white audiences are likely to be glad — at least covertly — to have the girl (Jenny Agutter) restored to her own washed-out civilization at the end. Tommy Lewis, the only other well-known Aboriginal actor, lacks the archetypal quality of Gulpilil and, although his main appearances have been in period films (*We of the Never Never, Robbery Under Arms,* and the title role in *The Chant of Jimmie Blacksmith*), he presents a more 'modern' *persona.* Where Gulpilil is frequently posed in ways that dominate the frame and the landscape, Lewis's Jimmie is characteristically a threatened figure — either by the hostile immensity of the landscape to which he no longer belongs or by the constriction of the white society which does not accept him. Only Lander's documentary-flavoured rock band odyssey, *Wrong Side of the Road,* really tries to come to terms with the Aboriginal in contemporary Australia, drawing into its episodic structure issues such as Land Rights and police harassment. It is perhaps the *start* of a new or counter-image of man in Australia, but white male supremacy, in terms of image manufacture, has as yet nothing to fear from its black predecessors. If women scarcely impinge upon the national myth-making, the Aboriginal has been utterly suppressed in the process, to the point where his absence becomes in itself a significant lacuna.

Mateship

The sentimental ideal of mateship may well be Australia's chief contribution to the history of human relationship. Like most images which together constitute a national identity, the image of men as mates derives from that blurred territory between myth and reality. The concern here is less with the origins of mateship — whether or not it is rooted in the early days of the country when men considerably outnumbered women, or in the pre-eminence of male-dominated activities, like agriculture and mining, and in the sheer loneliness of the settings in which these took place — than with how it has made itself felt in the new Australian cinema. It has been celebrated in the short stories of Henry Lawson, in the bush ballads of A. B. Paterson, and in the demotic verse narratives of C. J. Dennis whose *The Songs of a Sentimental Bloke* and *The Moods of Ginger Mick* were filmed by Raymond Longford for the Southern Cross Feature Film Company in 1919 and 1920 respectively. If mateship is no longer an important motif in Australian literature, several films of the last decade have helped to reinforce the myth.

Gallipoli, Igor Auzins' *High Rolling* (1977), and Richard Franklin's *The True Story of Eskimo Nell* (1975) are structured around inflections on the

Archy (Mark Lee) and Frank (Mel Gibson) in Peter Weir's *Gallipoli* (1981).

mateship theme, and further variants surface as narrative elements in *Wake in Fright, Sunday Too Far Away,* Phil Noyce's *Newsfront* (1978), Tom Jeffrey's *The Odd Angry Shot* (1979), Bruce Beresford's *Breaker Morant* (1980), and *The Plains of Heaven.* In the first group, the central characters are two men involved in a series of picaresque adventures, such coherence as the films achieve dependent on the growth of feeling between these characters. In each case, the pair consists of sharply contrasted types. Frank (Mel Gibson), in *Gallipoli,* is shrewder, more cynical, more realistic than the younger Archy (Mark Lee) who is ready to fight out of blind patriotism to a distant cause he scarcely understands. Frank joins up in the end because he does not want to be left out of things and because he does not want to be separated from Archy. Meeting first at a country sports ground, they race in friendly competition from Australia to Egypt to the cliffs of Gallipoli, their contrasting physical types reinforcing their divergent temperaments, and the latter dramatically justifying their different fates. Frank is a born survivor, Archy a sacrificial lamb; and no other relationship in the film is, in comparison with theirs, of any consequence. Perhaps it is at heart the male love story some have claimed it to be:[4] it is certainly distinct in spirit from American buddy movies such as *Butch Cassidy and the Sundance Kid* (1969); above all, it unequivocally celebrates the bond of mateship. Without being overtly interested in what that bond consists of, *Gallipoli* is an undeniably moving account of how it feeds into the national myth.

The mates in *The True Story of Eskimo Nell* are Dead Eye Dick (Max Gillies, in an enjoyably larger-than-life performance) and the much younger, womanizing Mexican Pete (Serge Lazareff). The film contrasts the former's sexual fantasy about the gorgeous Eskimo Nell with the latter's casual couplings. In the course of their adventures, Pete is more sympathetically

Mates, Mexican Pete (Serge Lazareff) and Dead Eye Dick (Max
Gillies), in Richard Franklin's *The True Story of Eskimo Nell* (1975).

drawn towards the ailing Dick; and the climactic act of mateship is in Dick's
sending Pete to enjoy the favours of Nell (the reality of whom is a grossly fat
whore) and Pete's reporting back on the experience with an enthusiasm that
ensures Dick's vicarious gratification. Richard Franklin's exuberant camera
style is not yet in full control, but his cutting between reality and fantasy,
between the older man's dream and the young man's prowess, offers a
reading of the mateship theme which, though often crudely comic, is also
inventive and touching. It is certainly more attractive than the sloppily-
made *High Rolling*, generically a road movie whose episodes fail to build.
Full of hip talk, it is relentlessly jokey, observing the Australian mateship
theme (in fact, one of the men is an American, Tex, played by Joseph
Bottoms) from a new, unattractive point of view. Tex, a travelling show
barker, and Alby (Grigor Taylor), a boxer, travel along Queensland's Gold
Coast, engaging in assorted tedious horseplay and sexual competitiveness.
The film founders on unsympathetic leads and on a curious sense that their
sort of mateship, at a remove from the usual stereotype certainly, does not
convincingly belong in the chosen ambience. There is in fact no sense of
relationship between them; they merely engage in a lot of caper-ish high
spirits.

   The bonds of mateship are tested in the isolating circumstances of *Sunday Too Far Away*, in which they are inadequate to assuage the real
loneliness of the situation; of *The Odd Angry Shot*, in which resilience and
boredom fight it out behind those other battle lines; of *Breaker Morant*, in
which the three men on trial (Edward Woodward, Bryan Brown, Lewis Fitz-
Gerald) are drawn closer together and closer to their defending counsel

(Jack Thompson) during their Boer War court martial; and of *The Plains of Heaven*, in which the two men (Richard Moir and Reg Evans) of different generations find different ways of dealing with the solitude of their relay tracking station on the Bogong High Plains of north-eastern Victoria. In the latter, mateship is scarcely an issue until an accident to the older man pushes the younger into a kind of emotional commitment to him. In *Newsfront*, there is an enduring bond between Len Maguire (Bill Hunter), top cameraman for Cinetone News, and his younger English soundman, Chris (Chris Haywood): this quiet endorsement of male friendship is the most satisfying in Australian films, placing it in a context of other relationships and of pleasure in working together. If it does not exactly provide a commentary on the mateship image (as *Wake in Fright* so harshly does), equally the image is not sentimentalized.

No One Tells Us What To Do

It has been suggested that 'the knowledge that life and victory over harsh nature could be won only by the strength of the individual's quality as a man'[5] accounts for the nineteenth century victory by the Australian Common Man over patriarchal control by an English-style landed gentry. The latter has indeed made its presence felt in pockets of the country, but it is the idea of the Common Man with his strongly anti-authoritarian leanings which feeds the national mythology. Being anti-authoritarian breaks down more specifically into being anti-rules and -laws, anti-boss, anti-European, and anti-British. It has concomitants such as affection for the underdog who suffers oppression by any of the foregoing objects of anti-feeling and love of a hero who breaks the rules. Not for nothing is a Ned Kelly or a Mad Dog Morgan who takes the law into his own hands accorded near-mythic status: there is a Robin Hoodish element here which evokes sympathy as these figures belabour the rich and powerful, but it is their daring disregard for the laws which distinguishes them as Australian folk heroes. If like Captain Starlight, the hero of Rolf Boldrewood's *Robbery Under Arms*, they have relinquished the privileges of English aristocracy to take on the adventurous gloss of Australian lawlessness, their image is only the more attractive. In later days, Pom-bashing has become almost a national sport as Australia loosens ties with Britain and moves slowly but inevitably towards Republicanism. The least endearing aspects of this anti-authoritarian image are a yahoo 'larrikinism', a mindless aversion to 'culture', and a suspicion of foreigners.

Some of the best films of the revival exhibit the varied manifestations of this image. *Gallipoli* is a film stuffed full of archetypal Australian images. Apart from those already noted — young men against daunting backgrounds, mateship — Weir's film presents the British in a poor light. They are either monocled silly-ass types like the mounted officers in Cairo, whom the Australians mock with cries of 'Tally ho! Tally ho! After the fox?', or the chilly upper-class officers at Gallipoli itself where, it is said, with perhaps dubious accuracy, the British used the Australian troops as cannon fodder.[6] The British are described as 'sitting on the beach and drinking tea': vague notions of Empire may have impelled Archy and others like him to head for Gallipoli, but the anti-British, anti-boss attitudes (in a war in which the British *are* the bosses) are nearer to the national mythology in which reverence for the mother country was always threatened by a determination not to be told what to do. Archy Hamilton, the fresh-faced under-aged Australian boy (breaking the rules to get to the war in the first place), is a victim, in Weir's film, to British exploitation of heroic young Australians.

If Peter Weir creates some striking images of Australia in this film, he is not temperamentally a polemicist. Neither perhaps is Bruce Beresford but his films pretty consistently reveal an anti-authoritarian approach. In *The Adventures of Barry McKenzie* (1974), this takes the form of anti-Britishness: the Poms, like the perverse Mr Gort (Dennis Price) and his shrewish wife (Avice Landon), are ripe for critical picking, and Barry's Aunt Edna (Barry Humphries) is used to pillory a certain middle-class Australian obsession with the Royal family and cosy English traditions. Never very funny, the film is crudely satirical at the expense of 'ocker' xenophobia, but it also reinforces the stereotype as well as criticizing it. Laura (Susannah Fowle), the schoolgirl heroine of *The Getting of Wisdom* (1977), finds herself constantly up against the authorities of the British-inspired boarding school to which her mother has sent her. Laura, a largely autobiographical sketch of the author, Henry Handel Richardson, has a capacity for intense feeling and an active imagination which are both suppressed by this seat of middle-class learning. Her rebellious approach to her snobbish peers, alternating with a fervid desire for acceptance, and her urge to know more than the dry-as-dust facts the school tries to cram her with, stamp her both as the Nietzschean free spirit of the original and as the embodiment of a peculiarly Australian anti-boss figure. Beresford's film loses its nerve somewhat towards the end when she is turned into a budding concert pianist winning the plaudits of the assembled school among whom the camera prowls unrevealingly. The point about Richardson's Laura *and* about three-quarters of the film's Laura is that she is indeed a square peg — and one too intelligent to value the plaudits of those she (rightly) regards as her intellectual inferiors.

Breaker Morant, Beresford's best film to date and one of the finest of the entire Australian revival, stamps him as more than a competent journeyman director and reinforces those 'anti' stances visible in his earlier films but here much more forcefully integrated into the film's narrative and imagery. The film begins and ends with the playing of 'Soldiers of the Queen', at first in a band rotunda in Pietersburg, Transvaal, and finally in ironic accompaniment to the lifting of the coffins containing the bodies of Morant and

Evelyn (Hillary Ryan) and Laura (Susannah Fowle) at the piano in
Bruce Beresford's *The Getting of Wisdom* (1977).

Handcock. That irony is a measure of the emotional distance travelled by
the film. In a marvellously composed scene, with Morant and Handcock
seated far right on the empty veldt and the firing squad at far left, the
execution watched by four British officers, an eloquent claim is made
visually about Australian fighting men being used as instruments of cynical
imperialism. This is intensified by Handcock's muttered, 'Shoot straight
you bastards, don't make a mess of it' *and* by the poem being read on the
soundtrack, about how 'Britons always loyally declaim/About the way we
rule the waves'. The British command is represented, in the performances
of Alan Cassell (Kitchener) and Vincent Ball (Colonel Hamilton), as stiff-
necked and opportunist: Kitchener claims that, 'If three Australians have to
be sacrificed to help bring about a peace conference [that is, to placate
Germany], it's a small price to pay'; and Hamilton lies at the court-martial to
protect the British position. It is not whether this is good history that matters here; what is striking is the way in which the British are identified as
coldly authoritarian and exploitative. One small episode in the narrative
encapsulates this attitude: the three prisoners are briefly released to help
repel a Boer attack, about mid-way through the film, and afterwards
returned to their cells. The irony of it being all right to kill Boers under
these circumstances is not lost on the three.

The hierarchy of command in *Breaker Morant*, with its shifting loyalties,
is comically reflected in Beresford's next film *The Club*, which deals with
anti-authority bickerings at various levels, from the dressing rooms to the
boardroom of a Melbourne football club. There are suspicions about a highly
paid newcomer to the club which lead to attempts to make him look foolish
at training, aggro about the possible displacement of Laurie (Jack Thompson) as coach, and a mixture of sentimentality and opportunism in the club

president's appeals to tradition to try to enforce his point of view; the film develops into a very Australian conflict between players (= workers) and committee (= management). The real thing in this respect (that is, workers vs management) is unequivocally but not simplistically presented in Richard Lowenstein's *Strikebound* (1984). It is surely curious that, in a professedly egalitarian country such as Australia, this should be the only serious feature film treatment of working class solidarity in the face of capitalistic bosses.

If the British and Britishness are consistently under attack in such films as Philippe Mora's *Mad Dog Morgan* (1976), Tim Burstall's *Eliza Fraser* (1976), Tom Cowan's *Journey Among Women* (1977), Carl Schultz's *Careful, He Might Hear You* (1983), as well as in some of the films already discussed, there is a small group of films which attacks Australian suspicion of foreigners as an ugly element of anti-European prejudice. The anti-British element in the national image is usually limned in terms of robust rejection of imperialist traditions, whereas the anti-European, perhaps implicitly rejecting a different, less fully understood, cultural superiority, is predicated on xenophobic bigotry. This is glimpsed in Paul Cox's *Kostas* (1979), in which a Greek migrant has difficulty establishing a romantic relationship in Melbourne and runs up against various kinds of hostility and ignorance; in Tom Jeffrey's *Weekend of Shadows* (1978) where small-town suspicions of murder naturally settle on a Pole; and, its amplest treatment to date, in Sophia Turkiewicz's *Silver City* (1984). In the latter, Europeans who came to Australia in the post-war migrant influx are harassed by customs officers, bullied by the migrant camp director who barks out orders in English over the loud hailer, and tormented by country-town yokels. It is ugly stuff but it is as much part of the anti-authoritarian image as those glamorous poses of heroic young men silhouetted against the skyline or sacrificed to imperialist ambition. 'No one tells us what to do' can signify admirable resistance to outworn authority structures; it can also signify a mind closed to otherness.

A Wide Brown Land

A later chapter will consider in more detail how recent Australian films have depicted the landscape and the way human life has adapted to it. Most effectively its representation has generated a powerful effect of menace: one thinks of the inscrutable, ancient monolithic outcrop in *Picnic at Hanging Rock*; of the raw, lonely, exposed mountains and forests of *The Chant of Jimmie Blacksmith*, and the inadequate, isolated huts; of the encroachment, of violated flora and fauna on the solitary camp of Colin Eggleston's *Long Weekend* (1978); or of some of the shots establishing country-town suspicions in Peter Weir's *The Cars that Ate Paris* (1974), Ken Hannam's

Nina (Gosia Dobrowolska) comes to the rescue of a fellow migrant (Wenanty Nozul) harassed by a customs officer (Russell Newman) in Sophia Turkiewicz's *Silver City* (1984).

Summerfield (1977), and *Weekend of Shadows*. These are not, however, the representations that most commonly feed the prevailing image of a big, open country as a repository for nationally formative rural values. The films which perpetuate and trade on this image are apt to be morally simpler — sometimes simplistic — films such as *The Man from Snowy River*, Peter Collinson's *The Earthling* (1980), John Richardson's *Dusty* (1982), *We of the Never Never*, and Henri Safran's *Bush Christmas* (1983).

These films, of varying pretensions, are full of handsome vistas of craggy mountain ridges and sweeping plains, and the narratives constructed against them are typically slender. *The Earthling*, for instance, charts the progress of a little boy, orphaned and lost in the Australian bush, finding his way to manhood with the help of a man who has come back there to die — and through a series of episodes of surpassing banality. Even the scenery which a schmaltzy camera celebrates comes to look less awesome than orchestrated as wild life appears on cue to punctuate the aphoristic claptrap of the dialogue. The bush as a crucible for distilling the manly virtues is of course a key motif in *The Man from Snowy River*, and in the achingly slow processes by which Mrs Aeneas Gunn comes to a better understanding of herself and the Aboriginals among whom she lives in *We of the Never Never*, the wide-screen rendering of the empty spaces of the Northern Territory strains towards an epic look which the human story cannot sustain.

There is a friendly expansiveness about the rural landscape in *Dusty* and, until old Tom (Bill Kerr) falls ill, he is able to live in the bush with his pet, the endangered dingo of the title. This sort of bushman's knowledge of the country, the pleasing sense of workaday farm lives (rounding up sheep, tightening fences, etc.), and the conflict between Tom's 'romantic' ideas of freedom and the idea of formal education to learn how to run a farm, give the simple story a satisfying dramatic texture. The kids in *Bush Christmas* track down a pair of comic horse thieves (John Ewart and John Howard), by means of their instinctive understanding of the landscape and with the help of an Aboriginal boy. It is essentially a children's film but, in its good-humoured way, is soundly structured around some basic oppositions: city ideas/bush knowledge; parents/children; Pom superiority/Aussie know-how; white/Aboriginal. It is an utterly indigenous film in its images and narrative, devoid of the pretty-pretty qualities with which Ross Dimsey endows the rural scenes of *Blue Fire Lady* (1977), a girl-and-horse story in which country values are simplified into sentimentality.

The image of the friendly little Australian country town, glimpsed in *Dusty, Bush Christmas*, and Carl Schultz's *Blue Fin* (1978), co-exists with that of the wide brown land. As the latter is subject to critical scrutiny in *Wake in Fright* where it assumes a terrifying emptiness, so the rural town is occasionally presented from an angle other than that which celebrates its homely virtues. Both Ken Hannam's *Break of Day* (1976) and Kevin Dobson's *The Mango Tree* (1977) respond to its destructive capacities for prejudice and the limitation of opportunity; John Duigan's disastrous *Dimboola* (1979) makes crude fun of its bucolic pleasures; and, most perceptively, *The Cars that Ate Paris* imbues it with horrifying potential. Like much of Weir's early work it reveals awareness that apparent ordinariness barely masks violence and terror. When the Mayor (John Meillon) of Paris, a town which gruesomely lives off road accidents, pursues Arthur (Terry Camilleri), the latest victim, into the countryside on a sunny Sunday afternoon, one gets a quintessential Weir image. A deceptively sleepy town nestling in the hills, it seems, but increasingly, one realizes, it is an inescapable death-trap for anyone trying to get in or out. What is exhilarating about the film is the way Weir spikes its mounting horror with black comedy, the latter often derived from some very un-Australian swipes at the nasty underside of a little country town. Susan Dermody has said of it: 'It becomes a Gothic horror story of the barely inhabited sparseness of our culture, the substitution of material fetishes for a lived culture.'[7] Weir's vision of the country town is a long way from the poet Kenneth Slessor's affectionate evocation of it:

Verandas baked with musky sleep,
Mulberry faces dozing deep,
And dogs that lick the sunlight up
Like paste of gold —[8]

Weir is interested in the possible horror behind the verandas; for him, the mulberry faces are only pretending sleep, and the dogs are more likely to be licking up blood.

Underdogs and Aussie Battlers

The sorts of heroes favoured in Australian folklore are those who either cock a snook at the law (like the bushranging fraternity) or who can be viewed in some way as underdogs. Dawn Fraser's triumphal progress from tomboy street urchin in the Sydney suburb of Balmain to international swimming star with three Olympic gold medals fits the underdog-into-hero pattern, and her constant brushes with the swimming authorities, leading to the ten-year ban imposed by the Swimming Union, satisfy the anti-authority element. Ken Hannam's film of her life, *Dawn!* (1979), unfortunately fails to capitalize on these exploitable aspects of his protagonist's life. The flash-back structure is curiously distancing; there is an over-all blandness in the narrative, as if one episode were as important as another, without the dis-criminations of dramatic shading; and the film's Dawn (Bronwyn Mackay-Payne), despite physical similarities to the original, is a gauche actress, in fact a total newcomer to films, who is unable to suggest the conflicting urges at work in Dawn's life and career. Dawn Fraser ought to have been the archetypal Australian hero but the film muffs its chances.

Much more successful, at least locally if not abroad ('another unexciting film about an exciting sport', said one reviewer)[9], is Simon Wincer's *Phar Lap* (1983). Framed by the news of the great horse's mysterious death in America, it does away with that kind of straightforward narrative interest to investigate how an under-horse, as it were, is turned into a hero. The Aussie battler element is there in the story of struggling trainer, Harry Telford (Martin Vaughan), whose faith in Phar Lap is not shared by the American magnate, Davis (a sharply knowing performance from Ron Liebman), and persists in the face of the horse's coming in last in his first five races. The rest, as they say, is history, but the film is emotionally engaging (certainly to many Australians) in its account of success for horse, trainer, and groom, Tommy Woodcock (Tom Burlinson), against unlikely odds, against opposi-tion from the snobbish Victorian Racing Commission, juxtaposing profes-sional obsession with subordinated private lives. Phar Lap becomes a hero in the teeth of opposition from those establishment forces, presented as unsympathetically at odds with the crowd's love of a champion. If the film shares some of the slow-motion indulgences of *Chariots of Fire* (1981), it also shares some of that film's exhilaration in physical effort and the triumph over obstacles.

But underdogs do not always grow into public idols, and films such as Donald Crombie's *Caddie* (1976), John Power's *The Picture Show Man* (1977), Crombie's *The Irishman* and *Cathy's Child* (1979), *Careful He Might Hear You*, Gil Brealey's *Annie's Coming Out* (1984), *Strikebound*, and *Robbery Under Arms*, a varied collection indeed, offer sympathetic accounts of those who find themselves at odds with the times they live in or with the prevailing hegemony. Crombie has in fact been designated 'Chronicler of the Underdogs'[10] and he has elicited fine performances from Helen Morse as Caddie, deserted and Depression-hit mother of two; from Michael Craig as Paddy Doolan, the Irish teamster, whose livelihood is threatened by more mechanized transport; and from Michele Fawdon, as Cathy Bakaitis, a Maltese immigrant who becomes a true battler in her efforts to retrieve the child her separated husband has taken back to Greece. These films are full of images that stay in the mind even when their somewhat straggling narratives need tightening. Crombie has a real sympathy for the underprivileged, and, in his latest film, *Robbery Under Arms*, co-directed with Ken Hannam and largely miscalculated in tone and short on narrative rhythm as it is, that sympathy is still apparent in the treatment of the Marston brothers and their families. However, he is more at home in the smaller-scale film, in which apparently unremarkable people find unexpected personal resources to deal with the vicissitudes of their lives.

In *The Picture Show Man*, our sympathy is retained for Maurice Pym (John Meillon), an itinerant rural picture show man who comes into competition with the brasher methods of Palmer (Rod Taylor), an American. Whereas Palmer has a motor-van, Pym can only manage a horse-drawn one; and Palmer beats him again by starting to show talking films. It is a film made with great affection (it was producer Joan Long's brainchild) but it moves at a snail's pace that undermines the narrative possibilities of its clash of showmanship methods and the generation gap that widens between Pym and his son. *Annie's Coming Out* is a special case: it dramatizes the true-life fight of a social worker to rescue a severely disabled but not retarded child from an institution, succeeding in spite of the obstacles erected by the institution, by bureaucracy, and by the law. The true story is inspiring but the film needs a warmer, tougher performance than Angela Punch-McGregor can provide as the crusading social worker. *Strikebound* is also special in the sense of institutionalizing the battler's struggles: Wattie Doig (Chris Haywood) is not just an individual up against uncaring bosses, but a member of a union which fights for the rights it believes management will deny to its members given half a chance. The miners win their strike after fifty-six hours down the pit, and after the Women's Auxiliary is founded by Mrs Doig (Carol Burns), who leaves the Salvation Army,

Taking the movies to the outback: Maurice Pym (John Meillon) and his son, Larry (Harold Hopkins) in John Power's *The Picture Show Man* (1977).

Aussie battler, Aggie Doig (Carol Burns), in Richard Lowenstein's *Strikebound* (1984).

the religion of the underdog, for what she regards as a more pressing cause. A beautifully and discreetly lit film (cameraman Andrew de Groot), *Strikebound* addresses itself seriously and without sentimentality to a form of underdoggery which is not always palatable to middle-class Australians.

The Aussie battler image is most memorably enshrined in Caddie, gradually shedding a useless gentility as she works as a barmaid to support her children, but it is also touchingly present in the characters of Lila and George (Robyn Nevin and Peter Whitford) in their struggle for custody of their small nephew in *Careful, He Might Hear You.* Every comfort in their Sydney shabby weatherboard house is hard-won, and the Depression in which George loses his job threatens the little they have. The cramped warmth of their lives is contrasted with the echoing, empty splendours of the house in which Lila's sister Vanessa (Wendy Hughes), for complex personal reasons, wants to bring up their dead sister's child. In Australian mythology, battling does not sour; it nourishes the affections when affections are all there is, whereas affluence may have too much else on its mind for the practice of affection.

Competitiveness

Perhaps the idea of competitiveness as an element of the national psyche seems at odds with the image of the apparently laconic, easy-going Australian, incarnated over several decades in the *persona* of Chips Rafferty, for instance. However, if competitiveness in the pursuit of excellence in serious matters is not the first image to leap to mind in relation to Australia, there is certainly a strong tradition of sporting rivalry, accompanied by a willingness to bet on anything that moves. This author does not include sport under the heading of 'serious matters' (although most of Australia would) and, since this is not intended as a purely personal history of the new Australian cinema, it should be noted that at least five recent films have addressed themselves to sporting competition: David Baker's *The Great McCarthy* (1975), *The Club, Gallipoli* (again — a comprehensive airing of national images), *Phar Lap* and *The Coolangatta Gold.* The first two focus on Australian Rules Football, the other three on running, horse-racing, and a triathlon event involving swimming, running, and surfboard-riding. Only the latter foregrounds the fierce physicality of athletic competition, which it presents in a series of memorably dynamic images with long tracking shots of the competitors running along beaches or silhouetted on cliffs. It is a good deal less persuasive in its discourse on the nature of the competitive instinct. With regard to the latter, it settles for the obsession of Joe Lucas (Nick Tate) with ensuring that his older son Adam (Colin Friels) retrieves the family honour by defeating in the Coolangatta Gold, Grant Kenny (played by himself), the son of the man to whom he lost the Gold Coast ironman contest twenty years before. He has to instil in Adam his own over-developed sense of competitiveness; he also sees himself still in competition with his sons: 'I can still run you fellows into the ground,' he boasts. His obsession with winning, with having Adam achieve what he has missed out on, has led him to undervalue his younger son, Steve (Joss McWilliam). On a fairly simple level, the film offers a critique of obsessive competition and sees it as injurious to family relations. Where the film falters is in the thinly written account of family tensions; where it succeeds triumphantly is in the overwhelming physical experience it offers as it presents a range of fiercely competitive activities.

The scene in which Joe urges Adam to go out there and beat Grant Kenny, and shows no patience with the idea of being a good loser ('Go through the race in your mind and find out where you lost it. Go to sleep knowing you are a winner'), recalls the opening scene from *Gallipoli*. In this, Archy's Uncle Jack (Bill Kerr) imbues him with the urge to push himself to his limits:

'What are your legs?' asks Uncle Jack.
'Springs. Steel springs,' shouts Archy.
'What are they going to do?' barks Jack.
'Hurl me down the track!' chants Archy.
'How fast *can* you run?' barks Jack again.
'As fast as a leopard,' chants Archy.

The first half of the film is full of people challenging each other, and others betting on the outcome. Later, Archy and Frank, stranded at a lonely railway siding, take up the challenge of the Aboriginal station-master who tells them they will not get to Perth for two weeks, 'unless you're game enough to cross the lake'. The challenge of war takes place in this context of competition and adventure. War offers a wider opportunity for the display of competition and sporting spirit, as well, of course, as mateship.

The football films make comparatively little of the game itself: *The Club* is more interested in its committee politics, but it does skilfully intercut staged shots of the game with actual news footage. The young player, Jeff (John Howard), on whose potential the drama centres, finally hands back the $10,000 he has been offered, having told the shocked committee, 'I'm sick to death of football. It's a lot of macho competitive bullshit'. *The Great McCarthy* wastes a talented cast on the foolish story of a country player who is kidnapped by a big Melbourne club, and, in the end, disillusioned by the machinations of those who run the club and by his experiences with women, returns to his country town. The film is full of witless vulgarities, and the football matches themselves are used for slapstick.

The first Australian-made film to be exhibited was Marius Sestier's *Melbourne Cup* (1896), and the *Bulletin* enthused: 'It is something beautifully appropriate that the first Australian picture presented by the new machine should be of a horse race. Of course it had to be either that or a football match.'[11] However, despite the implication that Australia is a nation of sports lovers, the films concerned with sport have not been more successful here than they have usually been elsewhere. The competitive impulse has made better drama in other settings. The shearing activities in *Sunday Too Far Away* become competitive between Foley (Jack Thompson) and the mysterious Black Arthur (Peter Cummins). Here the absurd rivalry grows out of the relentlessness of the work and the pressures of claustrophobic living conditions but, instead of providing some kind of relief, it merely exacerbates the tensions among the shearers. It functions not dissimilarly in *The Last of the Knucklemen* in which the isolation of the mining camp makes its own pressures. There is a willingness to bet on anything (as in *Gallipoli*), to make a competition out of anything, whether physical prowess or skill at cards. There is a particularly well-shot card game where the camera cuts adroitly to take in a variety of reactions as the stakes run high. And in *Wake in Fright*, the hero's undoing is the town's (illegal) two-up game which the local policeman (Chips Rafferty) allows to continue, partly because of the clout it gives him over many people and partly because he knows it to be the town's favourite sport and part of its unique appeal.

The images of Australia which the films of the revival have manufactured are, in general, conservative ones in the sense that they grow out of myth-

'Black Arthur' (Peter Cummins) and Foley (Jack Thompson) poised for action in the race for top shearer, in Ken Hannam's *Sunday Too Far Away* (1975).

ologies that have developed in much earlier decades. The bush, with the simple moral values associated with it; the mateship which is sometimes affecting, sometimes a brash or sentimental evasion of real feeling; the Jack's-as-good-as-his-master philosophy; the battlers and the rare heroes; the inveterate gambling and competitiveness; the overriding sense of a man's country — of a country for real men who disdain education and keep women in their place: it is startling to consider how traditional and how constricting these images are. They have their roots in the 1890s, re-inforced by the First World War and the Depression. Nothing since then has made quite the same claims on the national imagination and many of the best films of 1970s and 1980s — say, *Gallipoli, Newsfront, Breaker Morant, Strikebound* — offer re-workings of these structuring mythologies. Re-workings, but scarcely radical commentaries on them. For every film, such as *Wake in Fright*, that sets out to debunk the received wisdom enshrined in common images or, like *Picnic at Hanging Rock*, that is simply not interested in them, there are a dozen or more that espouse it.

[1] Sylvia Lawson, '*Gallipoli*', *Filmnews*, November/December, 1981, p.11.

[2] John Tulloch, *Legends on the Screen: The Australian Narrative Cinema 1919-1929*, Currency Press (Sydney) and the Australian Film Institute, 1981, p.351.

[3] Lawson, *op. cit.*, p.11.

[4] Phillip Adams, '*Gallipoli*: the great Australian love story', *The Age*, Melbourne, 22 August, 1981, p.24.

[5] A. A. Phillips, *The Australian Tradition*, Melbourne: F. W. Cheshire, 1959, p.48.

[6] There was considerable controversy in the British press about the film's presentation of the British role at Gallipoli for (example, from R. V. Rhodes James, M.P. for Cambridge, and his-torian, in *The Times*, 19 December, 1981, deploring the 'obviously intentional slur on the British soldier').

[7] Susan Dermody, 'Action and Adventure', in Scott Murray (ed.), *The New Australian Cinema*, Melbourne: Thomas Nelson, 1980, p.82.

[8] Kenneth Slessor, 'Country Towns', in *Poems*, Sydney: Angus & Robertson, 1957, p.71.

[9] Kim Newman, '*Phar Lap*', *Monthly Film Bulletin*, British Film Institute, Vol. 52, March 1985, p.88.

[10] David Stratton's title for Chapter 10, *The Last New Wave*, Sydney: Angus & Robertson, 1980, pp.140-155.

[11] *The Bulletin*, 28th November, 1896.

5 The Rural Landscape: Dangerous Idylls

When John Ford first used Monument Valley, Arizona, as the setting for *Stagecoach* in 1939 and thereafter many times over the next two decades, it became in his films something more than a background. The place undoubtedly exists — one can find it on a map or go there at certain times of year on a bus — but for most people it is Ford's filmic representation of Monument Valley that matters. And it matters because of the extraordinary narrative uses to which he puts its visual splendours. It is not for him a mere picturesque background (as 'beautiful scenery' so often is in films): he responds undoubtedly to the grandeur of its vast rock faces, but he is equally aware of its potential for danger. A sudden long shot of its mesas and buttes and dry valleys can reduce man to dwarfish ineffectuality; a silhouetted figure in the foreground can render his heroic possibilities in a landscape potentially inimical to man.

This kind of duality — this awareness of menace as well as spectacular beauty — has been a recurring characteristic in modern Australian films. To their credit, most film-makers have resisted the urge merely to exploit what is largely unknown to a generation of film-goers. That is, they have not simply used the strangeness of the landscape as an exotic prop for feeble narrative structures, counting on a ravishment of the senses to deaden the intellectual faculties. There are of course exceptions where Creeping Beauty seems to have won the day: Henri Safran's over-lyrical *Storm Boy* (1976), John Power's too-leisurely *The Picture Show Man* (1977), to name two widely liked but, to my mind, self-indulgent films, in which lingering over natural beauties is no compensation for lack of dramatic tension.

At its most individual it is a menacing landscape, even when this menace presents a seductive appearance, as so often has been the case in recent films. To the Europeanized mind of John Grant (Gary Bond), the schoolteacher hero of Ted Kotcheff's excellent *Wake in Fright* (1971), the landscape which stretches round the tiny railway siding of Tiboonda is menacing in its dreary, monotonous emptiness. There is nothing seductive about its empty vistas for him: it is the antithesis of his longing for Sydney and surf, and he is impervious to whatever harsh beauties it may offer. If what one makes of the landscape is partly a matter of whether the eyes and the heart are sympathetically attuned to it, then Tom (Bill Kerr), the ageing farmhand in John Richardson's *Dusty* (1982), provides a complete contrast to John Grant. *Dusty* is a charmingly unpretentious film, about an old man's

John Grant (Gary Bond) at the outback railway siding in Ted
Kotcheff's *Wake in Fright* (1971).

attempts to keep his dog which is part dingo; and one of its charms is in the
non-hostile expansiveness of the central Victorian landscape it presents. It
is essentially Tom's view, of dry rolling hills and forests that provide shelter
if not, in the end, protection. The film uses its setting as more than scenery
but does so unobtrusively: there is a benignity about it which dramatizes its
protagonist's view of it.

Recent films have tended to show a more sophisticated apprehension of
the bush than was the case in the earlier thriving period of the Australian
film industry in the 1920s and 1930s. Then, the bush was chiefly seen as
repository of specifically Australian values and challenges. It was seen as a
testing-ground for manhood (not in the subtle sense to which this applies to
the Aboriginal in Nicolas Roeg's *Walkabout*, 1971); as a site for struggles
between man and nature, where hard-working, decent men might live with
a peculiarly Australian dignity in an anti-city, anti-boss, anti-European
ethos; as the setting for simple, uncorrupted egalitarian values as compared
with the heartless capitalism of the cities. If by the 1930s this was no more
than a dream and an ideal, by the 1970s it was not even this. Australian
painters such as Arthur Boyd had synthesized the romantic dichotomy of 'its
beauty and its terror' (in poet Dorothea Mackellar's phrase); Patrick White
in *Voss* had created a hero who sensed the sublety of the inland; and poets
such as A.D. Hope and James McAuley, whose work frequently had nothing
to do with the specificities of Australian life, had arrived at more complex

71

conclusions about its nature. McAuley, in a poem of the 1940s, 'Envoi', speaks of the 'faint sterility' that emanates from the 'salty sunken desert/A futile heart within a fair periphery', but indicates as well a self-identification with the landscape ('and I am fitted to that land as the soul is to the body/I know its contractions, waste, and sprawling indolence'). Film-makers of the recent revival have, with exceptions such as George Miller in *The Man From Snowy River* (1982), approached the question of the landscape with a clearer-eyed, more comprehensive awareness of its capacity to alarm and delight that invites comparison with the poets rather than with the earlier film-makers.

At their most interesting they have addressed themselves to the country's surfaces to see what these might reflect about the nature of the human life lived on them. This may perhaps be seen as a short cut to establishing a distinctively Australian look and feel for their films, and to avoiding a second-hand European or American patina. Australian poet and literary critic, Chris Wallace-Crabbe, discussing the need for Australian writers of an earlier generation to come to terms with their non-native influences, writes:

> One way to escape the European ghosts that lean over one's shoulder and jog one's pen is by paying careful attention to the facts of immediate environment: the artist can forget mistletoe and oak in his observation of paperbark and pepperina.[1]

'... careful attention to the facts of immediate environment' might well describe much of the use of landscape in recent Australian films. Cameramen of international quality (Russell Boyd of *Picnic at Hanging Rock* and *Gallipoli*, Ian Baker of *The Chant of Jimmie Blacksmith*, Don McAlpine of *My Brilliant Career*, Vincent Monton of *Roadgames* and Brian Probyn of *The Mango Tree*) have collaborated with directors to provide such 'careful attention', with the result that there now exists in feature films a remarkably rich and varied representation of the Australian landscape more intimately known to more people through film than through all the other means of artistic representation put together.

One of the most seductive films of the 1970s was Peter Weir's *Picnic at Hanging Rock* (1975). Based on Joan Lindsay's banal and snobbish novel about the disappearance of a party of girls on the eponymous rock, Weir and his collaborators (particularly cameraman Boyd and composer Bruce Smeaton) have created a genuinely haunting experience. The film's meaning is organized around its presentation of two basic images: Hanging Rock and Appleyard College, two monoliths set down incongruously in the Australian bush. The incongruity of the College is established at first by a frontal shot which reveals it flanked by oddly exotic palm trees. The school's teaching and values are plainly those of middle-class English refinement and it is shortly to be defeated by the hostility of an alien environment. Rock and

College come together in the adventure of the picnic: the College is 'tested' by the Rock, and disintegrates under the strain, while the Rock remains wholly unmoved by the College's venturing upon it.

Joan Lindsay devotes considerable descriptive writing to evoking these two monoliths, between which — physically and metaphorically — the drama of both novel and film takes place. The College is 'an architectural anachronism in the Australian bush',[2] with gardens in which 'Heavy-headed dahlias flared and drooped in the immaculate flower-beds, the well-trimmed lawns steamed under the mounting sun.'[3] As for the Rock, it is introduced in full view as the school party gets its first sudden glimpse of it: 'Directly ahead, the great volcanic mass rose up slabbed and pinnacled like a fortress from the empty plain.'[4] The incongruity of the Rock is spatial rather than temporal: it has nothing to do with time, whereas the College is out of place and out of time. The film eloquently picks up the novel's suggestions in this matter and creates what is still one of the most visually arresting experiences in modern cinema, Australian or otherwise.

It begins evocatively with a bird call heard over a pale wash of trees and mist from which Hanging Rock emerges, at first distant and then in close-up, always ominous, in the way that Ford makes great rock faces threatening and mysterious in *The Searchers* (1955). By starting with the Rock, Weir's film ensures that the audience has that image — alluring, threatening — in mind during the subsequent scenes at the College. The connection is enforced by the way the brooding rock face is replaced by an exquisite girl's face on a pillow. Both Rock and College acquire a powerful physical presence in the film, camera angles accentuating the way they dominate their landscapes. Tactfully, each comes to acquire a pervasive sexual connotation as well: the smothered sexual yearning of the College (the film begins on St Valentine's Day, 1900, and there is a susurration of sexual excitement in shots of girls washing, dressing in flimsy white, sighing over their lushly-worded cards) is about to be let loose for some of the girls in answer to the phallic invitation of the Rock. Weir has claimed, in answer to a question about the film's exploitation 'of sexuality in an environment which represses it',

> I was never really interested in that side of the film. I didn't see it as part of its theme. I remember when I went to London for the promotion, that was the area that most interested the British critics. Comments ranged from talk of repressed sexuality to the less subtle, talking about lesbianism and so on. But it didn't interest me. For me the grand theme was Nature, and even the girls' sexuality was as much a part of that as the lizard crawling across the top of the rock. They were part of the same whole; part of the larger question.[5]

Whatever Weir's conscious awareness of what he is doing, the film insistently links the sense of sexual repression to the College, that of sexual liberation to the Rock; and in the failure of some of the girls to return, including Miranda (Anne Lambert), the most beautiful of all, it seems to suggest that sexual awakening is as potentially dangerous as it is irresistible.

The large metaphorical significances which attach to both Rock and College are carefully articulated at local levels. As the picnic party draws towards it, the Rock is seen as the only outcrop on the yellow, summer-dry plain; up close, the party succumbs to a post-luncheon drowsiness at the foot of the Rock, as if its influence has begun to exert itself; and there are striking close-ups of the natural life on the Rock, all of it seen as effortlessly belonging there in a way that the girls necessarily do not. And during the girls' climb, the camera tilts and lifts and pans to suggest, in collaboration with the effect of Gheorghe Zamphir's pan pipes, a place both enticing and threatening. In the case of the College, the sun-filled opening sequences gradually give way to a gathering darkness as it takes on the grim knowledge of what Hanging Rock has done. Inside, there are numerous shots of the Headmistress (Rachel Roberts) losing nerve and dignity in pools of light surrounded by gloom; outside, in the College hot-house, Whitehead (Frank Gunnell), the gardener, asks, 'Did you know that there are plants that . . . that can move?', and illustrates by touching a leaf which suddenly closes, 'as if touched by the withering rays of the sun'. The screenplay notes: 'The demonstration has a chilling effect on Tom [the handyman], even if he doesn't quite know why. Whitehead has made his point about nature and he moves away, a trace of a smile on his lips.'[6] And the film cuts to a low-angle view of the 'sharp twisted stone peaks of Hanging Rock'. Weir and his screenwriter Cliff Green have registered in micro- and macro-terms the kinds of threat that nature contains for them, and the film finds in its chosen physical settings forces profoundly disturbing as well as compellingly beautiful.

Picnic at Hanging Rock is an important and rewarding film from points of view considered elsewhere in this book, but it is crucial to this chapter because it provides some of the most eloquent visual statements about the physical nature of Australia and its relations to man's place in the continent. A picnic in the Australian bush is an idyll that should be undertaken cautiously: the landscape may look passive from a distance but up close it may be fraught with danger for the uninitiated. Nicolas Roeg's *Walkabout* had perceived these dangers five years earlier in his adaptation of James Vance Marshall's children's novel, from a screenplay by Edward Bond. The latter credit ensures that *Walkabout*, far form being a children's film, is a wholly sophisticated extrapolation from the novel: Roeg and Bond offer a re-working of the noble savage myth in a visually stunning evocation of the Australian desert. Like Weir's film, it takes a picnic as its starting point. Perhaps the very notion of the picnic, defined by the *Oxford English Dictionary* as originally, 'A fashionable social entertainment in which each

Jenny Agutter and Lucien John as the sister and brother lost in the
Australian desert in Nicolas Roeg's *Walkabout* (1971).

party contributed a share of the provisions; now, a pleasure party in which
all partake of a repast out of doors' is alien to the Australian landscape. The
O.E.D. (noting that the word is adapted from the French) seems to be suggesting a pleasure for more reliably civilized landscapes. The picnic in
Walkabout never really gets underway: a father (John Meillon), having
driven his fourteen-year-old daughter (Jenny Agutter) and six-year-old son
(Lucien John), clad in their school uniforms, into the Australian desert for
this purpose, goes abruptly berserk; he starts to shoot at them, sets fire to
the car, then kills himself, and the children are left to find their own way
back to civilization. They do so with the help of a young Aboriginal (David
Gulpilil) who travels with them, guarding them from dangers, and keeping
them alive by his hunting skills.

This drama is framed by sequences set in a washed out, etiolated urban
society, suggestive of modern man's dissociation from the mythically
enshrined roots of human thought and action. The journey itself acquires a
rich texture through its examination of inter-sexual and inter-cultural tensions, when civilized man is faced with circumstances in which civilized
codes are irrelevant if not, in fact, destructive. The Aboriginal boy destroys
himself when the girl ignores his courtship; years later, married to a city
businessman, she can only recall — wistfully — a lost innocence in a land-

scape as beautiful as she had first found it terrifying. The Aboriginal's understanding of the land — his organic connection with it is reinforced by the way Roeg's camera frames him against it — had revealed to her not only its capacity to sustain them but its awesome beauties as well. All this is achieved without simplistic generalizations about natural man, but through a 'foreign' director's wholly cinematic response to the landscape's changing terrain. As the children gradually shed the vestiges of their European-style school uniform, they come nearer to sharing the Aboriginal's instinctive insight into the land. For him, as for them, the journey is a matter of survival: as a tribal adolescent he must survive the desert alone for six months; in poignant irony, having taught *them* to survive, he destroys himself because of the girl's civilized refusal to understand.

The half-caste Aboriginal no longer attuned to the timeless mysteries of this continent is repeatedly presented as being dwarfed by the landscape in Fred Schepisi's passionate and under-valued *The Chant of Jimmie Blacksmith* (1978). Undervalued in Australia, that is: it was highly praised by British and American critics, including Pauline Kael who thought it 'magnificent' and found its use of landscape 'very sensual'.[7] In a film of powerfully suggestive images, those that haunt the mind most tenaciously offer solitary figures dwarfed by a harsh and indifferent terrain. English reviewer John Pym quibbles about 'Ian Baker's Panavision camera lingering sometimes a little too fondly on the seemingly new-discovered beauties of the Australian countryside'.[8] In fact, the images work primarily towards thematic rather than picturesque effect: Jimmie Blacksmith (Tommy Lewis), betrayed by the white society to which he has aspired, is lost in the grim, majestic landscape to which he flees, just as he is 'lost beyond repair somewhere between the Lord God of Hosts and the shrunken cosmogony of his people'.[9] For Jimmie Blacksmith is a 'hybrid' and the film's imagery shows him adrift from both the worlds the film presents. In the 'white' world he is either cramped or kept at a remove from social intercourse; in the natural world of his ancestors, he finds concealment but not comfort.

Appropriately, Jimmie never seems quite at one with this unyielding landscape of sullen blue-grey bush and the sudden arbitrariness of great rock heaps that fill the screen with a sense of undefined terror. Unlike the Aboriginal in *Walkabout* who truly belongs to the grim glare and unexpected beauties of Central Australia, Jimmie does not belong to the mountain crags and forests of eastern New South Wales. And it is part of the film's meaning that he should not. Where the grace and strength of the Aboriginal establish his place in the desert landscape (and, indeed, in the more sentimentally-treated beauties of South Australia's Coorong area in *Storm Boy*), the characteristic images of Jimmie against the landscape stress his estrangement. Jimmie and his half-brother Mort (Freddie Reynolds) edge around a rocky outcrop, as if menaced by the physical scene, and this impression persists as they run along a blue-lit, early-morning ridge lined

Jimmie (Tommy Lewis) strides through the bush in Fred Schepisi's
The Chant of Jimmy Blacksmith (1978).

with dead trees. No noble savage silhouettes here, just desperate fleeing
boys, 'displaced persons' in every sense of the word. Mort is a full black,
unlike Jimmie, and 'still had his nearly intact black soul',[10] and the difference
between the two is distinguished when they come upon what was once
sacred ground now desecrated by white intruders. In this place, where vast
trees suggest cathedral architecture, Mort flays his body 'to divert the
foreign spirits', while Jimmie, as much associated with the white desecra-
tions as with the original sites, is again adrift in the scene, wearily insisting,
'Yer'll never fix it. It'd take bloody days and yer still wouldn't fix it',[11] as
Mort tries to restore the place.

John Pym may speak of the 'seemingly new-discovered beauties of this
landscape', but Schepisi and Baker, not unaware of this pictorial splendour,
are more concerned with its terror potential. It matters more to their
theme: Jimmie has been encouraged to leave the huddled, squalid black
encampment to make his way in the white world; when that world frustrates
his proper ambitions and intentions, he lashes out murderously, and is
forced to flee to this natural world which might once have been sacred to his
forebears but is now merely hostile to him. Australian poetry is full of
attempts by poets, with 'European' education and images, trying to come to
terms with this landscape ('part of my blood's country', Judith Wright
affirms); few have been more eloquent than Schepisi in catching the lure of
its inhospitable contours.

Like Jimmie Blacksmith, the eponymous hero of Philippe Mora's *Mad
Dog Morgan* (1976) finds no place in society and takes revenge on it, as a
bushranger. After serving twelve years' hard labour for stealing a man's
clothes, Morgan (American actor Dennis Hopper) joins forces with an Aboriginal, Billy (David Gulpilil), and learns to *use* the empty, threatening landscape to his own purposes. 'He disappears like a bloody black', one of his

pursuers claims, and, like Billy, acquires a measure of adaptation to the scene. The most impressive aspect of this episodically structured film, which was largely shot on those actual locations near the Victoria–New South Wales border in which the real-life Morgan had practised his criminal trade, is the landscape itself, as handsomely photographed by Mike Molloy's Panavision cameras. One striking composition reveals a gun-barrel at low centre of the screen as it picks off McLean (David Brooks) riding to the police across the vast echoing landscape, before cutting to his bloody body lying in a field of purple flowers.

*Mal*adaptation to the landscape is what does for the trendy young city couple who repair to a lush green coastal retreat for a camping weekend in Colin Eggleston's *Long Weekend* (1979). Not all Australian landscape is threatening, for those who know how to deal with it, as Morgan learns to or as Gulpilil's Aboriginal instinctively knows how to. But Peter (John Hargreaves) and Marcia (Briony Behets) are messy, careless people, their private lives marked by bickering self-interest, and if the bush takes on a hostile character it is, one gathers, because their attitude to it is purely exploitative. They unnecessarily litter their camping area; Peter mindlessly hacks at a tree, shoots a dugong, and fires randomly into the bush; and Marcia smashes an eagle's egg against a tree. Ultimately the bush strikes back. Scott Murray in *Cinema Papers* claims that the 'lack of any major injustices being visited on the bush leaves the strong sense of menace evoked at the start basically unexplained'.[12] Perhaps, but from the beginning the film has evoked a tense relationship between suburban man and the natural world: the film opens superbly as the camera (Vincent Monton) pulls back from a close-up of a crab on a rock to reveal a vast and lovely stretch of coast, before cutting to a city street where there is a flutter of birds as a car starts; there is a news report that white cockatoos are attacking houses, and Marcia closes the curtains as if to shut out the threat of nature, and takes a frozen chicken from the refrigerator. The film occasionally over-signals its thematic intentions (for example, an eerie response in the night bush, like a baby crying), but such explicitness is compensated by the steady imagistic build-up as friction grown between Peter and Marcia and as nature begins to respond with increasing malevolence to their presence. Their camp-site, a small pool of light, begins to look threatened by the foliage; an eagle attacks Peter, and a possum eats their food; and the beauty of the sunset mocks the increasing ugliness of their relationship and the danger of the situation. *Long Weekend* is essentially concerned with, and coherently intelligent about, the extent of suburban man's ignorant response to the natural world. Marcia's refusal to accommodate herself to its challenges and Peter's romanticized view of reality are both scrutinized; and her flight and death, the breaking of Peter's nerve and his being run down by a truck driver whose attention is distracted by a bird bring the film to a violent but poetically apt conclusion.

Two films which contrast a peaceful-looking natural setting with human events of appalling violence are Peter Weir's first feature, *The Cars That Ate Paris* (1974), and George Miller's *Mad Max* (1979). Paris is an apparently cosy little country town which happens to live off the road accidents that it regularly causes. It is not that there is anything inherently sinister in the image of green hills and snug little town: rather, the dramatic effect lies in the contrast of the landscape with the violence and terror of the human behaviour, barely masked by the apparent ordinariness. In its apprehension of the extraordinary hovering at the edges of the everyday, *The Cars That Ate Paris* anticipates Weir's next three films, *Picnic at Hanging Rock, The Last Wave* (1977) and the telefeature *The Plumber* (1979), and its genealogy, in this respect at least, could be traced back to such Hitchcockian ventures as *Shadow of a Doubt* and *The Birds*. In *Mad Max*, there is from the start an imminence of violence that may be about to take over; and part of the film's mesmeric effect derives from its use of gently rolling countryside as visual counterpoint to violent movement and a pounding score. A beach retreat begins to look threatened rather than peaceful, as a result of what one begins to fear about human possibilities. As Max's wife Jess (Joanne Samuel) goes to swim, the camera tracks her through the woods, then summarizes the whole threatened idyll in an overhead shot, later tracking her back through the woods, teasing the audience about who or what is pursuing her. With the deaths of his off-sider Jim Goose (Steve Bisley), then of his wife and child, Max (Mel Gibson) takes to the roads, and cameraman David Eggby again and again catches the drama of powerful machines splitting a peaceful landscape. In *Mad Max 2* (1981), George Miller was working with a budget nine times that of the earlier film which had been shot, largely for economic reasons, on the plains round Melbourne. The locations for the sequel are the much more desolate country near Broken Hill, in south-west New South Wales, and this time the setting is used to create a hopeless, violent future. Almos Maksay, reviewing the film, describes it as a 'sci-fi setting',[13] and Dean Semler's camera evokes from it a terrifying sterility which reinforces the progress of the dehumanization process at work in its protagonist.

Semler also contributed to the strikingly surrealist treatment of the outback setting in Russell Mulcahy's shocker, *Razorback* (1984), about the depredations wrought on man and property by the grotesque wild boar of the title. In a film full of sadistic narrative touches — kangaroos shot but not to kill, so as to prolong their agony, and worms making a banquet of what is left of the head of the Ahab-figure (Bill Kerr) who has pursued the razorback, are but two — it is the stylish images of the landscape that account for its power. When American Carl Winters comes to Kamulla, 600 miles west of Sydney, to investigate the death of his wife Beth (Judy Morris), an animal rights campaigner, he finds himself embroiled with a pair of vicious 'yobbo' brothers (Chris Haywood and David Argue) in a desert landscape which exudes a nightmare beauty and menace. *Razorback* is a schlocky long way from *Picnic at Hanging Rock* but it does share this duality in its representation of place.

In an utterly different mode, Ken Hannam's *Sunday Too Far Away* (1975) is an important film for its sustained picture of people actually working. It also offers a 'critical examination of the Australian bush ethos, along with an understanding of it'.[14] The landscape here is not merely peaceful but empty and monotonous ('A telephone line wends its way across a plain of salt bush and occasional mulga . . . a soft lonely ridge over which a red earth road appears, heading directly for us',[15] the published screenplay records), and the lives the film explores are irrevocably marked by that loneliness. The physical horizons may be vast, but the vistas of the shearers on whose lives the film is focused are short and narrow. (Tim Burstall's *The Last of the Knucklemen*, 1979, a study of day-labourers on a wildcat mine in the far outback, makes some similar points about constricted lives in a remote place.) Although there is beauty in the representation of this severe landscape, it is also true that 'the film . . . illustrates the various tyrannies the harsh, distant environment imposes on everyone in remote areas'.[16] While it is true that the camera can only record what is there before its lens, that (for instance) a photographed landscape can, strictly, neither menace nor beckon, one of the powers of narrative is to show the interaction of person and place, so that the latter by implication ceases to be a merely passive element in the dramatic contract.

The films discussed so far in this chapter have been among the most intelligent of their decade and their response to the environment has been a potent source of their strength and appeal. There are, as well, other films less explicitly concerned to diagnose the strangeness and complexity of the landscape but which nevertheless draw on it for memorable images. The dry emptiness of the Western Australian countryside offers not merely some of the most potent images from Peter Weir's *Gallipoli* (1981) but also prefigures the Egyptian desert and the Anzac Cove, Gallipoli, in its bleak, craggy slopes. In fact, although some of the film is set in Western Australia, the scenes of Archy's (Mark Lee) home life, the stunningly shot empty salt lake which Frank (Mel Gibson) and Archy cross on foot, having been stranded at a railway siding, and Gallipoli itself, were located respectively in the Lower Flinders Ranges, Lake Torrens and Port Lincoln, all in South Australia. (The other main location was Cairo and its environs.) Russell Boyd's camera shows remarkable feeling for the empty spaces, not so much hostile as indifferent to man, and this very indifference serves to highlight the growing bond between the two young men who will ultimately arrive at Gallipoli by separate paths. The emptiness of the landscape has a thematic significance in stressing Australia's physical isolation in 1915, marvellously encapsulated in Archy and Frank's meeting with the old man (Harold Baigent) as they cross the empty lake. They are on their way to fight in a war thousands of miles away; in this vast salt pan they meet someone who has never heard of the war. During this trek their mateship grows and their attitudes to the war are crystallized.

Another film which deals with the relationship between two men in a remote setting is Ian Pringle's *The Plains of Heaven* (1982), which won a prize at the Mannheim Festival in 1983. It is set in the Bogong High Plains of north-western Victoria, not far from where *The Man from Snowy River* was shot. Barker (Richard Moir), in his twenties, and the much older Cunningham (Reg Evans) are employed on an isolated relay transmission station, getting on each other's nerves and devising different ways of coping with the loneliness. Cunningham's feeling for the landscape, in an unexpected turn of plot, fails to save his sanity, whereas Barker's indifference to it and his immersion in the technology of the station protects him. The astonishing beauties of this mountain country, stunningly shot by Ray Argall, are used to emphasize the men's isolation and to assume a dramatic function in the way they discriminate between the two men's responses to their situations.

Four films which offer spectacular exploitation of the beauties of the Australian countryside without adequately integrating them into their narrative structures are Kevin Dobson's *The Mango Tree* (1977), George Miller's *The Man from Snowy River* and Igor Auzins' *We of the Never Never* (both 1982), and Auzins' *The Coolangatta Gold* (1984). The luxuriance of the Queensland sugar cane plantations forms the background to *The Mango Tree*. In vivid contrast to the desert settings for *Gallipoli*, the tropical lushness of this scene carries with it a suggestion of debilitation for man (for example, the fanatical preacher who goes mad, the remittance man long since given over to drink) as well as a fertile setting for burgeoning youth. *The Mango Tree* is a slackly structured piece but Brian Probyn's images of a different sort of outback ravish the eye even when the film's human drama scarcely detains the mind. Dobson has clearly responded to the re-creations

Barker (Richard Moir) in the Victorian high country, in Ian Pringle's *The Plains of Heaven* (1982).

of time and place which are the chief strengths of Ronald McKie's shapeless source novel. Bundaberg in 1917 looks an idyllic place to grow up in. There are misty morning riverscapes, marvellous shots of red paths cut through the green abundance of cane fields, sandy streets with lonely-looking verandah posts, and weatherboard houses of unpretentious beauty or paint-flaking dilapidation. Scene after scene is unerringly composed and lit, credit no doubt due in varying degrees to director, cameraman and art director (Leslie Binns). In general, they have resisted the temptation to linger over Queensland's natural beauties, but they have been unable to conceal the fact that the gorgeousness of the film's patina covers an exceedingly rickety structure.

Queensland's famous Gold Coast, to which the geriatric South makes annual winter pilgrimages, is wittily used in Carl Schultz's cod private-eye thriller, *Goodbye Paradise* (1982), a *Big Sleep*-ish spoof with some handsome tracking shots of beach and river. However, it is Igor Auzins and his superlative cameraman, Keith Wagstaff, who have unequivocally celebrated the beauties of this strip of Australian coast in *The Coolangatta Gold*. The film has been much despised by local critics: newspaper reviewer Neil Jillett listed its ingredients as 'Beefcake, bombast and boredom, in roughly equal proportions',[17] and in general the most it was allowed was that it was good to look at. The point is that it is so sensationally good to look at that it leaves one pondering the screen's function as purveyor of sheer sensuous pleasure. There is, for instance, a breathtaking tracking shot of a motor cycle speeding along a coastal road, which cuts into a close-up of a wheel, then to a medium shot of swimmers in the surf before the camera pulls back for a wide shot of a vast stretch of beach. The symmetry of the shots and the excellence of the cutting, allied to the sheer physical beauty of the place, create their own excitement. The drama of family tensions which is played out against this background of surf beaches and banana plantations is never worked out in enough detail; but again and again the exhilaration deriving from colour, camera angles, and editing, abetted by a derivative but still exciting score (Bill Conti) acts as compensation. At its best the film (which must be seen on a wide screen) contrives through its visual panache to give some vitality to its human relationships and to the competition which gives the film its name.

The Coolangatta Gold is immensely more entertaining than Auzin's previous film, *We of the Never Never*. Apart from the near-epical sweep of the physical setting, the latter is a numbingly slow and dramatically pointless account of the attempts of a white woman, Mrs Aeneas Gunn (Angela Punch-McGregor), to come to terms with outback life and its inhabitants, both white stockmen and Aboriginals. Here the wide-screen beauties of northern Australia, and its daunting potential for extremes of physical hardship, do little more than provide a picturesque background for a series of unrealized thematic possibilities. Tom Ryan rightly draws attention to 'the glorious tracking shot across a vast empty landscape behind the opening credits', and sees in it 'a movement forward, morally and emotionally, into a new world'.[18] The rest of the film, unfortunately, fails to sustain this high promise.

The same complaint — picturesqueness devoid of drama — is almost true of *The Man From Snowy River*. It offers stunning vistas of rugged mountain country but its makers have succumbed to every cliché of horsemen against the sky so that the actual rigours of the mountain country are romanticized. A. B. Paterson's ballad on which it is based, though scarcely great poetry, does give a much firmer sense of the harsh individuality of the bush. It is difficult country and Paterson catches this in suggestions of 'flint-stones flying' and 'fallen timber', and he also catches a laconic, necessarily adventurous response to the physical surface of the place that is a long way from his anglicizing predecessors (such as Henry Kendall) and nearer to the stiff challenges of the bush. *Snowy River* is often wonderful to look at; in fact, it would be a splendid film for deaf people, since almost every spoken word is a platitude, and this has the effect of reducing the environment to mere scenery. Further, during the climactic search through the mountain country for the missing colt, despite incidental felicities (for example, as the camera catches horses making near-vertical descents), the editing does not always work in the interests of narrative clarity. As a narrative, the film is careless and banal in its account of the boy finding his manhood (etc.); it is content to rely on its great natural advantage: the awesome countryside itself.

Filming George Miller's *The Man from Snowy River* (1982) in the Australian Alps.

The Man from Snowy River is in fact unusually old-fashioned in its use of the landscape, presenting the sort of story of bush hardihood more common in the 1920s and 1930s. The bush virtues were more unequivocally celebrated then than in the more sceptical 1970s and 1980s. In the earlier period, the Sydney-or-the-Bush dichotomy was easily settled by reference to the manly virtues engendered by rural life; in the later, while city life has been increasingly the site of concern and disillusion on the part of Australian film-makers, the bush is no longer generally seen as a simple romantic alternative. The Nullarbor setting for the long central section of Richard Franklin's *Roadgames* is just as dangerous as the urban edges of the film and the continent. The notion of the bush as offering any sort of pastoral escapism has never been seriously countenanced in Australian literature. An Anglo-Australian author, Martin Boyd, tries to reproduce a European idea of pastoral in an Australian setting in several novels (for example, *Outbreak of Love*), but the Australian landscape cannot generally accommodate it. Essentially urban films such as Michael Pattinson's *Street Hero* (1984) and Gil Brealey's *Annie's Coming Out* (1984) can suddenly surprise by long, lyrical overhead shots of the countryside, as their protagonists make brief sorties away from the pressures of their everyday lives. However, there is no suggestion of a genuine rural alternative to those lives; these are just fleeting moments between one place and another.

Films such as *The Man From Snowy River* and *We of the Never Never* present a landscape which is demanding as well as rewarding but, generally, they are not successful in integrating this perception with the kinds of human dramas enacted in the spectacular settings. Part of the success of one of the major films of the revival, Gillian Armstrong's *My Brilliant Career* (1979), is due to the very intelligent way in which the landscapes depicted become external indices for the ups and downs of the heroine, Sybylla (Judy Davis). Yearning for a place in the world of art and culture, stifled by the dusty rigours of life at her father's poverty-stricken property, Possum Gully, she is transported to the verdancy of Caddagat where her grandmother (Aileen Britton) and Aunt Helen (Wendy Hughes) lead lives of gracious, if complacent, serenity. In this gentler landscape, Sybylla's burgeoning spirit has room to breathe and grow, and the process continues when she visits Five Bob Downs, the still grander home of Harry Beecham (Sam Neill), her 'one and only love'. In these two places, man has brought nature to heel: there are elegant gardens that act as a buffer between the homestead and the bush. At the lowest ebb of her life, she acts as governess to the children of a slovenly but prosperous selector, and she returns from there to Possum Gully where nothing has changed except herself. She refuses the possibility of a rich marriage, committing herself voluntarily to the arduous ways of her home, as if in coming to terms with it she will find the means to be herself, and to achieve the potential she believes she has.

The quietly optimistic ending shows her tapping her fingers in suppressed excitement, as another dawn comes up over the landscape whose beauties and austerities she has thoroughly internalized.

The most perceptive film-makers have not found the Australian land-scape one to be taken for granted or to be used as a mere background. They have seized on its contradictions — its great age only very recently the object of white endeavours; the hostility of its emptiness and craggy bush as well as its sudden splendours — and made drama of them and of the lives that have had to come to terms with them. To do so was both shrewd and necessary in the growth of an indigenous film industry whose products might interest Australians and others.

1   Chris Wallace-Crabbe, *Melbourne or the Bush*, Melbourne: Angus & Robertson, 1974, p.8.

2   Joan Lindsay, *Picnic at Hanging Rock*, Melbourne: Penguin Books, 1970, p.8.

3   *Ibid.*, p.7.

4   *Ibid.*, p.19.

5   'Peter Weir — Towards the Centre', interviewed by Brian McFarlane and Tom Ryan, *Cinema Papers*, No.34, September-October, 1981, p.325.

6   Cliff Green, *Picnic at Hanging Rock, A Film*, Melbourne: Cheshire, 1975, p.72.

7   'Pauline Kael and the Australian Cinema', interviewed by Sue Mathews, *Cinema Papers*, No. 40, October, 1982, p.421.

8   John Pym, '*The Chant of Jimmie Blacksmith*', *Monthly Film Bulletin*, London: British Film Institute, London, March 1979, p.41.

9   Thomas Keneally, *The Chant of Jimmie Blacksmith*, Melbourne: Penguin Books, 1973, p.148.

10   *Ibid*, p.148.

11   Fred Schepisi, *The Chant of Jimmie Blacksmith* (unpublished screenplay, p.193), Australia: The Film House.

12   Scott Murray, '*Long Weekend*', *Cinema Papers* No.20, March-April, 1979, p.305.

13   Almos Maksay, '*Mad Max 2*', *Cinema Papers*, No.36, February 1982, p.75.

14   Geoff Mayer, 'Comedy', in Scott Murray (ed.), *The New Australian Cinema* Melbourne: Thomas Nelson, 1980, p.54.

15   John Dingwall, *Sunday Too Far Away!* Melbourne: Heinemann Educational Australia, 1978, p.1.

16   Keith Connelly, 'Social Realism', in Murray, p.29.

17   Neil Jillett, 'Silly and careless mixture of beefcake and boredom', *The Age*, Melbourne, 20 November, 1984, p.14.

18   Tom Ryan, 'Australian Films of the Year' in Al Clark (ed.), *The Film Year Book: Volume Two*, Melbourne: Currey O'Neil Ross, 1984, Australian Supplement, p.5.

6 The Cities: The Way We Live Now

And her five cities, like five teeming sores,
Each drains her: a vast parasite robber-state
Where second-hand Europeans pullulate
Timidly on the edge of alien shores.

A. D. Hope: 'Australia'

Highway by highway the remorseless cars
Strangle the city, put it out of pain,
Its limbs still kicking feebly on the hills.

Chris Wallace-Crabbe: 'Melbourne'

Safe behind shady carports, sleeping under
the stars of the commonwealth and nylon gauze ...
... safe behind lawns and blondwood doors, in houses
of glass. No one throws stones.

David Malouf: 'Suburban'

Poets, as the above quotations ranging over thirty-odd years suggest, have not dealt kindly with Australian cities. One can expect nothing vividly Australian, Hope implies, in the site of 'second-hand Europeans'; Wallace-Crabbe sees Melbourne as having succumbed to anonymous (and, elsewhere in the poem, platitudinous) over-development; and Malouf indicts the unreflecting conformity of the suburbs. Playwrights from Ray Lawler to David Williamson have stressed the shabby, alienating, and dangerous aspects of city life; novelist Patrick White has never ceased to pillory the suburbs for their pursuit of materialism and mediocrity; and the painter John Brack in his *Collins Street 5 pm* (1965) depicts the uniform pallor, the erasure of individuality, in a soulless metropolis.

Nevertheless, most Australians now live in the cities at the edges of the continent, huddling on the coast as if for a quick getaway, looking outward (Europe, America) rather than inward (the awesome emptiness behind the coastal mountains) for the signs by which to organize their lives. For better and/or worse, the cities are where Australians live and a film industry in touch with the 'national life' can hardly afford to ignore what goes on in them. If the rural landscape so brilliantly interpreted in films such as Nicolas Roeg's *Walkabout* (1971) and Fred Schepisi's *The Chant of Jimmie Black-smith* (1978) offers images that are at once intransigently Australian, the cities — and the films set in them — produce a life showing more in common with cities elsewhere. Shopping malls and office blocks, plushy hotels and suburban sprawl are internationally recognizable; so are the problems (of unemployment, of homelessness, of a competitive, capitalistic society) that assume high visibility in the city scene.

Because the best-known films of the recent revival have been set in rural Australia, this has tended to obscure the fact that there has been, through-out the past fifteen years, a steady trickle of 'city films'. The two notable outback films of 1971, *Wake in Fright* and *Walkabout,* each presented an overseas director (Ted Kotcheff, Nicolas Roeg), excited by the empty inland on which most of Australia turns its back; and the two films that really launched the revival, critically and commercially — Peter Weir's *Picnic at Hanging Rock* and Ken Hannam's *Sunday Too Far Away* (both 1975) — were set in wide rural landscapes, as was the 1976 box-office success, Henri Safran's *Storm Boy.* Yet, it is important to note that there were some important urban films from the start of the revival: Brian Kavanagh's *A City's Child* (1971), Tim Burstall's *Petersen* (1974), Donald Crombie's *Caddie* (1976), Bruce Beresford's *Don's Party* (1976), Michael Thornhill's *The FJ Holden* (1977), Peter Weir's *The Last Wave* (1977); and so the trickle goes on until in 1982 when eight worthwhile urban films were re-leased: David Stevens' *The Clinic,* Michael Caulfield's *Fighting Back,* Phil Noyce's *Heatwave,* Paul Cox's *Lonely Hearts,* Ken Cameron's *Monkey Grip,* Michael Pattinson's *Moving Out,* Henri Safran's *Norman Loves Rose,* and Gillian Armstrong's *Starstruck.* These films may not have much more in common than their setting (and their use of and response to it are notably diverse) but that in itself is important in the context of the new Australian cinema. It is not just, or even mainly, a cinema in retreat from the way life is lived by most of the country's population: its insights into and exploration of that life provide a valuable record and reflection of late twentieth century urban Australian people. And 'cities' in Australia means essentially the large metropolitan centres, since Australia, unlike England or the US, is not rich in provincial cities which have a thriving life of their own.

In most of the films to be considered here, the city has been the site of realist fictions. Urban life and the *milieu* which produces it have not elicited the elements of the romantic or the epic one finds still in those films set in rural landscapes. There is no Australian film such as Woody Allen's *Man-hattan* (1979) or David Lean's *Summer Madness* (1955). No one has yet sung a cinematic hymn to an Australian city: even the obvious visual invi-tation of Sydney's Harbour has been only tentatively, even perfunctorily, accepted: there is no film that does for Sydney what Kenneth Slessor's most famous poem, 'Five Bells', does. And no film does for a city what Roeg's *Walkabout* does for the outback or matches Igor Auzins' celebration of Queensland's Gold Coast in *The Coolangatta Gold* (1984).

*

It is possible to distinguish between those films which have engaged with city life in ways that present the city as a protagonist in their dramas and those which make other uses of it. The *distinctiveness* of city life is more emphatically felt in the former; the latter have in mind ideas other than the explicit examination of man's relation to his urban environment. This chapter will be chiefly concerned with the former group in which one finds certain key recurring elements; but, first, it will be worth looking at those other films which in one way or another make use of a city setting. These include:

- those which use the city as a background for period pieces;
- intimate films and genre films which take it for granted as the setting for most contemporary Australian lives and therefore do not foreground its documentation;
- those in which it is felt as a presence and a pressure even when not physically especially obtrusive.

Those films which use the city as a background for period pieces are, not surprisingly, in view of the extra difficulties and expense of authentic staging, comparatively few. Donald Crombie's *Caddie* (1976) and *Kitty and the Bagman* (1982), and Kevin Dobson's *Squizzy Taylor* (1982) are the only full-scale city period reconstruction pieces. Phil Noyce's *Newsfront* (1978) and Sophia Turkiewicz's *Silver City* (1984) both offer the authentic feel of the cities in which they are partly set, but they are set in a past so recent (late 1940s, early 1950s) as not to make such major demands in matters of production design and location, in which both, incidentally, excel. They also open up important historical and sociological issues that remove them from the limiting category of 'period piece'.

Not that *Caddie's* interest is exhausted by such a description either. It appeared at a time when several important films were set in the past: *The Devil's Playground* (1976), *Eliza Fraser* (1976), *Break of Day* (1976), *The Getting of Wisdom* (1977), *The Mango Tree* (1977), and *The Picture Show Man* (1977) among others. This led many reviewers to be 'critical of the period boom, arguing that the films were an escape into the past and that Australia needed film-makers who were prepared to confront the present [ignoring the fact] that several film-makers were intelligently tackling 'modern' issues in these films'.[1] *Caddie,* for one, is eloquent about the position of the single woman in a male-dominated society, as well as offering a loving re-creation of Sydney during the Depression: cable trams, job-seeking queues, itinerant rabbit-salesmen, and the notorious 6 o'clock swill of the pub where Caddie works as barmaid. Crombie's other urban period film, *Kitty and the Bagman*, is a lively account of the rivalry of two underworld Czarinas (Liddy Clark and the splendidly bellicose Val Lehman) and of assorted racketeers in 1920s Sydney. Its re-creation of the period, though carefully selective, suffers somewhat from the budget restraint that inhibits a fuller, firmer sense of the city at large. Further, it is a little over-long: a tighter narrative structure might have made more of its play on loyalties and trust and betrayal among whores, cops and a corrupt judiciary. However, its big scenes, such as the raid on the 'illegal casino' (= brothel) run by Kitty (Clark), are well-staged; and John Stanton as the Bagman, whose protection Kitty finally accepts for good, reveals a striking star presence too little used in Australian films. *Kitty and the Bagman* is a minor piece but it exhibits Crombie's characteristic attention to detail of place and character.

The best of Kevin Dobson's *Squizzy Taylor* is in its picture of seedy alleys and warehouses, offering an unromanticized look at the back streets of big city crime. Taylor, a notorious gangster who terrorized 1920s Melbourne, was the subject of a documentary by Nigel Buesst in 1967. In the newer film, Dobson, whose previous directorial credit was *The Mango Tree*, shows himself again adept at evoking an earlier period, claiming in an interview that: 'There is not one little piece that is not absolutely correct. Some of the places might have been moved around but that is what Melbourne looked like in the 1920s.'[2] However, as in his early film, he also shows himself deficient in pulling together a slack-minded screenplay (by Roger Simpson). As demystification of the gangster hero, small, mean, and vicious, the film needs a more compelling central presence than David Atkins'; as a gangster melodrama, it fatally lacks pace and drive, as much a fault of

Gangster Squizzy (David Atkins) dances with his girlfriend Ida (Kim Lewis) in Kevin Dobson's *Squizzy Taylor* (1982).

lethargic editing as of a director whose forté is his feeling for time and place and not for narrative rhythms.

Among those films identified above as taking the city setting for granted, one finds intimate films like Paul Cox's *Lonely Hearts* (1982), *Man of Flowers* (1983), and *My First Wife* (1984), and Brian Kavanagh's *A City's Child* (1971). Cox's films are primarily small-scale studies of somewhat bizarre relationships but they offer, almost incidentally, the spectacle of a director in love with Melbourne's Edwardian suburbia, all but fetishistically obsessed with the beauties of lead-lighting and wooden tracery. The influence of suburban mores is not a negligible narrative element, but the real interest of these three striking films is in how they dramatize certain kinds of sexual relationships. Brian Kavanagh, in *A City's Child*, uses suburbia as a commonplace setting for a tense examination of the fantasy life of a lonely spinster (Monica Maughan). Suburbia may be felt as an alienating influence but the film's chief concerns are psychological, not sociological.

The genre films take their city ambience for granted (although they are not necessarily perfunctory in its representation) because their interest lies in the re-activation of various conventions in a new setting. Only Phil Noyce's *Heatwave* really exploits the thriller potential of a large city in ways that recall such masterworks as *The Maltese Falcon* (1941) or *The Asphalt Jungle* (1950), or even such lesser urban thrillers as Peter Yates's *Bullitt* (1970), John Farrow's *The Big Clock* (1947), and Jules Dassin's *The Naked City* (1948), which so effectively created a sense of the dangerousness of a huge city sweltering in the heat, or, more recently, Australian Richard Franklin's dazzling use of San Antonio, Texas, in *Cloak and Dagger* (1984). By comparison, Australian genre film-makers have failed to make striking use of urban tensions and paranoia, of criminal underworlds, or of the visual threat of burgeoning high-rise development. The excellences of Franklin's Australian-made thrillers, *Patrick* (1978) and *Roadgames* (1981), really lie in other directions, although each makes marginal use of city landscapes to good, sinister effect.

Bruce Beresford's efficient heist film, *Money Movers* (1978), involving the complexly master-minded robbery of a counting-house money van, contrasts its chilly interiors with some effective city scapes, as trucks loom over elevated roads. As a thriller, it cuts effectively among drivers, police, crooks, and counting-house workers, and its slick, economic narrative procedures employ several sequences which thoroughly understand the power of parallel editing. It hints at, but disappointingly does not pursue, connections between crime and a brutally 'ocker' macho aggressiveness (glimpsed in derisive talk among the gang about 'poofters' and someone's girlfriend as a 'little sort'). *Money Movers* scarcely extends Beresford, one of the ablest craftsmen of the Australian revival, but it does display his capacity to present a conventional story, with conventional characters (disenchanted

90

ex-cop, flabby master-mind, etc.), with brisk narrative control and an un-obtrusive sense of how the operations of a large city generate crime.

There is less to be said for Simon Wincer's *Snapshot* (1979) or Terry Ohlsson's *Scobie Malone* (1975). In *Snapshot*, just after the credits, a girl (Sigrid Thornton) is running through busy city streets, the camera working to imbue buildings with eloquent menace as she runs. It is a neat anti-climax that she is only late for work, and, although the rest of the film lacks such a firm tone or narrative control, its one persistent virtue is its use of the city as a source of potential excitement and of escape from the dreary little suburban houses which epitomize the life from which its heroine wants to escape. If it is not the gritty urban thriller one would like to see an Aus-tralian film-maker tackling, it offers a marked advance on Ohlsson's shoddy *Scobie Malone* (based on *Helga's Web*, a Jon Cleary *roman policier*) which adopts a numbingly simple-minded approach to its hearty mixture of viol-ence and sex, corruption in high places and thuggery in low. Centring on the murder of an avaricious and notably unsubtle call-girl, Helga Brand, it engages in a specious moral sententiousness: 'Is there one rule for them the rich and mighty and one for the Helga Brands?' asks the eponymous detec-tive-stud (Jack Thompson). Unlike, say, *The Maltese Falcon* which wore its urban morality with organic laconicism, as much a part of its dark view of the way things are as the sleazy streets and sleazier people, *Scobie Malone* merely *imposes* it on a rickety narrative structure, mouthed piously by a thuggish hero. The film (incredibly, co-written and produced by Hollywood veteran Casey Robinson) fails either to take its city settings quite for granted or to use sun-drenched Sydney to contrast the moral squalors of its story.

The comedies, *Norman Loves Rose* and Michael Robertson's *The Best of Friends* (1982), and the musical, *Starstruck*, are all set in Sydney, each offering a different perspective on it. *Norman Loves Rose*, one of the most underrated films of the revival[3] and its *only* graceful comedy, is firmly set in well-upholstered middle-class suburbia. Its chief characters are Jewish and well-do-do, and, though it uses its Sydney locations unemphatically, it is distinctively a city film in its evocation of the pressures that bear on the emotional lives of its characters; pressures aggravated by family tensions, played for comedy but, underlying this, touching and serious. *The Best of Friends* is a largely witless go at a swinging comedy in which a twenty year old friendship founders when it turns sexual. The camera pans elegant ter-races, tracks the car of the friends (Graeme Blundell and Angela Punch-McGregor) through streets and freeways, lingers over Sydney skyscapes, and tries — haplessly — to conjure up a world of trendy professionals. The film unfortunately has no more feeling for place than people, neither scriptwriter nor stars having much gift for sophisticated comedy.

Much more likeable is *Starstruck*, which is an engaging attempt to breathe new, *Australian* life into venerable clichés: the kids-putting-on-a-

Angus (Ross O'Donovan) and Jackie (Jo Kennedy) in Gillian Armstrong's *Starstruck* (1982).

show, the singer-getting-a-big-chance, and the saving-the-old-home-from-the-receivers narrative elements are all there, and given the kiss of life by Gillian Armstrong. The fourteen-year-old entrepreneur, Angus (Ross O'Donovan), determined to make a star of his cousin Jackie (Jo Kennedy), is an amusing invention, and it is a nice touch that the 'old home' is a rather run-down pub near Sydney's Circular Quay. The pub is set more or less under the Harbour Bridge, and that other Sydney icon, the Opera House, represents the show biz goal of the young. In a climactic alternation between pub and Opera House, Jo wins the $25,000 that will keep the pub out of the brewery's hands while the clientele watch it all on television. The pub — lavatory tiles and red laminex — and the cutting-down-to-size dialogue ('You wouldn't give this to a Jap on Anzac Day' says a customer of his counter-lunch) establish one aspect of the Sydney scene, the lively use of exteriors suggesting a place where anything might happen (unlike staider Melbourne) is another.

Tony Petersen (Jack Thompson), the electrician who aspires to University education, in Tim Burstall's *Petersen* (1974).

Among those films in which aspects of the city are felt as pressures on the lives of those who live there, but in which the city is not physically obtrusive, one might include *Petersen, Don's Party, The Last Wave*, Jim Sharman's *The Night the Prowler* (1978), and *The Clinic*.

Petersen received an unwarranted critical mauling when it first appeared, reviewers deciding that director Tim Burstall was ploughing the same 'ocker' sex territory he had so successfully exploited in *Alvin Purple* (1973). Several years later, David Stratton considered that 'apart from one or two relatively minor lapses, *Petersen* is a very fine film indeed':[4] the truth lies somewhere between this and the earlier diatribes. In fact, Burstall's account (from a screenplay by David Williamson) of an electrician, Peterson (Jack Thompson) who is studying for an Arts degree at the University of Melbourne manages some trenchant commentary on the dissatisfactions of a suburban life which hems in aspiration and of an academic world with little understanding of such dissatisfaction. That is, it offers by implication a picture of a city in which categorization by class and education is the norm. The representation of sexual relationships certainly takes advantage of the easing of censorship in the 1970s, and the film does dart about among contemporary issues (women's lib, abortion) without examining them seriously. *But* it does take its hero and his dilemmas seriously: the ideology questioned and criticized is equally that of the educated middle classes and of the beer-drinking suburban 'ockerdom' from which Petersen tries to escape. His values are tested in two jaunts to the country (to an old friend whose horizons are wholly material and to his clergyman father) but his problems are essentially those of a sprawling, alienating city, and neither jaunt offers any answers.

Apart from an early morning scene in a polling booth on Election Day, 25 October 1969, and a brief scene in a motel, *Don's Party* is wholly set in and around the suburban home of Don and Kath Henderson (John Hargreaves and Jeanie Drynan). Bruce Beresford, while resisting the temptation to 'open out' David Williamson's play (Williamson also wrote the screenplay), and his brilliant cameraman, Don McAlpine, have prowled in and out of rooms and into the yard, with such ease that the film acquires a fully cinematic life, avoiding criticisms of staginess. This is nevertheless a film of city life, of people whose aspirations have been moulded in a metropolitan ideology, whether it has made them trendily leftist or timidly conservative like Simon (Graeme Blundell), the inhibited Liberal wimp in a safari suit at a party of raucous Labor voters. Their backgrounds are the University, the professions, suburban affluence and city modishness, and the *mise-en-scène* is perceptively worked to establish this. The city itself is scarcely seen, but its formative influence on their lives is firmly present: the parallel between Labor's defeat in the election, recorded on the television and increasingly ignored throughout the evening, and the growing disenchantment of the guests at the party (between Party and party, as it were) is distinctly the product of a city phenomenon. In Australia at least, Don's kind of party and guests would scarcely be expected outside a large city, which is not to say that some of the film's thematic concerns (for example, the confrontation of various kinds of failure) are limited to the *milieu* in which Williamson's screenplay enacts them. The film has a fine, rancid atmosphere and, in Philip French's words, 'captures those peculiar rhythms, that alternation between periods of dim lassitude and sudden frenetic action one associates with lengthy drunken parties.'[5]

Like *Picnic at Hanging Rock* which preceded it, *The Last Wave* also dramatizes a seemingly stable society about to disintegrate under the threat of unknown fears hovering at its edges. In the later film, the suburban comforts of a professional middle-class home in Sydney prove unequal to the challenge offered to the lawyer David Burton (Richard Chamberlain) by the disturbing intimations of his connection with a pre-European civilization. His tasteful home and agreeable wife (Olivia Hamnett) and children cannot save him from increasingly perilous intervention in the killing of a tribal Aboriginal in Sydney. And the shadowy, rain-shrouded streets and skyscrapers of the city become inadequate bulwarks against the irrational but profoundly disturbing sense of the primitive, irrational forces at work in man and nature. In terms of conventional narrative, *The Last Wave* loses some of its impetus towards the end. Weir has said: 'My interest itself lies in those unknown areas, not so much in finding neat endings. There are no answers; there is no ending'.[6] Indeed, there was no money for the more elaborate ending Weir wanted; however, the film, despite some confusions

Chris Lee (Gulpilil) and his tribal elder Charlie (Nandjiwarra Amagula) explain tribal laws to David Burton (Richard Chamberlain) in Peter Weir's *The Last Wave* (1977).

and pretensions, is an often-unnerving exploration of civilized urban man pushed beyond the usual safe parameters of his life of work, home and leisure.

The Night the Prowler impugns a stultifying middle-class urban culture. Since it is adapted by Patrick White from one of his own short stories, it is no surprise to find that the film flays almost everyone except its lumpish heroine, Felicity (Kerry Walker), and the handful of oddly assorted initiates privy to White's vision of a life beyond that of respectable, aspiring suburbia. It is the satire of the latter which is best done in the film: White is an old hand at this sort of thing and Sharman's flashy direction is reverently at his service. The *sense* of a large city's informing the thinking and lives of the heroine, 'liberated' by an assault that did not happen, and her family and friends, is quite powerfully felt; when Felicity takes to the Sydney streets and parks on her nocturnal prowlings, the film fleetingly suggests the potential terror of the city. However, whatever is dramatically promising in the situation is in the end vitiated by a screenplay and direction more concerned with making points than understanding people.

'Understanding people' is precisely the strength of *The Clinic*. It adopts a day-in-the-life-of approach to a busy VD clinic, unwisely trying to pull together an episodic narrative by stressing the growing respect of a young medical student, Paul (Simon Burke), for Eric (Chris Haywood), the humane gay doctor at the clinic. The film scarcely leaves the clinic and does not need to give a firm sense of its being part of a large city. There are glimpses of

95

Medical student, Paul (Simon Burke), and gay doctor, Eric (Chris Haywood), in David Steven's *The Clinic* (1982).

busy streets, certainly, but it is the sharply observed come-and-go of patients that imbues the film with an unexpectedly rich vein of human warmth, so that the clinic becomes a reluctantly-sought but gratefully-reached haven in a busy, impersonal metropolis. The film is concerned with more helpful, more sympathetic sex education, and its ample comedy is at the expense of neither problem nor sufferer.

*

The films considered so far have not so much specifically *engaged* with the city as been aware of it as a presence, sometimes cheerfully bustling, sometimes oppressive in relation to man, a presence which, however, they have more or less taken for granted. The most important films from the point of view of this chapter are those which address themselves directly to some of the key pressure points in urban living. They show a striking awareness of both city man's lack of solitude *and* of his increased difficulty in forming and sustaining relationships. There is no sense of people pulling together in these films: the urban films arrive at no sort of cross-sectoral consensus. The characters in these films remain clearly blocked out, estranged, from other groups of the society in which they live. There is, for instance, no *rapprochement* between those who seek to preserve threatened terrace houses, in either Donald Crombie's *The Killing of Angel Street* (1981) or *Heatwave,* and the business interests which want them down to make way for high-rise growth. Nor is there any suggestion of intersection between the shifting liaisons of inner suburban life in *Monkey Grip* and the middle-class background from which the heroine comes; or between the haves and have-nots in John Duigan's *Winter of Our Dreams* (1981).

If there is no suggestion of understanding between urban classes in these films, in those which focus on city *youth* there is, characteristically, open hostility between the young protagonists and the representatives of middle-class authority: 'parents, teachers, and the law' to whom generations of Australian schoolchildren used to promise weekly allegiance. If these three sources of authority are not necessarily middle-class in origin, the values they espouse tend to be so, and to be seen as such by disaffected youth. A closer look at some of the city youth films will reveal several other aspects in common; and in the disposition of their sympathies these films recall that famous batch of British realist films of the late 1950s and early 1960s (*Room at the Top, A Kind of Loving, Saturday Night and Sunday Morning* and others): these were also the product of middle-class, mostly university-educated men directing their sympathetic interest to the urban working-class young.

The most significant interpreter in cinema to date of the harsh realities of Australian cities is John Duigan, whose *Mouth to Mouth* (1978) struck a very refreshing note of immediacy in relation to urban problems of youth, homelessness, unemployment, and neglected old age. When it first appeared, the films exciting most attention were the period films, which, whatever their contemporary relevance, displayed this at a cushioning remove in time. The contemporary setting of a large city geared to the lives of a remote uncaring bourgeoisie (affluent hotel guests, employment officers, etc.) confronted audiences directly with the plight of homeless youth on the dole, without the distancing glow that inevitably attaches to, say, the heroines of *Caddie* or *My Brilliant Career* (1979). Those are films relevant to aspects of present-day Australian life but they offer in a sense *illustrations* of contemporary problems rather than the urgency of the problems themselves. This is not to make Duigan sound like Stanley Kramer: There is nothing portentous about *Mouth to Mouth* and no suggestion that its significance is merely being imported into the film. Rather he has a filmmaker's eye for what will create an air of social immediacy; he knows how to use his young actors (and the alcoholic old derelict played by Walter Pym) and his *mise-en-scène* to achieve the contrasts between, say, affluence and poverty, between indifference and cautious relationship. The four teenagers, with nowhere permanent to live and no prospect of satisfying employment, are treated with sympathy and a subtle sense of dramatic alternations by Duigan. The two girls, Carrie (Kim Krejus) and Jeannie

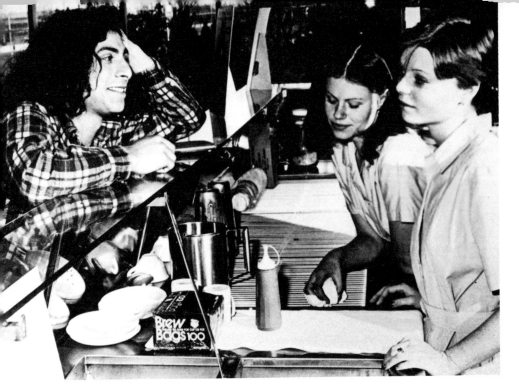

Serge (Sergio Frazetto) chats up Carrie (Kim Krejus) and Jeannie
(Sonia Peat) in John Duigan's *Mouth to Mouth* (1978).

(Sonia Peat), are city-wise girls who have been 'inside', and are now on the
run from an institution: Carrie, dark and pinched with experience, Jeannie,
fresh-faced and fair, are attracted to their physical opposites, and, with
hindsight, the outcome for each seems to have been written in their faces.
The boys, Serge (Sergio Frazetto) and Tim (Ian Gilmour), are from the
country ('the wild men of Wonthaggi', Carrie mocks them): shy, Anglo-
Saxon Tim finds sexual relationship with Carrie difficult, whereas the less
inhibited Serge and Jeannie have an easier rapport. Both relationships foun-
der on the girls' money-making ventures — shop-lifting and 'escort work'
— and the future for all four is bleak. But the film, curiously, is not: Tom
Cowan's fluid camera work, tracking and panning through streets and cafes,
brilliantly observing both cramped interiors and a beach scene which begins
like a British realist film idyll but ends more soberly. The film was shot in
four weeks, on a very tight budget; it nevertheless remains the Australian
cinema's sharpest perception of the drab hopelessness at the fringes of
urban life.

Michael Thornhill's *The FJ Holden* shares with *Mouth to Mouth* a sympathetic interest in the uninviting vistas of urban youth, the setting this time
being the desolate Western suburbs of Sydney. It is a less shapely film than
Duigan's, less formally interesting, but in its episodic, slice-of-life approach
to a few months in the life of a wrecking-yard worker, Kevin (Paul Couzens),
it offers sharp insights into an alarmingly sterile round of work, boozing, sex

Kevin (Paul Couzens), Anne (Eva Dickinson) and car in Michael
Thornhill's *The FJ Holden* (1977).

and brawling. His affair with Anne (Eva Dickinson), a shop assistant in a
large, characterless urban mall, begins in the back seat of the eponymous FJ
(in 1953, the first all-Australian car), and founders on his insensitivity to her
needs. Eva Dickinson, seventeen at the time, is remarkably fine as the girl
already bearing in her face and eyes and voice a lifetime's experience of
boring work — both in the shop and at home where she is surrogate mother
to two small brothers and housekeeper to her deserted father (superbly
sketched by Ray Marshall).

The FJ Holden loses little by its narrative looseness because its real
strength lies elsewhere. First, in the way the film's relationships are developed and made to comment on each other: Anne and Kevin have little to say
to each other, except for laconic exchanges of information; Kevin's parents,
despite his mother's efforts, suggest a similarly empty relationship. There
are yawning gaps between sexes, between generations, between classes,
and between youth and authority (the omnipresent police are their natural
enemies); and the nature of these gaps is tellingly dramatized in a crowded
party scene where *mise-en-scène* and tracking camera authoritatively
reveal the barriers to relationship in this environment. Second, in its observation of a suburbia which ranges only from tacky to tasteless: the film has a
very sharp eye for the social discriminations that can be made wordlessly
through the *mise-en-scène*. Kevin's family, a rung or two further up the
ladder, live in comparative comfort (kitschy decoration, candles and wine to

impress Anne at 'tea'), whereas Anne's runs on minimal lines. This suburbia may be dreary but it achieves an authentic note of poignancy when David Gribble's camera catches it at sunset or dawn in a series of wide-reaching crane shots. That these do not seem gratuitously 'lyrical' but, instead, touching in the contrast they offer to the limited suburban lives beneath those red tiled roofs says something for the skill and feeling with which Thornhill has evoked those lives. Further, the brightly painted yellow FJ represents the level of aspiration in an urban wasteland in which the potential of youth hardly stands a chance of realization.

Those two films — *Mouth to Mouth* and *The FJ Holden* — set the pattern for the youth-in-the-cities films which proliferated in the 1980s. There is an ideological consistency about these films. The environment of drably industrialized suburbs, garish streets, flashy threadbare entertainment, and quick carnal exchanges, properly attracts the film-makers' sympathies. They are almost invariably focused on working-class lives, observed with a shrewdness and compassion that do credit to their largely middle-class makers. The almost inevitable drift into petty crime, either because of the lure of easy money or because society offers no workable alternative; the fragility of family structures, offering little to support teenagers, either through parental unawareness of their problems or through the peculiarly urban pressures at work on the family unit; the essentially middle-class attitudes and consequent irrelevance of the schools; the shoddily enticing world of the streets and their violent potential: these are recurring narrative elements in these films. Formally, they are apt to be episodic in their approach, aspiring to slice-of-life verisimilitude rather than to structural niceties or to the diegetic causality of the classic Hollywood realist texts. Their ideological positions are often established through alternation between sequences showing teenagers relaxed in their own worlds and those depicting the pressures of, say, home or school. And this alternation is underscored stylistically by the contrast between the pervasive tracking shots as kids take to the streets and the cramped cutting of the sequences in their homes. There is, as well, a characteristic use of long shots of industrial works which act as a sort of visual metonymy for the grimly charmless world in which these dramas of youthful frustration and rebellion are acted out.

The critical success of *Mouth to Mouth* in 1978 did not inspire a rush of similar films. Esben Storm's *In Search of Anna* (1977)[7] makes skilful use of a film-long process of alternation to contrast the journey north of its hero Tony (Richard Moir) with a liberated young woman called Sam (Judy Morris) and the big-city menace which has led to his spending five years in gaol. Its chief interest is in the growth of the relationship but it achieves some dramatically telling scenes of the fringes of urban crime and the grimness of Tony's suburban home where his mother has committed suicided during his term in gaol and where his Greek-speaking father is afraid of and for him.

Don McLennan's *Hard Knocks* (1980) also adopts a distinctively fragmented narrative style in pursuing the development of its central character, Sam (Tracy Mann), as she moves between the world of fashion-modelling and that 'shadowy no-man's-land where the police practise their bloodhound instincts by hunting those who are already marked by society as victims'.[8] Despite resourceful performances from Richard Moir and Tracy Mann as their respective protagonists, neither of these films, formally more ambitious than most of the city and youth films, enjoyed the commercial success of Bruce Beresford's *Puberty Blues* (1981). In the latter, the anti-authority aggression takes in parents and teachers as well as the law. In their desire for acceptance by the surfing fraternity of Cronulla Beach, Sydney, the two girls, Debbie (Nell Scofield) and Sue (Jad Capelja), are scornful of parental suggestions of finding 'friends at Fellowship' and utterly unimpressed by the headmaster (Charles Tingwell) who says: 'I don't understand you — you've a good IQ. You come from a good home.' Why, he implies, do they want to turn their backs on this to seek out the dangerous allurements of the city's streets and surf beaches? It is an intelligent, lively film in which the girls arrive at a dramatically satisfying decision to repudiate the male-dominated mores that have pushed them into increasingly dangerous territory.

From 1982, there was a steady stream of city-and-youth films, including *Fighting Back, Moving Out,* Haydn Keenan's *Going Down* (1982), Michael Pattinson's *Street Hero* (1984), and Ken Cameron's *Fast Talking* (1983). The best of these is *Moving Out* which introduces an ethnic element into the films of the youthful hazards of city life. Its title is ambivalent: it refers partly to the Italian family's move from the dreariness of inner Melbourne to the middle-class respectabilities of the other suburbs (the old home to be taken over by new arrivals from Italy); and partly to the young hero Gino (Vince Colosimo) who needs to move out from the family and who wants to stay in the area they are leaving in their search for the suburban good life. In an effectively sober ending, the family's ambition is achieved: the removal van is loaded and the family heads for the middle-class suburbs — with Gino, who hasn't yet reached the stage of moving out. Along the way, the film is very sensitive to his resentment of his parents' staying 'Wog', objecting to their talking Italian at home when he wants to be an Australian, and being an Australian for him is strutting down the streets to the pinball parlour, or smoking and drinking with his friends in an abandoned car. *Street Hero* has the same director, producer (Julie Monton), screenwriter (Jan Sardi) and cameraman (Vincent Monton), and again stars Vince Colosimo, this time as Vinnie, a seventeen-year-old rebel against any authority that stands in his way. He is a product of the hideous high-rise flats which disfigure parts of Melbourne's inner suburbs, of the streets they loom over, of the cramped tedium of the government school he attends, of the gambling headquarters of the local mafia, where the money to be made from crime makes education seem a laborious and unrewarding process, and of the 'Champion' coffee shop-cum-disco. These oppressive physical settings are represented with varying degrees of realism and stylization. The over-all effect is to romanticize street-wisdom at the expense of, say, formal education. There is also a jaunt to the country, when the Western City High School Orchestra visits the town of Romsey, and the film suggests an interesting shift in Australian values. It is no longer a case of corrupt city types and honest rural folks: the latter are 'yobbos' who get deservedly done by the WCH lads in their orchestra uniforms. The handsome views of the countryside on the way to Romsey have nothing to do with either the city kids or the local louts. The country, that is, provides no viable retreat from the scruffy world of the streets and petty crime which exert a major pull on Vinnie's aspirations.

Fighting Back's chief concern is with the efforts of a young teacher, John Embling (Lewis Fitz-Gerald), to reclaim a mentally and emotionally disturbed student, Tom (Paul Smith). The source of Tom's disturbance is his brutal father's desertion of him and his mother (a touching, detailed performance from Kris McQuade), and the site of its display is, variously, home, school, and the city streets. There is a shot of Tom walking in a suburban street with a grim city-scape behind him that suggests an intelligent understanding of the power of *mise-en-scène*. Ultimately, however, and in spite of the film's opening statement, 'What follows is a true story', *Fighting Back* is an old-fashioned and simplistic piece. Its intentions are exemplary but its treatment lacks the motivating complexity that would make it seem *dramatically* true.

Going Down ploughs familiar fields of inner city life — dope, discos, unemployment, messy communal living, prostitution, sex shops, poolrooms — and records it in an incessant flow of profanity, and with a rather more adventurous camera (Malcolm Richards) than usual. There is very little interest in its story of four young girls going on the town the night before one of them, Kylie (Tracy Mann) is due to fly to New York. Kylie is leaving 'because I'm scared of what's happening to me' and one is nagged by the feeling that she has too much intelligence and resourcefulness to have put up with the boring *milieu* the film presents. The film is worth noting only for the almost surreal quality it brings to its presentation of the city streets. In its use of colour, and in its compositions of skyscrapers which seem to drift and which at points dissolve into faces, it achieves a highly conscious encapsulation of the city's essence rather than the more usual realistic images. Steve (Rod Zuanic), the fifteen-year-old hero of *Fast Talking*, is already well away on a life of petty crime (he sells 'grass' at school, for instance); his father (Peter Hehir) is an alcoholic bully who poisons Steve's dog; his mother (Julie McGregor) has gone off 'with a man who makes cakes'. The combination of parents, teachers, and the law, has given up on him, and the only one who tries to help him is Redback (Steve Bisley) who runs a motor-bike wrecking-yard — and in the film's last scene provides the means for

102

Steve to ride off into a future whose lines are clearly laid down. This account makes the film sound more solemn than it is: it is in fact often amusing (for example, the supermarket theft in which Steve replaces the contents of a Weeties packet with cigarettes), and avoids the temptation of sentimentalizing Steve's situation.

Perhaps it is an excess of kindly feeling for those they see as deprived that sometimes leads the makers of these films into caricaturing the enemies of youth: parents, police, employers, teachers. For example, the English teacher in *Moving Out*, Mr Aitkin (very well played by Brian James), is written with simplistic crudity. His one concern seems to be ensuring that Gino learns to recite 'My Country', recalling (for Gino's inspiration) a boy he had met again after twenty years who could still intone this famous piece of chauvinistic doggerel. One registers the ironies of getting an Italian-born, city-dwelling teenager to memorize lines about 'sweeping plains' and 'rugged mountain ranges' at the same time as responding to the unfairly 'loaded' representation of the teacher. Apart from the committed liberal on the staff in each case — trendy Sharon Hart (Tracy Mann) in *Fast Talking*, the art teacher in *Moving Out* and the music teacher in *Street Hero* (both played by the excellent Sandy Gore), and John Embling in *Fighting Back* — teachers are depicted as out of touch with the realities of urban life. Apart from the Students' Friend figure, the rest are variously cynical, lazy, cowardly and sadistic. Parents, police, and employers fare no better. Police naturally want to rough up teenagers on the streets; parents are always timidly fearful and distrustful of the hazards of city life, unreasonably wanting to know where their sixteen or seventeen-year-olds are going, for how long and with whom; and employers, like the dress shop manageress (May Howlett) in *The FJ Holden* who talks sneeringly to Anne about 'girls of your type', can hardly wait to dismiss their teenage staff.

This imbalance is common to most of these films, and while it may be socially pardonable — that is, the film-maker's sympathy is directed to where it is most needed — it is often dramatically less defensible. The drama of youthful rebellion against various kinds of authority would sometimes be more compelling if the authority figures of modern urban life were presented less one-dimensionally. Abetted as they usually are by a pounding and banal rock score, these films are apt to settle too easily into ill-considered sympathy for youthful aggro and too-easy blaming of adults. Another kind of imbalance is exhibited in the way the middle classes, appearing on the edges of the films, are invariably made a butt of. Perhaps such aspirations as epitomized in Kevin's mother's table-setting in *The FJ Holden* or the parents' fuss over a new car in *Puberty Blues* deserve criticism, and so perhaps does the kind of respect for authority favoured by and largely administered by the middle classes. It would be refreshing, however, to see a film which seriously examined middle-class life in an overwhelmingly middle-class urban society.

Disadvantaged youth is not the only element of city life with which the new Australian cinema has engaged. Two thrillers, Donald Crombie's *The Killing of Angel Street* (1981) and Phil Noyce's *Heatwave*, have both made drama from the uglier aspects of urban development. Crombie's film involves the murder of an elderly academic, Simmonds (Alexander Archdale), who refuses to leave his Sydney suburban terrace to make way for its demolition by a large, semi-crooked building company which pays hoodlums to terrorize older residents into vacating their houses. Simmond's daughter Jess (Elizabeth Alexander) and a union official Jeff (John Hargreaves) refuse to accept his death as an accident when his house catches fire and in investigating the death, and the disappearance of an earlier protester, come perilously into conflict with the development company. In balancing the personal drama of the growing accord between Jess and Jeff with the public, the film is not without interest, but it rarely does more than scratch the surface of the oppositions it sets up: young/old, conservationists/developers, private needs/community demands. Further, it is apt to be simplistic in its ranging of liberal sympathies (unionists, students, working-class stay-puts, the prosing academic Simmonds), in its depiction of the police (they smile as the Angel Street house falls), and its final banal formulation that 'It's not the winning or the losing; it's the fight that counts.'

Noyce's film (as might be expected from the director of *Newsfront*, also partly city-set and one of the most significant Australian films) is altogether

The demonstration in Donald Crombie's *The Killing of Angel Street* (1981).

tougher, tighter and more subtly intelligent. Steve (Richard Moir), the architect of a vast housing scheme optimistically named 'Eden', to which he has an artists's commitment, is scarcely at one with the money behind the development run by a boorish English magnate Houseman (Chris Haywood), ' a two-bit Pommie [come] to the sunny South'. As he comes to know Kate (Judy Davis), who is organizing the opposition to the project, it is clear that his increasingly troubled conscience is the real site of the film's drama. *Heatwave* ranges its antagonists more complexly than *Angel Street*: the central importance of Steve's position (and Moir plays him with a very compelling intensity) prevents the simplistic confrontation of ruthless capitalists and liberal trendies. Even the bullying Houseman is made comprehensible in terms of his ambitions and his relations with his wife (Lynette Curran) and children, and the opposition is presented as having a thought-out, if opportunistic, position. The thriller element, set in motion by the disappearance of Mary (Carole Skinner, one of Australia's best character actresses) to silence the voice of her militant news-sheet, winds in and out of the film's thematic interests. These are not just a matter of urban conservation versus progress, but the rights and dangers of individuals, of the conflicting claims of private feelings and professional pride. Further, *Heatwave* is not a thesis film: it is highly skilful in marshalling its narrative elements and deployment of cinematic techniques. Its most striking sequence — Steve's pursuit of Kate through the crowded streets of Sydney's King's Cross — is a virtuoso triumph in the Hitchcock manner. The celebrating crowd jostling in the summer heat of the night-time streets on New Year's Eve becomes infused with a sense of menace that reaches its

Architect Steve West (Richard Moir) and journalist Freddy Dwyer (John Meillon) in Phil Noyce's *Heatwave* (1982).

Middle-class Rob (Bryan Brown) and hooker Lou (Judy Davis) in John
Duigan's *Winter of Our Dreams* (1981).

climax in a shooting, and ends with the rain that breaks the oppressiveness
of a large city sweltering in a heatwave. The city is throughout an ominous
presence, threatening always to close in and swallow up those who resist its
pressures. This threat is reinforced by a very eloquent use of music, and by
an inquisitive camera which ensures that the *mise-en-scène* is persistently
giving crucial information about the various levels of life that are caught up
in the film's central drama.

Two other important films with overlapping interests in their portrayals
of city life are *Winter of Our Dreams* and *Monkey Grip* which both touch on
the alternative life-styles and the drug culture to be found in the inner
suburban life of Sydney and Melbourne respectively. *Winter of Our
Dreams* is a more ambitious and formally sophisticated film than *Mouth to
Mouth*, but again it is concerned with life at the city's edges: metaphorically,
that is, since this is an inner-Sydney drama, whose protagonist is Lou (Judy
Davis), an aggressive, vulnerable King's Cross hooker and drug-taker. Lou
enters the life of bookshop-owner Rob McGregor (Bryan Brown) when a
mutual friend, Lisa, commits suicide. Lisa has belonged to Rob's militant
university days; he has long since put these behind him and established a
comfortable 'open' marriage with Gretel (Cathy Downes) in the trendy
middle classes. The film is not simple-minded about this: Rob is not presented crudely as having sold out to greater affluence. There is, of course, a
strong element of that, but he is also simply *older* and the film acknowledges

Nora (Noni Hazlehurst) and her junkie lover Javo (Colin Friels) in Ken Cameron's *Monkey Grip* (1982).

that maturity as well as affluence brings changes. However, Lou's 'razor-edge existence' (in Duigan's own phrase),[9] in a very unsentimental view of a prostitute's life, has a raw, demanding honesty that gets under the faint moral flab that has grown about Rob's attitudes. The film alternates perceptively between *milieux* (Rob and Gretel's elegant flat and Lou's squalid room) and relationships: Rob and Lou's, Rob and Gretel's, the one reluctant, the other a shade complacent, each working on the other. Duigan's control of the *mise-en-scène* is vividly and intelligently at the service of discriminating between these alternations: Rob and Gretel's flat is full of sophisticated music equipment, liquor and furniture, around which the camera prowls critically; Lou's room is a mess, minimal and grubby, with a television set on which a quiz programme, with furs offered as prizes, makes an ideological comment on the acquisitive society that pushes the likes of Lou — and the dead Lisa — to its edges. (In her brilliant analysis of Duigan's *Far East* (1982), Debi Enker notes his continuing concern 'with individuals condemned to dwell on the fringe of affluent societies'[10] although the later film both extends his range and destabilizes the centre of this concern.) *Winter* is a political film, not only in the explicit sense of questioning Rob's earlier involvement with causes and in Lou's final, hesitant commitment as she joins a group of anti-nuclear demonstrators, but also in its observation of and distaste for a brutally divided society. People like Rob and Gretal *owe* that society more than their relaxed, agreeable life-style ever prompts them to pay.

Monkey Grip shares with *Winter of our Dreams* an interest in alternative life-styles, although on a grottier level of inner suburban terraces where the come-and-go of the inmates is as casual as their relationships, and an interest in lives caught up in the drug habit. Helen Garner's source novel is a deceptively shapeless, episodic account of a year in the life of Nora and her junkie lover, Javo, held together by Nora's first-person narration which gives a colouring warmth and a consistent but imaginatively mobile point of view on the shifting lives of those around her. The *film* is given coherence by Noni Hazlehurst's rich, complex performance as Nora and what, in relation to the novel, it loses in terms of her inner response to people and places, it gains through its superb exploitation of the *mise-en-scène*. The sense of a population in flux, drifting from swimming pool, to bars, to experimental theatres, to coffee shops, is established through director Ken Cameron's attention to detail, to highlighting the vulnerability of lives lived in restless retreat from the middle classes, and through cameraman David Gribble's images of a city at different times of day and year. Ambience is of course an element in which a film ought to have least trouble in the enterprise of adaptation from a novel; and Cameron, in his first feature, has succeeded to a remarkable extent in making the *mise-en-scène* replace Nora's narrative voice in the novel. Unclamorously but surely, Cameron and Gribble have captured those aspects of Carlton life (at the northern fringes of the city) that neither the National Trust has an interest in preserving nor the developers in developing. Against this seedy view of Melbourne, the film accurately places the messy, painful lives of its protagonists who draw comfort and desolation in varying proportions from what it offers.

Of all the city films, *Heatwave* is perhaps the shapeliest in narrative terms. It engages significantly with urban life but does so through a coherently structured screenplay (co-written by director Noyce and Marc Rowley), eschewing the slice-of-life open-endedness of films such as *Monkey Grip* or *The FJ Holden*. These, and most of the others, place their observation of the city scene in a looser dramatic structure, taking their shape less from a carefully worked out plot than from gradual character changes wrought in relation to the pressures of the environment. The city films have tended to be in the mould of social realism, displaying contemporary problems and eschewing nostalgia, even in the few urban period films. For instance, in *Newsfront*, the difficulty of maintaining integrity in the face of inducements to personal advancement, of a kind most commonly found in urban concentration, gives a sharp edge to Phil Noyce's brilliant reconstruction of the late 1940s and early 1950s. And Sophia Turkiewicz's *Silver City*, although set in the 1950s, offers a critique of Australian urban and country town manners which is still, too often, shamingly accurate.

As suggested earlier, Australian cities no doubt have much in common with cities of most countries: the *mise-en-scène* of the best films under discussion conveys these common elements of urban experience (pressures, threats, and opportunities). What is distinctive about life in Australian cities is less clear — a quality of light, a monotonous sprawl, perhaps. However, in these films, the city is not just a setting but a narrative and thematic determinant. If, by and large, they are less firmly associated in the international mind with the new Australian cinema than are the rural films, the reason is probably less to do with relative quality than with relative distinctiveness.

[1] Scott Murray, 'The Australian Film Industry', in Al Clark (ed.), *The Film Year Book: Volume Two*, Melbourne: Currey O'Neill Ross, 1984, (Australian Supplement, p.14).

[2] 'Kevin Dobson', interviewed by Scott Murray in *Cinema Papers*, No.36, February 1982, p.11.

[3] Almost the only detailed and complimentary accounts of its are Brian McFarlane's review of it in *Cinema Papers*, No.40, 1982, p.465, and Tom Ryan's article in Al Clark (ed.), *The Film Year Book: Volume Two*, Melbourne: Currey O'Neil Ross Pty Ltd, 1984, Australian Supplement, p.8.

[4] David Stratton, *The Last New Wave*, Melbourne: Angus & Robertson, 1980, p.32.

[5] Philip French, *The Observer*, London: 23 April 1979.

[6] Quoted in Stratton, p.77.

[7] For me, this film has improved greatly on re-viewing, and I now think much more highly of it than when I complained of its pretensions and 'fouled-up narrative habits' in 'Horror and Suspense', in Scott Murray (ed.), *The New Australian Cinema*, Melbourne: Thomas Nelson, 1980, p.76.

[8] Almos Maksay, '*Hard Knocks*', *Cinema Papers*, Issue 29, October-November 1980, p.379.

[9] In interview with Sue Mathews, *35mm Dreams*, p.197.

[10] Debi Enker, '*Far East*', *Cinema Papers*, Issue 39, August 1982, p.363.

7 Men and Women: Personal Matters

Like Australian novels, the films of the recent revival have largely avoided the full-scale treatment of romantic love between men and women (let alone between members of the same sex). Only a few films have actually concentrated on such relationships and scarcely any have followed them through to a hopeful ending. It is not just a matter of wondering where the local equivalent of Ingmar Bergman is with his sustained and powerful examination of the wars between — and sometimes within — the sexes. At the lesser but still honourable level of that Hollywood staple — the romantic melodrama — there is virtually no Australian director who exhibits the all-stops-out approach of a Douglas Sirk or a Vincente Minnelli. Carl Schultz's *Careful, He Might Hear You* (1983) is the nearest contender in this field and stands almost alone; moreover, it is the small boy rather than the adults who provides the film's narrative linchpin. And there are two exotically set pieces, Peter Weir's *The Year of Living Dangerously* and John Duigan's *Far East* (both 1982), which offer love stories against a background of political turmoil at a remove from Australian life. However, if the romantic melodrama is scarcely a flourishing concern in Australia, the romantic comedy is virtually a non-starter: Michael Robertson's *The Best of Friends* and John Lamond's *Breakfast in Paris* (both 1982) are titles to chill the bones of the few who saw them. Paul Cox's gentle *Lonely Hearts* (1982) is both comic and touching but does not quite fit the generic label.

*

The reasons for the shyness of Australian film-makers in dealing with the kinds of experience one would have supposed common to people everywhere presumably lie buried deep in the national psyche. No doubt professionals in various fields could provide scholarly explanations. Anyone who ever attended an Australian country town dance in the 1940s or 1950s might not be surprised at such evasiveness. While the girls sat on the seats around walls of the dance hall, the men stood in a cluster smoking near the entrance, making forays out to choose partners for each dance, then returning them to their seats (or abandoning them on the floor) at the end of the dance before retreating to the male camaraderie near the entrance. Having little to say to each other, the sexes came together for the ritualized steps of the dance then separated for the single-sex talk they enjoyed better, and possibily left the dance for other rituals conducted in parked cars or uphol-stered 'lounge rooms'. It was not a situation to encourage the challenges of relationship but it may be symptomatic of certain aspects of Australian-ness which account for the failure of most Australian films to take the emotional life seriously. By this I mean a reticence in expressing feeling, not on grounds of British reserve but because you might feel a fool if you tried to be articulate. Also, the men's attitude to the women, as the latter sat round the walls, reflects the high value placed on mateship in the national identity and its concomitant relegation of women to subordinate roles.

These are large generalizations and, as such, perhaps untrustworthy. Australian life has changed since the 1950s (country dances probably have, too) but on the basis of the films of the 1970s and 1980s one wonders if the articulate feminist movement of those decades has much informed the dis-course on sexual relationship to be found in the recent film revival. There is scarcely any evidence of film-makers' being concerned to confront personal relationships as the central theme, the *raison d'être*, of their films. The notion of love between the sexes as challenging, exciting, or rewarding is barely visible. Perhaps this is partly a reflection of a male-dominated society, in which the national myths and the historical situations which pro-moted them are essentially male-centred. Partly, though, it may also reflect an international tendency: that is, there have been few major female stars anywhere in the film-making world during the period of the new Australian cinema; and the days of the powerful romantic drama or of the romantic comedy passed with the fading and ageing of the great female stars (Davis, Stanwyck, Colbert, etc.). There may then be both social and industrial explanations for why the Australian cinema has failed to develop a major body of films about men and women coming to terms with each other: not only would such a development seem unlikely in the Australian cultural climate but the international film industry as well seems no longer inter-ested in such an enterprise.

Nevertheless, it is not feasible to suppose that a film industry could ignore the relations between men and women: if there is little celebration of such relations and little sense of their centrality to Australian narrative film, one might ask just how the sexual/emotional life *is* presented in the films. There are several responses which need considering:

1   In place of celebration, there is a strong emphasis on the negative pos-sibilities of relationship;

2   There is some preoccupation with the stranger manifestations of the sexual impulse;

3   The representation of men and women in recent Australian films has been constrained by existing stereotype images;

4 The exploration of relationship has been contextualized in various ways, either thematically or generically;

5 Sex has been made the subject for raucous comedy and for soft-porn enterprises;

6 There is indeed a handful of films which address themselves to male-female relations; and

7 There is some, usually far from radical, attention to male-male and female-female relationship.

A closer look at this motley collection of answers will suggest something of the strengths and limitations of those films which in some degree are concerned with the intimate lives of grown-up people.

1 Accentuating the Negative

There has been recurring stress on the frustrations, inequalities, and destructive patterns at work in relationships rather than on the more positive possibilities. Once again one is reminded of Australian novels which have rarely celebrated the marriage of true minds but which have often, as in the works of Henry Handel Richardson, Patrick White, and Martin Boyd, presented male/female relationships as elements in a larger pattern of disintegration. In Boyd's 'Langton' novels, for instance, successive generations of marriages inevitably lead to a weakening of the values and traditions on which the Langton family has been founded in Australia, opportunism and lassitude proving equally destructive. Films which evince similar preoccupations — the etiolation of feeling in ill-matched liaisons — include Tim Burstall's *Petersen* (1974), Bruce Beresford's *Don's Party* (1976), Ken Hannam's *Break of Day* (1976), Stephen Wallace's *Love Letters from Teralba Road* (1977), Colin Eggleston's *Long Weekend* (1978), Ken Cameron's *Monkey Grip* (1982), and Paul Cox's *My First Wife* (1984). No one lives happily ever after in these films: if couples are together at the end, they can look forward either to bored frustration or further rancorous exchanges. The modern Australian film has shown little confidence in the building and sustaining of relationships; and, with the odd exception of, say, *Lonely Hearts*, optimistic, let alone happy, endings tend to look merely cobbled together rather than *earned* in the films' rendering of personal matters. 'Cobbled together', that is, when not merely absurd like the final reconciliation between Ian (Robert Coleby), just released from gaol for a rape he may or may not be guilty of, and his boutique-owning wife, Jess (Cheryl Ladd), in Adrian Carr's *Now and Forever* (1982). Here the full treatment of rural setting, soupy theme song and freeze frame negates what little sense there was in the foregoing ninety minutes. Love does not easily find a way in Australian films and when it does credulity is often stretched. The con-

112

vincing happy ending derives from less divided times than these in which moody acceptance of stasis or decline seem more the order of the day; have, indeed, been characteristically the order of the day in Australian fiction of this century.

2 The Wilder Shores ...

A small group of films has addressed itself to some of the stranger manifestations of sexuality and feeling. These include Brian Kavanagh's *A City's Child* (1971), Jim Sharman's *Summer of Secrets* (1976) and *The Night the Prowler* (1978), Ken Hannam's *Summerfield* (1977), Michael Pate's *Tim* (1979), and Paul Cox's *Man of Flowers* (1983). Only the first and last of these are really worth noting, the first chiefly for Monica Maughan's detailed, thoughtful distillation of the lonely spinster's life, a life which hovers between drab suburban reality and sensual fantasy. When her domineering invalid mother (Moira Carleton) dies, she meets a young man (Sean Scully) who becomes her lover (or does he?) and lives with her. When he goes, she is again alone, left hovering dangerously on the edge of a fantasy world in which she believes herself to have a child. *A City's Child*, shot on 16mm, was well-received at the 1971 London Film Festival, but, despite the seriousness of its approach to the theme of loneliness and its potentially bizarre results, and despite the excellent playing of its major roles (Maughan won an Australian Film Award for hers), the film failed to find satisfactory commercial distribution. By the time *Man of Flowers* appeared,

Monica Maughan as the lonely spinster in Brian Kavanagh's *A City's Child* (1971).

Paul Cox was well on the way to becoming the cult director of the new Australian cinema, and this stylish account of a repressed aesthete's sexual — and other — proclivities won generally enthusiastic reviews at home and in Britain where it arrived shortly after his earlier romance, *Lonely Hearts*. Cox is, of course, a major figure to consider in this chapter: his absolute engagement with the emotional lives of his characters sets him apart from most Australian directors, and his films will receive fuller treatment later.

Oddest of all the films in this group is *Summer of Secrets*. It offers a schematic account of sets of memories, with two sets of characters united by their attempts to recapture the past. A young student and his girlfriend are caught up in the baroque activities of a Dr Beverley Adams (Arthur Dignam) who engages nightly in a weird, multi-media ritual in which he recalls the great love of his life, Rachel (Kate Fitzpatrick). The film is so inept that it cannot even play its trump card — the resuscitation of Rachel — with any flair, and as an exploration of the more arcane reaches of human relationship the film is both flashy and empty. Sharman's *The Night the Prowler*, discussed elsewhere, is just as flashy, but it does have at least a strong central performance from Kerry Walker as the heroine (liberated by a failed rape) and some insight into family tensions.

Michael Pate, as writer, producer, and director, must shoulder the blame for *Tim*, which charts the relationship between Mary, a plain, middle-aged spinster (played by glamorous, youthful-looking Piper Laurie), and Tim, a

Mary Horton (Piper Laurie) and retarded Tim (Mel Gibson) in Michael Pate's *Tim* (1979).

retarded twenty five-year-old gardener (Mel Gibson). A high point in the film's astonishingly foolish screenplay has a psychiatrist (Michael Caulfield) recommend that, to help Tim most, Mary should marry him — which she does. Set firmly in the realm of the novelette (and based on one by Colleen McCullough), *Tim's* essential stupidity did not prevent it from doing well at the box-office when better films were failing. Gibson won an Australian Film Award for his playing of dim Tim and a career was launched, but the real acting in the film comes from Alwyn Kurts and Pat Evison — two stalwart character players — as his parents, properly suspicious of Mary's interest in him.

Summerfield tries to combine elements of conventional mystery thriller (what became of Flynn, the missing school-teacher in a quiet coastal town?) with a more unusual mystery surrounding siblings, Jenny and David Abbott (Elizabeth Alexander and John Waters), who live at the secluded house of the title. New teacher Simon (Nick Tate) becomes involved with both: the solution to the Flynn mystery is no more than narrative cop-out. As to the Abbotts, the audience is asked to be excited about incest between brother and sister, and Jenny's daughter, Sally (Michelle Jarman), is revealed as the result of this union. This shocking revelation is signalled by some heavy-handed references: Jenny, we are told, went away ten years ago and came back with the child; David has just killed some new kittens because 'the cats on this place are a pretty poor lot; they're all inbred'. The film finally erupts in a horrifying but oddly uninvolving bloodbath. From the moment Simon peers at Jenny and David's love-making, the film begins to fall apart. It is as though scriptwriter Cliff Green has no way of reconciling the interests of mystery-thriller and psychological drama, and one feels cheated by the hints of connection the film has strewn so liberally.

3 Stereotypes and Questions

Australian male and female stereotypes are occasionally submitted to critical scrutiny in the films of the past ten years or so, but more often the narratives are content to exploit the commonly accepted images. Certainly, recurring images of men and women emerge in their dealings with each other, and in their perceptions of themselves as individuals and in relation to each other. One characteristic image of the Australian male is aggressive, conscious of the need to assert his virility, sexually confident or sexually obsessive, and wary of tenderness. The characters played by Bryan Brown in such films as *Far East* and *Love Letters from Teralba Road*, a short perceptive account of a marriage which has foundered on the husband's brutal, 'ocker-ish' insensitivity, or by Jack Thompson in Michael Thornhill's shoddy *The Journalist* (1979), in Terry Ohlsson's *Scobie Malone* (1975), in Donald Crombie's *Caddie* (1976), and in *Petersen* exude sexual confidence. There are underlying elements of self-doubt at work in some of these characters and they are not exempt from pain, but the appearance they present to the world, and to women in particular, works to conceal such elements. Like the sexually obsessed characters, such as Alvin Purple or Barry McKenzie or the men who attend *Don's Party*, they do not seem actually to *like* women very much, and, except when making love (and not always then), are uneasy in their company. There are films which offer some critique of the preoccupation with male virility, with varying degrees of perception: for instance, against the mindless 'ocker' chauvinism of the Alvin Purple and Barry McKenzie films, one finds in Ted Kotcheff's *Wake in Fright* (1971) David Baker's 'The Family Man' segment in *Libido* (1973), *Petersen, Don's Party*, and Rivka Hartman's short film, *A Most Attractive Man* (1982), some quite trenchant criticism of male exploitation of and insensitivity towards women. Unless he is lame, like Tom (Andrew McFarlane) in *Break of Day*, or the town simpleton, like 'Rabbit' (John Waters) in Tom Jeffrey's *Weekend of Shadows* (1978), or retarded, like the hero of *Tim*, or a junkie, like Javo (Colin Friels) in *Monkey Grip*, the hero of an Australian film in which there is an important man-woman relationship is likely to be conceived in terms which perpetuate the virile 'ocker' *persona*. Sometimes, mercifully, as noted above, the image is undermined by criticism; more often one seems expected to find it engaging as in *Far East* or *The Journalist* or Igor Auzins' *Coolangatta Gold* (1984). The last-named may imply some criticism of Australian male competitiveness but more pervasively it celebrates the icon of the bronzed surfing jock whose women are a subsidiary interest when there is no race to train for or plantation to chop down.

Marriage is rarely seen as other than an impediment to true minds, certainly not as offering a situation within which two people are likely to find a relationship capable of growth. In John B. Murray's 'The Husband' episode from *Libido*, Jonathan (Byron Williams) is made absurd by jealousy — well-founded, as it happens — of his Nordic wife Penelope (Elke Neithart); Jack Thompson's *Petersen* is trapped with his pretty little wife who wishes he would talk to her about his university course but he is sure there would be no point in doing so; Ray (Mike Preston) in Tim Burstall's *Duet for Four* (1982) is caught between demanding ex-wife and increasingly dissatisfied mistress, the latter resenting the claims of the former whose official status she longs for; the young husband, Peter (John Hargreaves) in *Long Weekend* finds himself locked in a round of abrasive exchanges with his sulky wife Marcia (Briony Behets); the husbands in *Don's Party* feel sexually deprived and professionally handicapped by their wives, their resentments fanned by the apparent successes of their bachelor mate Cooley (Harold Hopkins); and, most acutely and painfully observed, John (Hargreaves, again) in *My First Wife* barely understands what has gone wrong with his marriage.

As to the women involved in these relationships, they are either anxious and put-upon, merely used by and subsidiary to the men in their lives, or

116

more sexually aggressive, in which case they are likely to end unhappily or to be presented as somehow reprehensible, if not indeed sluttish. In the former category, there have been memorable performances from Jacki Weaver (as the dim wife in *Petersen* and the battered Marilyn in Tom Jeffrey's *The Removalists*, 1975); from Pat Bishop and Jeanie Drynan as two of the fed-up wives in *Don's Party*; from Kris McQuade, gaunt and disillusioned, in *Love Letters from Teralba Road*; from Helen Morse in *Caddie*, though she is allowed a certain resilience as a result of the blows dealt her; and from Judy Davis as the emotionally repressed wife in Claude Whatham's *Hoodwink* (1981). Perhaps because the images of women represented by these characters are more in tune with the traditional roles of women in Australian society, writers and actors have been able to fill in their contours with more convincing detail than has been the case with the more obviously sexual, assertive women.

Among the latter, Helen Morse's Jo in *Far East* and Sigourney Weaver's Jill in *The Year of Living Dangerously* are potent sexual *presences* but it is hard to construct a complex sense of their inner lives; Margot (Diane Cilento) in *Duet for Four* is presented unsympathetically because she wants money from her estranged husband and has a younger lover (Warwick Cober); Sara Kestelman's Alice, in *Break of Day*, is doubly suspect as artist and city woman, an exotic in rural Victoria; and the two sexually aggressive women in *Don's Party*, Susan (Clare Binney) and Kerry (Candy Raymond), are presented as promiscuous and calculating respectively. In their various ways they evidence the failure of Australian cinema to come to terms with a fully sexual woman whose sexuality is an active element of her nature. Only when their sexual frankness causes women unhappiness — for instance, Noni Hazlehurst's Nora in *Monkey Grip*, or Briony Behets' Marcia in *Long Weekend*, or Judy Davis's vulnerable hooker in *Winter of our Dreams* (1981) — have their roles in male-female relationships been realized with any emotional resonance. Australian films have generally been more at home with the ill-used or with the sexually inhibited (such as the two strikingly different roles played by Wendy Hughes in *Lonely Hearts* and *Careful, He Might Hear You*), than with women who make claims to some sort of sexual parity with men.

4 Among Other Things ...

Rather than make relationship the central issue of the narrative, many Australian films have chosen to place it either in a recognizable generic framework or subsume it in a more comprehensive social discourse. In the former category one finds the political melodramas, *The Year of Living Dangerously* and *Far East*, and films such as *Hoodwink*, *Now and Forever*, and *Summerfield*, in which the romantic element is subordinated to criminal or mysterious events. In the second category is a batch of interesting films in which male-female relationship is but one element of the film's discourse. This group includes such films as *Petersen, The Removalists, Long Weekend*, Paul Cox's *Kostas* (1979), *Winter of our Dreams, Monkey Grip*, and Sophia Turkiewicz's *Silver City* (1983). In these films, the issue of sexuality and emotion between men and women jostles for place among issues such as class and educational inequality, police brutality, the environment, inter-cultural difficulties, the drug scene, the shifting messiness of alternative life-styles, and the opening up of Australia to European migration. The external elements affecting relationships in these films are of at least as much narrative significance as the nature of the relationships themselves.

Among the melodramas in the first group, *Hoodwink* is a proficient enough thriller (without actually being very thrilling) of a criminal's escape from prison by pretending to be blind and performing the eponymous deception. The experiences leading to his imprisonment, including fleeting sexual encounters with two women and the episode with his family, are perfunctorily handled. What gives the film its distinction is the way English director Claude Whatham has handled the relationship between the con, Martin (John Hargreaves), and Sarah (Judy Davis), wife of a lay preacher attached to a church near the country prison to which Martin is sent, and the performances of Hargreaves and Davis. There is a trim, still, repressed quality about Sarah, and when she comes to visit Martin in prison she is clearly sexually disturbed as, pretending blindness, he asks: 'May I see what you look like?' and runs his hands over her face. The scenes between these two and her beaming husband Ralph (well played by Dennis Miller) are very shrewdly observed, drawing skilfully on the background of all three to create a tension which is partly good conventional 'thriller' tension but more importantly the tension of lives awkwardly impinging on each other. The way Sarah wears her innocuous clothes, the way she sits and stands, the way she doesn't quite meet Martin's eyes, blind as she at first believes them, and the inhibited delivery of the lines that establish her relations with Ralph ('Things aren't right between me and Ralph') work towards a remarkable characterisation. This carefully restrained performance plays off — and *pays* off — brilliantly against the calculations of Hargreaves' deceitful con gradually falling in love when he'd only meant to prepare the ground for escape.

Hoodwink is a minor piece compared with the two exotically set melodramas but the relationship between Sarah and Martin is realized with more subtlety and concern for emotional nuance than those between either Guy (Mel Gibson) and Jill (Sigourney Weaver) in *The Year of Living Dangerously* or Morgan (Bryan Brown) and Jo (Helen Morse) in *Far East*. In each of these the starring pair plays with appropriate star gloss but the feeling between the man and women in each case is more conventionally derived. Guy Hamilton and Jill Bryant are, respectively, a foreign correspondent and

118

Casablanca revisited: Jo (Helen Morse) and Morgan (Bryan Brown) rekindle sparks in John Duigan's *Far East* (1982).

British Embassy official in Jakarta in 1965 when an aborted left-wing coup is followed, in turn, by the installation of a new right-wing hero, Suharto. Whereas in Christopher Koch's novel the romance between the two is more unobtrusively subsumed into the larger context of the country's political volatility, it occupies a more privileged position in Peter Weir's film version. The latter opts for being a romantic melodrama like *Casablanca* (1942) and *un*like Costa-Gavras' *Missing* (1982) which kept Chilean politics and the *rapprochement* of its characters on an equal footing. It is, in fact, a stirring example of the genre, in an unusually exotic and well-realized setting. The film is well-served by the attractive performances of Gibson and Weaver, but David Williamson's screenplay makes claims for them which it fails to substantiate. For instance, Billy Kwan, the Australian-Chinese dwarf cameraman (superbly played by Linda Hunt), describes himself and Guy as 'divided men . . . not quite at home in the world': the script does not make Guy interesting enough to justify such a cryptic utterance, and Gibson's *persona* is not complex enough to fill in the lacunae with reserves of his own. Similarly, Billy's file on Jill records that she has 'little real feeling, yet has a reverence for life. Could lapse into the promiscuity and bitterness of the failed romantic.' Weaver's Jill has a lovely, sexy elegance but cannot bear the weight of such characterizations. Within these limits; however, the love story develops satisfactorily, generating on occasions a persuasive aura of sexual hunger. The lovers are associated with a rather lushly romantic score (by Maurice Jarre) and are placed against a range of picturesque backgrounds so as to command at least as much, if not more, attention than the political events.

The ghost of *Casablanca* hovers in the background of *Far East* as well. In fact, its director John Duigan has said, 'As I was writing the script I created a series of similarities with *Casablanca*, an old favourite of mine. I set the initial character dynamic along similar lines, namely a triangular situation, with the female walking into the nightclub with her husband some years after a love affair, to find the old lover running it'.[1] He then goes on to discuss ways in which the political and moral issues in *Far East* are less distinct than those faced by the characters in *Casablanca* in which the Nazis were 'evil without qualification'. In the undefined Asian country in which the film is set, it may be the multi-nationals and an aggressive military who are the villains and less obvious ones than *Casablanca's* Nazis, but when Jo Reeves and her journalist husband Peter (John Bell) arrive at the 'Koala Klub' run by Morgan Keefe, the air is thick with resonances of Rick's Bar. Jo and Morgan have been lovers in Saigon during the Vietnam war and the old sexual sparks are re-kindled. The language of romantic love has changed in forty years (when Jo turns up next day, Morgan the 'ocker' gentleman, says, 'I thought you'd come round for a quick grope'; 'God, you've got class' is her reply) but at least some of the same old fundamentals still apply. Morgan treats his current mistress, Nene (Sinan Leong), with casual but presumably irresistible brutality; however, when Jo turns up with Peter, who has a serious cause, both she and Morgan are shaken out of a somewhat affectless sensuality and into the birth of conscience and commitment. While Brown and Morse are both accomplished players with, what is more, the gloss of stardom, the moral growth of their characters needs — for the sake of the film's coherence — to be worked out more complexly in terms of the political situation in which they find themselves. It is not just that the film's villains are less clear-cut than the Nazis; they are simply too shadowy to provide a convincing basis either for Jo's decision to return to the husband she admires, or for Morgan's emergence from the sleazy Klub to the (for him) fatal reality of the outside world. Unsurprisingly, the film works better on the romantic level than the political, but, as a film from the director of *Mouth to Mouth* (1978) and *Winter of our Dreams*, *Far East* offers a disappointing slickness in the place of the earlier, more austere social commitment.

Among the films which consider relationship in socially significant contexts one of the most intelligent is *Monkey Grip*. As noted in the chapter on city films, it is interested in alternative life-styles and the ambience found/created by them in inner suburban Melbourne in the 1970s. A notable human aspect of the *milieu* so convincingly suggested in the film's *mise-en-scène* is the restless, unpredictable relationships which are characteristic of it. In escaping the entrapment of bourgeois suburbia, the protagonist Nora (award-winner Noni Hazlehurst), single mother of a young daughter Gracie (played with marvellous matter-of-factness by Alice Garner), drifts out of one affair and into another, potentially destructive one, with junkie Javo (Colin Friels). The film sounds thin to talk about — it chronicles the on-and-off course of this affair and the drifting lives of those it touches — but it is rich in detail. Detail, that is, of people as well as of place and time, and detail about the nature of relationships, and in the film's sympathically div-ided view of the lives that accommodate them.

Director Ken Cameron, greatly helped by the screenplay which he co-wrote with Helen Garner, author of the source novel, balances a clear sense of rootless, itinerant camaraderie, stressing the supportive aspects of its drifting non-nuclear households, against the emotionally-draining, unfulfil-ling relationships of people who feel able to come and go at will. Nora's apparently cheerful 'I'll-see-you-when-I-see-you' approach is touching as it becomes increasingly clear that she would like something more dependable. She and her friends talk so much about their emotional lives and needs that it becomes clear how inadequate to them are the uncommitted relationships in which they mostly find themselves. The endless talk along the lines of 'I love you, but I can't handle it' strikes again and again authentic notes of unhappiness and banality. Against Nora's bleak prospects of anything per-manent with Javo ('I can't just stay with you all the time', he tells her), and 'placing' these, is the warmth of affection between her and Gracie. Nora knows what steady love is like when shorn of sexual complication, and some of the scenes between her and her friends reinforce this. Good or bad, however, Javo is currently what she needs and the film is sensitive *and* candid about the limitations of sexual love, even at its most urgently neces-sary, in the absence of other aspects of relatedness. Hazlehurst's fine, unmannered performance makes us accept Nora's final comment about her life as 'a complicated dance to which the steps hadn't quite been learnt' as she 'through the ebb and flow of her existential summer-to-summer journey flounders toward a sort of self-knowledge and ongoing transcendence'.[2] The dance is complicated because Nora and her friends are who they are and because the time and place are what they are. *Monkey Grip* will gain stature as a social document as well as for its eloquent portrayal of one dancer practising her steps.

The other films in this group have different social contexts but what they share is their way of showing how context can become determinant in shaping relationship. For instance, in *Winter of our Dreams* the failure of middle-class bookshop owner Rob (Bryan Brown), comfortably settled in 'open' marriage with Gretel (Cathy Downes), to respond to the plea of help from the King's Cross prostitute Lou (Judy Davis) is a function of the social gap that separates them. The failure in fact draws attention to this gap and to how far Rob has moved from the political commitment of his university days, a commitment towards which Lou tentatively moves in the film's last scene. Peter and Marcia (John Hargreaves and Briony Behets), the bickering suburban trendies of *Long Weekend*, become more alienated from each other as they become more alienated from the natural world of their coastal camp-site which they variously despoil. In *The Removalists*, the battered wife, Marilyn (Jacki Weaver) is subjected to another kind of battering from the police to whom she complains. The analogy is clear: her husband's brutality stands as synecdoche for the larger society. The relations between men and women of course surface in many Australian films; it is curious, however, that so few films regard the nature of relationship itself as engrossing or important enough to build a whole film on.

5 Nudges and Titters

The most lamentable surfacings occur in the appalling bunch of sex comedies and the still worse soft-porn ventures. In the comedies (don't expect them to be funny) sex is the recurring subject of a witless, numbing jokiness. Some of these, such as Bruce Beresford's *The Adventures of Barry McKenzie* (1972) and Tim Burstall's *Alvin Purple* (1973), made money and spawned sequels; others such as Terry Bourke's *Plugg* (1975) and John Lamond's *Pacific Banana* (1981), less technically proficient, did not; and the spin-offs from television series, Peter Benardos' *Number 96* (1974) and Paul Eddey's *The Box* (1975), were as abysmal as such projects usually are. *The Adventures of Barry McKenzie* is a crude satire (to use the term loosely) on the theme of the boisterous Fosters-swilling Aussie at large in England, teaching Pommie sheilas a thing or two about real men; *Alvin Purple* is a one-joke piece about a young man (Graeme Blundell) who, despite or perhaps because of his diffidence, is irresistibly attractive to women; *Plugg*, possibly the worst Australian film ever made (though the competition is tough at this level), is an astonishingly inept sex — and private eye — spoof set in Perth, dealing with the activities of the Pussycat Escort Agency; and *Pacific Banana* stars again the hapless Blundell, this time as a pilot whose ill-timed sneezes interrupt his coitus, as it were. There's wit for you. These films are invariably sexist: the women either legitimate objects of pursuit or, if pursuing, objects of heartless derision; and they are as subtle as a poke in the ribs with a sharp stick. *Number 96* and *The Box* were based on two early 1970s 'adult' television serials (adult in the sense of each having a resident homosexual and much exposed flesh), in which an improbable cross-section of character types revolved around, respectively, a Sydney apartment block and a Melbourne television studio. Dire weddings of opportunism and smut, they met with critical opprobrium but, one is sorry to add, some commercial success. Some of the greatest American films are comedies of sexual manners: think of Leo McCarey's *The Awful Truth* (1937), or Howard Hawks' *Bringing Up Baby* (1938) or George Cukor's *Adam's Rib* (1949). The Australian cinema has not come within, as they say, a bull's roar of understanding what this genre may achieve: its output in the genre makes the 'Carry on . . .' series look like Restoration comedy, and remains at the level of the smoke-light entertainment.

At an even lower level of achievement is an assortment of soft-porn enterprises which purport to be either 'serious' explorations of the sexual impulse or which exploit the format of sexual enquiry to use it as a means of providing a range of voyeurist treats. John Lamond's *Felicity* (1979) belongs in the first category as it dramatizes the sexual odyssey of a boarding-school girl initiated into the erotic mysteries of exotic Asia. Like Lamond's *ABC of Love and Sex — Australia Style* (1978), it adopts a tone of didactic tolerance about sex (the importance of acknowledging and gratifying desire, the danger of repression, etc.), as if to lend respectabilty to its squalid banalities. These are elaborate peep shows and so are the immensely successful *Fantasm* (1976), directed pseudonymously by the very talented Richard Franklin, and the suavely titled *Fantasm Comes Again* (1977), directed by 'Eric Ram' (that is, Colin Eggleston). Each of these remorselessly smutty Austro-American co-productions uses a flimsy framework (a 'Freudian' lecture about the need for fantasy in the first; in the second, case studies from the Advice to the Lust-lorn column of a newspaper) on which to hang ten anecdotes of the sexual life. All these films, and another John Lamond piece, *Australia After Dark* (1975), an allegedly documentary account of Australian sexual habits, are witless, sexist, and shoddy, catering to the lowest and commonest of denominators. Presumably every national cinema, at least where censorship permits, has its squalid underbelly; and presumably the makers of these wretched (and tedious) films know to what audiences they are directed. Sadly, these audiences have often proved much larger than those for a film of real merit, such as Richard Lowenstein's *Strikebound* (1984), to choose one at random.

6 Something Like It

Among the few films which centrally concern the nature of male/female relationships and the function of sexuality within them, Paul Cox's are the most significant. This is not to say that other films have not offered, in various narrative contexts (as the foregoing discussion has indicated) an at least intermittently intelligent discourse on the way men and women behave towards each other in this society. Cox, however, places his explorations of emotional life centre-stage, confident that this will be enough in itself to hold audience attention. After a string of short films from 1965 on, the Dutch-born director achieved his first real notice when *Kostas* opened the Melbourne Film Festival in 1979, the first Australian film to do so.

Kostas is an earnest, intelligent attempt to chart a romance between Greek Kostas (Takis Emmanuel), a refugee from the régime of the colonels (1967–74), now working as a taxi driver in Melbourne, and a trendy young middle-class woman, Carol (Wendy Hughes), who maintains a small daughter and a job in a commercial art gallery. The film has some effective swipes at national prejudice (as in Dawn Klingberg's dim landlady to whom Greeks and Turks are all one, or Maurie Fields as Kostas's boss who warns him: 'Don't play funny buggers with me'), but Linda Aronson's screenplay is insufficiently detailed about the central relationship. Neither Kostas nor Carol is a quite full-bodied enough characterization to overcome a sense of (honourable) schematism about the film: one responds to them more as representatives of cultures, of ways of life, rather than as individually complex figures.

However, if *Kostas* enjoyed only limited success, it notably began Cox's association with Wendy Hughes who, at her best, is one of the most imposing stars in the new Australian cinema. A classically beautiful woman, able to suggest passion and intelligence, Hughes has given two finely perceptive performances for Cox — in *Lonely Hearts* and *My First Wife.* In the former, she suppresses her beauty to play the dowdy Patricia, an inhibited bank clerk, who meets Peter Thompson (Norman Kaye, another Cox regular), through the services of a dating agency. Peter, a fifty-year-old bachelor whose mother has just died, is a piano-tuner and occasional shoplifter, who wears a wig and goes in for amateur dramatics, in which he

Peter (Norman Kaye) and Patricia (Wendy Hughes) on the verge of love in Paul Cox's *Lonely Hearts* (1982).

persuades Patricia to join, urged on by the camp producer, George (Jon Finlayson). The lives of Patricia and Peter are curtailed both by lack of personal assurance and by restrictive family influences, and the film sketches these lives economically and wittily, and in such a way as to account for their growing *rapprochement*. Peter's bossy sister, Pam (Julia Blake), nags: 'You're nearly fifty you know. You've got to do something with your life' and quarrels with him about putting their aged, vegetable-like father in hospital. Patricia's parents come storming into her neat little flat, father demanding to know: 'What's going on? Why haven't you rung? Your mother has been worried sick. etc., etc.'. Each has to break free from a lifetime's subservience to the wishes of others before taking the first cautious steps towards independence and relationship.

This account makes the film sound more schematic than it is. It is intended to suggest the film's firm structure, but it does not suggest its tenderness or its comedy. The tenderness is certainly there in the writing (screenplay by Cox and John Clarke) and in the performances of Hughes and Kaye. Each resists the temptation to be, respectively, merely twitchily neurotic (although there *is* a neurotic element in her sexual fears) or merely idiosyncratic (although there is a real quirkiness in some of the details about Peter). Above all, in the genre of gentle romantic comedy they create very touchingly and credibly a growing sense of two people feeling their way towards relationship. This is a film which constantly surprises and delights by the sharpness of its observation which in turn fleshes out a sturdy dramatic framework. Made on a small budget, *Lonely Hearts* succeeded at local and overseas box offices, proving 'at the end of 1983 that there was also room in the American market for the occasional "little" Australian film'[3] (That is, as distinct from blockbusters like *The Man from Snowy River*.) It is, in fact, one of the most heartening films of the entire revival, both for its sensitivity and for what it suggests about the possibilities of small-scale film-making in Australia.

It has not too much in common with Cox's next film, *Man of Flowers*, except that, as *Sight and Sound* has noted, 'the commitment to genuine feelings ... is equally apparent'.[4] The titles unfold over a background of statues and paintings, with classical music on the soundtrack, before cutting to a squalid back alley from which a girl emerges, gets into a waiting car and drives off. In the long take which follows, the girl, Lisa (Alyson Best), is seen undressing, shaking out her hair, looking out into the off-screen space behind the camera which gradually pulls back to reveal a man, Charles Bremer (Norman Kaye), watching as she undresses. An operatic duet on the soundtrack accompanies this ritual: when the girl is naked, the man goes out, crosses a busy road to a church and begins playing the organ. This is a more enigmatic opening than is usual in Australian films and *Man of Flowers*, a more teasing film than most, does not let it down. From these opening scenes, it sets up an opposition of high culture and sexual oddity.

Charles, it appears, is trying to make life imitate art: his pleasure in watching Lisa undress is not mere voyeurism but an attempt to create a live art work, and it is also connected with his childhood response to seeing his mother undress. Our sympathies are with Charles, not with Lisa's crudely chauvinistic artist boyfriend, David (Chris Haywood), who asks: 'What about this bloke you take your knickers off for while he plays Beethoven? . . . What's wrong with the bloke?' And David, whose art is produced by the violent squeezing of paint tubes over canvas, then jumping on it (in a somewhat easy tilt at 'modern art'), will become Charles's final macabre attempt to make art out of life.

Man of Flowers is not especially a profound film but its interest in the bizarre life at its centre is more than merely exploitative. Charles's incapacity for relationship is elaborated and explored, and is seen as being a subject worth putting at the centre of a film. The flashbacks to his childhood — Cox moves fluently in time and space (see also *My First Wife*) — invoke a stern, repressive father (film director Werner Herzog) and over-protective mother (Hilary Kelly), but without the pat psychologizing that might have attended these. What the flashbacks achieve is a basis for our understanding Charles's proclivities in regard to art and sex and to their inter-dependence. (One is reminded of the use of the flashbacks in Michael Powell's *Peeping Tom* in helping to explain a hero for whom art and sex have become dangerously entangled.) 'Imagination is a word people use when they don't know what they're doing, says a bullying art teacher (Julia Blake, another of

Lisa (Alyson Best) performs for Charles (Norman Kaye), a kind of artist, in Paul Cox's *Man of Flowers* (1983).

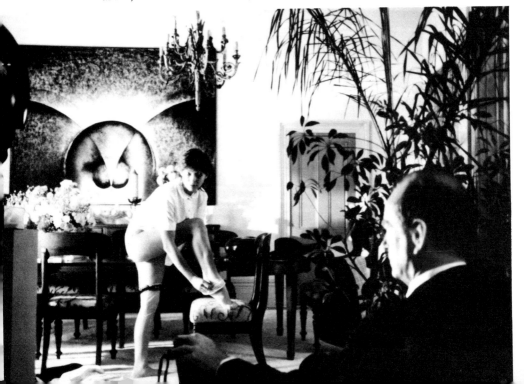

Cox's stock company). The anti-Cox faction which dismisses him as 'ornate', 'self-conscious', 'arty', as if anything other than linear realism were an offence, might take up the art teacher's comment and turn it on Cox. Wrongly, in the present author's view: Cox has more ideas than most Australian film-makers and a restless visual flair and energy that sometimes threaten to shake his structures, but in *Lonely Hearts, Man of Flowers* and *My First Wife* there is a sufficient grasp of the central narrative concern to keep his potential excesses in control. Or, at least, to provide a stimulating tension between the film's handsome, sometimes florid surfaces and the sense of incipient disruption that always seems about to threaten those surfaces.

My First Wife, more complex than *Lonely Hearts*, less baroque than *Man of Flowers*, shares with them a structuring interest in the relationship between men and women and how these are worked upon by what has happened between parents and children. A marriage foundering on emotional negligence and infidelity; an older couple — parents of the wife — complacent and ineffectual, a third couple — the husband's parents — whose marriage has survived an early affair of the mother's; and the relationship between each set of parents and their child: this all sounds like the basis for a Sirkian melodrama of middle-class emotions on the edge. But Cox has moved away from the more or less naturalist treatment of *Lonely Hearts* and *Kostas*: he is prepared to be ambitious, to risk charges of floridness and pretension (and sometimes to deserve them) and to make use of screen space in quite daring ways.

A family at odds: John (John Hargreaves), his daughter Lucy (Charlotte Angwin), and his wife Helen (Wendy Hughes) in Paul Cox's *My First Wife* (1984).

'In the end the family is important', says the husband's dying father (Robin Lovejoy); 'in the end the family is everything', and the film moves towards an unemphatic affirmation of this belief. In the last scene, as the mourners move away from his father's grave-side, John (John Hargreaves) and his wife Helen (Wendy Hughes) are together, not with any certainty of reconciliation perhaps, but taking tentative steps towards it. It has cost a death and John's failed suicide. The film's structure depends on the parallels and contrasts between the couples concerned, the relationship between each partner and the other, and that between each set of parents and its offspring. Though Hargreaves (now a major Australian actor after recent successes in films such as *Careful, He Might Hear You* and the television series, *The Dismissal*) and Hughes are both excellent in the central roles, the presentation of their marriage is the least convincing. It is never wholly clear why and how their marriage has reached the breaking point which is the linchpin for the film's narrative. The actual scene in which Helen confronts John with the fact that she wants to leave him signally fails to maintain the tensions so far built up with economy and a Coxian enigmatic quality. What lets this crucial scene down is the dialogue which Cox and co-screenwriter Bob Ellis have provided: it is consistently banal ('For God's sake say what you're feeling for once', 'We never make love anymore', 'Oh dear. I just can't believe this'). Cox, *the director,* on the other hand, shows in this scene that he knows when to keep his often restless camera still and concentrates on the faces here in a long two-shot, but he is let down by the inadequacy of the screenplay which suggests that the background to the break has not been fully imagined. In an interview, he has claimed that: 'It is totally unimportant to make up a reason for a separation these days ... We live in a society where these things happen'[5]. Maybe. If, however, one accepts the break-up as a narrative *donnée,* then much of the rest of the film is an affecting account of John's attempts to achieve a reconciliation.

There is less comedy than in the two preceding films, although there are some satrirical swipes at Helen's parents as the camera prowls round their expensively upholstered house, full of the artifacts of bourgeois prosperity. Even this is serious in its function in the film: the emotional inadequacy that accompanies this cushioned life is contrasted with the rawness of feeling enacted elsewhere. This rawness is exposed in John's Russian mother's incoherent grief at her husband's funeral and, of course, in the film's central relationship in which the painful attempts at reconciliation are seen as being just that — painful.

Cox is a highly self-conscious film-maker and highly conscious of what film can do that other narrative media cannot. His methods foreground the artificiality of film as a system (for example, in his use of a choric image of trees rushing past as if viewed from a moving train) rather than seek to suppress it in the classic Hollywood style. More than any other Australian film-maker he has been insistently concerned with relationships, between men and women, parents and children; and he is clearly interested in the erotic and its power to disturb orderly, cultured surfaces. *Lonely Hearts* is his most *achieved* film to date but the later two, despite lapses into pretension and worse, are more important.

The only other Australian feature films persistently concerned with the male-female relationship are John B. Murray's *The Naked Bunyip* (1970), a fictionalized documentary about a market researcher's survey of Australian sexual mores; Chris McGill's *Maybe This Time* (1980), a wry comedy-drama of a twenty-nine-year-old woman, Fran (Judy Morris), looking for emotional fulfilment with several men of unprepossessing sexual manners; two romantic comedies, *The Best of Friends* and *Breakfast in Paris*; and *Duet for Four*, in which the demands of business impose pressures on emotional pairings. The romantic comedies require a closer look — partly because they are so rare, partly because they are so awful.

The Best of Friends, first feature for director Michael Robertson, traces the decline of a 20-year-old friendship between television 'personality' Melanie (Angela Punch-McGregor) and accountant Tom (Graeme Blundell) when they become lovers. The film seems to aspire to Hollywood screwball comedy of the 1930s but, in the absence of, say, Carole Lombard and Cary Grant and with the loss of subtlety that seems consequent upon the increased permissiveness in matters of dialogue and situation, the edge, charm, and inventiveness appear to have deserted the genre. There are incidental pleasures — Tom's and Melanie's parents are nicely discriminated as to social and religious affiliations — but the protagonists resolutely fail as a team. Punch-McGregor is sour and strident; Blundell in comedy still resonates (unhelpfully) with Alvin Purple; and, as Geoff Mayer has pointed out, in an article comparing this film with Norman Jewison's *Best Friends* (1982), based on a comparable situation, with 'the males in both films, unlike the women, . . . eager for marriage . . ., the changed social context has also reduced the impact of the role reversal'.[6] In the 1980s it is no longer especially funny to find the man fussing in the kitchen or being peeved when the woman has not come in to dinner.

Still, *The Best of Friends* is *Bringing Up Baby* compared with the relentless stream of clichés let loose in *Breakfast in Paris*. The sparring pair inevitably headed for a happy fade-out has a long and honourable tradition in film comedy (think of *It Happened One Night*, 1934, or *Pat and Mike*, 1952 for two prime examples), but the tradition depends on the charm and light touch of the protagonists and a screenplay that knows wit when it sees it. Here, she is a dress designer, Pauline (Barbara Parkins), one of the most aggressively unattractive romantic comedy heroines in film history — and Parkins plays her as a graduate of the Joan Collins School of Dramatic Art. He is a restorer of Carlton terrace houses, Michael (Rod Mullinar), described as 'a lovely witty sensitive man', though nothing else in the film would bear out such a characterization. After meeting not so much cute as boorish at Melbourne airport, then squabbling all the way to Paris, they conduct their on-and-off affaire before many a familiar landmark in the city of love, beguiling each other if not us with lines like, 'You can't take money to bed with you. You can't talk to it.' Sophisticated romantic comedy has never been an Australian staple; *The Best of Friends* and *Breakfast in Paris* will do nothing to disturb the status quo.

Tim Burstall has never been a critics' director (and would probably scorn to be so) so that films such as *Petersen* and *Eliza Fraser* (1976) have been undervalued, perhaps as a way of getting back at him for the vulgar success of *Alvin Purple*. What all his films of the 1970s had was a kind of libidinal energy which distinguished them from their more decorous, more kindly received contemporaries. In view of this it is disappointing to record that *Duet for Four*, based on a screenplay by David Williamson, lacks the vigour, abrasiveness, and warmth of his best work. Ray (Mike Preston), a toy manu-facturer, is separated from his wife Margot (Diane Cilento) and living with Barbara (Wendy Hughes) who would like to be married and resents the inroads Margot continues to make on their lives. He has troubles not only with Barbara and Margot, but with his pregnant teenage daughter, Caroline (Sigrid Thornton), with his business partner (Gary Day) at whose wife Dianne (Vanessa Leigh) he makes a perfunctory pass, and with a visiting American (Michael Pate) who is aiming at a takeover of Ray's firm. The film's problem is not so much that it is overplotted (Sam Rohdie's review of the film convincingly argues for the way the '"thematic" of split, division, moral indecisiveness'[7] exercises a pervasive internal coherence) as that it is under-detailed about the participants. Only Thornton suggests a complex character, as the daughter: hurt, vulnerable, flailing emotionally, deserted by her boy-friend, unable to count on her father, but with a touching moral honesty. The rest of a competent cast has too little to work on: neither Burstall nor Williamson has caught the feel of these middle-class lives with the gritty exactness that distinguished much of *Petersen*. There is some criticism of the ideology of selling and of manipulating in both business and personal lives, but too often the characters are left mouthing platitudes about, say, double standards or wallowing in the contemporary *angst* of 'Nothing matters . . . in the long term'. The film has to it a professional gloss that owes more to American soap opera series than to observation of any real ambience. Nothing in it is as sharply delineated as the plight devised by Burstall and Williamson for that earlier protagonist, Petersen (Jack Thomp-son), caught in suburban marriage to a nice dim little wife, Susie (Jacki Weaver), and aspiring inarticulately towards university education and his coolly elegant tutor, Trish (Wendy Hughes). If in the end one hates Petersen for the brutal rape of Trish who is ready to drop him in order to take up a job at Oxford, one also feels for his pain and for the failure implicit in his return to mindless sexual availability.

7 Scarcely Daring To Speak Its Name

Those films which have sought to explore relationships between members of the same sex have been very thin on the ground. Male camaraderie not surprisingly has been frequently canvassed and, indeed, may be described as central to Richard Franklin's *The True Story of Eskimo Nell* (1975), Tom Jeffrey's *The Odd Angry Shot* (1979), Bruce Beresford's *The Club* and *Breaker Morant* (both 1980), Stephen Wallace's *Stir* (1980), Peter Weir's *Gallipoli* (1981), Ian Pringle's *The Plains of Heaven* (1982) and Arch Nicholson's *Buddies* (1983). To describe the issue of male friendship as 'central' to such films is not, however, to suggest any serious exploration of what makes Australian men cluster round the dance hall floor together. Links between mateship and suppressed homosexuality never surface explicitly; for all that *Gallipoli* is apparently regarded in some quarters as a gay love story, there is no sense of this being other than a submerged motif, probably unconscious on the part of the film's makers. *Eskimo Nell* amusingly and sometimes touchingly comments on mateship as a compensation for sexuality: its hero can only experience sex vicariously through the exploits of his youthful stud companion. In *Stir* the question of sex in prison is briefly highlighted but the film as a whole, excellent as it is in creation of suspense and of the tensions between prisoners, registers this as only a minor element in the film's narrative structure. As with *Stir; The Club, Breaker Morant, The Odd Angry Shot* and *The Plains of Heaven* are all set chiefly in male preserves: respectively, a football club, a Boer War court-martial, a pocket of the Vietnam war, and a remote relay tracking station on the Bogong High Plains; and they all have points of interest in their observation of male behaviour. The two Beresford films explore shifting loyalties in hierarchies of male command, and they share with *The Odd Angry Shot* a typically Australian anti-authoritarian spirit. The latter is less a war film than a study, often played for comedy, of a group of soldiers coping with boredom and each other. *The Plains of Heaven* plays off youthful casualness against middle-aged obsessiveness, with the former coming to some understanding of the latter.

None of these films, however, constitutes a serious examination of male friendship and the kinds of emotional rewards that this might offer. Representations of male homosexuality, apart from the fleeting exception noted in *Stir* and, with surprising lack of prurience, in Frank Brittain's otherwise trashy *The Set* (1970) scarcely exist. It provides an ugly element in Igor Auzins' buddies-on-the-road movie *High Rolling* (1977) in which wealthy homosexual Arnold (John Clayton) propositions Alby (Grigor Taylor), who knocks him out and steals his car; and the two television serial spin-offs, *The Box* and *Number 96*, perpetuate their respective flamboyant and sensitive gay types. In contrast, at least two films, Tom Cowan's *Journey Among*

The convict women in Tom Cowan's *Journey Among Women* (1977).

Women (1977) and Paul Eddey's *The Alternative* (1978), offer a more or less radical approach to the possibility of relationships between women as their chief preoccupation, and a number of others, such as *Caddie, A Most Attractive Man*, and *Monkey Grip*, dramatize the kinds of comfort and support which women offer each other even though their narratives are essentially constructed around male-female relationships.

Journey Among Women (1977) uses its historical setting — the earliest days of convict Australia — to explore the possibility of feminist organization. The convict women, freed by a young upper-class woman, find a degree of independence in the wilderness: away from the oppression of male authority, they find in each other a warmth and supportiveness strikingly at odds with the abuse to which they have been subjected in the colony. The women's commune is short-lived but its spirit has subtly and perhaps permanently altered the attitude of Elizabeth (Jeune Pritchard), the judge's daughter who is returned to the colony with a less tractable response to the idea of male dominance. Though sometimes simplistic, as in its equation of woman with an intuitive life-force, *Journey Among Women* is one of the few films which bears the marks of 1970s feminist thinking in its depiction of relationship.

Though this book is not concerned with television, it is worth noting that the most serious, unsensationalizing treatment of homosexuality has been in Paul Eddey's telefeature, *The Alternative* (1978). Here, the dominant ideology, with heterosexual marriage as its norm, is challenged in this story of a career-woman and single mother who opts, not for marriage to the child's father, but for a lesbian relationship. And yet, as Lesley Stern points out in a very long review of the film (its length is a measure of the rarity of what the film attempts), 'The issue of lesbianism is subordinated to the primacy of the discourse on the family'.[8] That is, when Melanie (Wendy Hughes) decides at the film's end to create a life for herself and her son with her former secretary, Linda (Carla Hoogeveen), who has resigned to become full-time baby-minder and housekeeper, the film is endorsing not so much a lesbian relationship as the establishment of an inflection of the model of heterosexual marriage. One partner will go out to work, make decisions, feel important, the other will be the little homebody who will have pipe and slippers (as it were) ready for her at the end of the day. This is not to undervalue what *The Alternative* achieves — a good deal, in the context of Australian film culture — but to regret that it does not go further in challenging the stereotypes.

Mainstream Australian film-making, despite the presence of strongly individual actresses such as Wendy Hughes, Judy Davis, Noni Hazlehurst, Helen Morse, and Judy Morris, has nevertheless tended to uphold the values of male-dominated, heterosexual, monogamous family life. This may well be due to the scarcity of women scriptwriters and directors in Australian mainstream film-making. As suggested above, there have been occasional forays into more adventurous fields but in general casual affaires are shown to lead to unhappiness, adultery is punished, and departures from the prevailing hegemonic structures are both few and unwise. Within these structures, a healthy pleasure in sexuality is less common than its thwarting and inhibition. Decorum and reticence distinguish the cinematic representation of Australian men and women (more markedly in fact than in Australian life) and there are plenty of incidental felicities of observation, moments when accepted values are subjected to scrutiny. But boldness and outspokenness, thematic and stylistic, might produce more *exciting* films about how the sexes engage with each other in Australia. They might even produce films which not merely reflect but influence such engagement.

[1] Quoted in Sue Mathews, *35mm Dreams*, Ringwood; Penguin, 1984, p.204.

[2] Peter Kemp, '*Monkey Grip*', *Filmnews*, June 1982, p.15.

[3] David White, *Australian Movies to the World*, Melbourne: Fontana Australia and Cinema Papers, 1984, p.112.

[4] "On Now", *Sight and Sound*, British Film Institute, Vol.53, No.4, Autumn 1984, p.338.

[5] 'Paul Cox', Interviewed by Debi Enker, *Cinema Papers*, July, 1984, p.129.

[6] Geoff Mayer, 'Best (of) Friends', *Cinema Papers*, April 1982, p.169.

[7] Sam Rohdie, '*Duet for Four*', *Cinema Papers*, April 1982, p.169.

[8] Lesley Stern, '*The Alternative*', *Cinema Papers*, No.32, May-June 1981, p.185.

8 Growing Up Was Never Easy

At the end of Carl Schultz's *Careful, He Might Hear You* (1983), the small boy (Nicholas Gledhill) who is the 'He' of the title demands to know from his assembled relations, 'Who am I?' P.S., the name by which he has always been known, no longer answers his need for a full sense of self. He has been called P.S. since his late mother described him as 'a postcript to her ridiculous life'. On being told that his name is 'Billy' he acquires a new sense of his own wholeness, his *own* identity, regardless of how other people see him or to what uses they put him. This movement towards an individual identity, with varying degrees of conscious awareness on the part of their protagonists, has underlain most of the nearly thirty films of the new Australian cinema which have addressed themselves to the process of growing up.

Just as questions of *national* identity have preoccupied film-makers in films with historical themes and settings, so in films focused on burgeoning youth the issue of *personal* identity has taken centre stage. The issue has been characteristically located in fictions which emphasize the painful aspects of growing up: the adjustment to Australian mores of children under the influence of other national backgrounds; the rebellion against repressive institutions; the difficulties of coming to terms with parental authority and expectations; the frustrating search for suitable adult models of ways of thinking, feeling, and behaving; and the challenges of adult sexuality. In their various ways, these aspects of growth constitute pressures, tensions, and obstacles that must be taken into account in the move towards self-realization, which is, in so many of the films in this category, the dominant narrative motif. Virtually none of these films offers a celebration of the joys of youth; what joy there is tends to be hard-won, those who achieve it bearing the scars of struggle.

*

This may simply suggest that growing up was never easy but it may also be argued that the process as depicted has some peculiarly Australian difficulties. For one thing, until well after the Second World War the education available to Australian children was very much dominated by English traditions, often at odds with the more relaxed social modes of this country. Films such as Bruce Beresford's *The Getting of Wisdom* (1977), Peter Weir's *Picnic at Hanging Rock* (1975), Kevin Dobson's *The Mango Tree* (1977), Gillian Armstrong's *My Brilliant Career* (1979), and Weir's *Gal-*

lipoli (1981) reflect quite strongly the presence of English ways of thinking in the influences on young people.

In the first two named films, the school building and gardens might just as easily be English; the girls are rigorously disciplined in the interests of their behaving like English young ladies; and the brief glimpses of curriculum suggest little concession to antipodean location. In *The Getting of Wisdom* Laura (Susannah Fowle) is worried that Cromwell's foreign policy will appear on an examination paper, is laughed at for her appalling French accent, and pounds away at Schubert and Beethoven on the piano. The girls in *Picnic at Hanging Rock* are full of smothered excitement about St Valentine's Day; the headmistress, Mrs Appleyard (Rachel Roberts), speaks yearningly of Bournemouth, the English middle-class fount of all her aspirations which, in turn, govern her approach to the girls; and Miss Lumley (Kirsty Child) hammers out 'Men of Harlech' for gymnastic exercises in one of the film's key scenes. These random examples are indicative of a pervasive un-Australian-ness about the two young ladies' colleges. The information and attitudes they seek to instil attempt to replicate English educational experiences, and Australian-ness is apt to be equated with hoydenism and signified by a broader Australian accent than is common among the girls.

The two films set during the First World War, *The Mango Tree* and *Gallipoli*, present their respective teenagers, Jamie Carr (Christopher Pate) and Archy Hamilton (Mark Lee), as subjected to the patriotism of Empire. Both films are set in very distinctive Australian locations — Bundaberg, Queensland, and outback Western Australia — so that the influence of loyalty to a distant imperial power is more striking. In *The Mango Tree*, the idea that 'Your Country Needs YOU' (and Jamie is too young to fight) is qualified by the impassioned cry for national pride which his grandmother, Mrs Carr (Geraldine Fitzgerald), makes as a patriotic rally. However, this national pride is to be displayed in the service of a European war which threatens not Australia but Britain. In one charming domestic episode in *Gallipoli*, Archy's Uncle Jack (Bill Kerr) reads to his nieces and nephews and, while the Australian wind whistles round their isolated farmhouse, the children listen rapt — to Kipling. The point is unobtrusively made that Kipling is as much part of this scene as the kerosene lamp. At the sportsground where Archy is running, a soldier with a drum is led forward on a wooden horse bearing the legend 'Join the Light Horse', while another poster proclaims 'The Empire needs You'. Distant England, however vaguely apprehended, is a determining influence in Archy's growth, a process never completed before service in England's cause cuts him down at Gallipoli — in a final freeze-frame which, for once, means something, as it leaves the viewer with a clear sense of lives cut short in utter futility.

It is notably in the films of the 1970s that the English influence on youthful aspiration and in shaping childhood modes of thought is most strongly

P.S. (Nicholas Glenhill) between warring factions, aunts Vanessa (Wendy Hughes) and Lila (Robyn Nevin) in Carl Schultz's *Careful, He Might Hear You* (1983).

felt. Sybylla Melvyn (Judy Davis), the heroine of *My Brilliant Career*, arrives at a firm commitment to the demanding landscape she lives in, but she also yearns for the culture of the great world (that is, for England and Europe). It is an unspecific yearning, but when she finally writes her book it is sent off to a British publisher — Blackwood's of Edinburgh. P.S., the little boy in *Careful, He Might Hear You* is the victim of a custody struggle between two aunts, homely Lila (Robyn Nevin) and sophisticated, Anglophile Vanessa (Wendy Hughes). Significantly, the latter is presented not as one who might open up new vistas to P.S. but as a threat to his security. Vanessa, who was taken to England as 'a great opportunity', when her mother died, wants to do the same for P.S., saying (absurdly, in view of his being six years old): 'In London, he'd have the world at his feet.' Her reasons for wanting custody of P.S. are complex, involving her feeling for his father, Logan (John Hargreaves), but all that her efforts mean to the child are a break from the happy past he has known in Lila's now-Depression-hit home. Her first appearance is in an aureole of light as she stands by the porthole of her cabin in the ocean liner bringing her back to Sydney. She is at once, by contrast with Lila, presented as belonging to another — European, romantic — world; ironically in the film's structure, this light-shrouded figure will prove to be a force of darkness and pain in P.S.'s life. Although the theme of Anglo-Australian influences on young lives has been common in Australian literature, most persistently in Martin Boyd's 'Langton' novels (*Outbreak of Love* and *A Difficult Young Man*, particularly), it has not so far been the central concern of an Australian film. However, in the ways suggested above, it has been a frequent narrative strand in films set in the earlier years of this century.

As the Australian film revival gathered momentum, towards 1980, the films about children and teenagers have become more obviously Australian in their representation of youthful difficulties. In this respect, *Careful, He Might Hear You*, in which a pretentious Anglophilia is an inhibiting pressure on a child's growth, is an exception. The 1980s youth films have taken their lead, it seems, from John Duigan's *Mouth to Mouth* (1978) rather than from, say, *Picnic at Hanging Rock*. It is tempting to suggest that, as the revival has gained confidence, it has turned away from representations of the past, with its strong pull towards England, and addressed itself more directly to what it is like to be young in Australia today. However, if the English influence is no longer as dominant in Australian life, and in the 1980s less commonly a narrative component of Australian films, at least two of the youth films, Michael Pattinson's *Moving Out* (1982) and *Street Hero* (1984), reflect another sort of ethnic influence at work on the lives of their protagonists. In each case, the hero is played by Vince Colosimo. In the earlier film he is Gino, the adolescent son of Italian immigrants bent on working their way out from Melbourne's inner suburbs to join the ranks of the eastern suburban bourgeoisie. Gino's life is doubly dislocated. First, he has had to 'assimilate' and be 'assimilated by' his high school friends, with little enough help from his teachers apart from the sympathetic art teacher, Miss Stanislas (Sandy Gore), but every time he goes home he is confronted by an alien 'wog' culture and refuses to speak Italian with his parents who speak little English. Second, though he wants to 'move out', to leave home as a step towards establishing an independent identity, he is in the end forced to join his parents in their 'moving out' to the balustrades of brick-veneered Doncaster, thus cutting him off from what security he has found among his inner suburban contemporaries. 'The pangs of the alienated adolescent are overlaid with the pangs of the alienated immigrant' as Geoffrey Gardner's review[1] of the film notes, and this double set of pressures is

137

treated with unaffected sympathy and sociological accuracy by director Pattinson and scriptwriter Jan Sardi.

Pattinson, Sardi and Colosimo have opted for a flashier approach in *Street Hero*. This time Colosimo plays Vinnie, again an alienated teenager of Italian immigrant parents, but the ethnic issue is less central to the film than it in in *Moving Out*. Vinnie's growth towards manhood is aided and abetted by a variety of individuals (mother, teachers, girlfriend, mates) and by contact with school, home, the local mafia, and the 'Champion' disco-coffee bar. These influences are frequently juxtaposed in a series of montage sequences, but the film's quite sophisticated visual sense is often undermined by the banalities of the screenplay ('He was always a good boy,' intones Mama) and by Colosimo's inexpressive performance. The camera dotes on him in lovingly held close-ups of moody profile or bared torso and he is in virtually every scene, but he is not a flexible enough actor for the demands made on him. The film is eclectically derivative: there are echoes of *Rebel Without a Cause* (rebel hero, girlfriend, friendly side-kick), *The Corn is Green* (teacher hoping to reclaim youth through fostering talent, this time for music), *The Godfather* (alley killing), *West Side Story* (the character of old George, who runs the coffee bar and trains Vinnie as a boxer), and of any number of more recent youth movies in its use of a pounding rock score, in ill-considered sympathy for youthful truculence, and a simplistic view of adult influences. The Italian-ness of Vinnie's background and the pressure it places on him is only one strand of an overcrowded and under-nourished screenplay. It is, the film suggests though it does not develop the point, basic to his adolescent *angst*, but *Street Hero* lacks both the seriousness and the sharpness of *Moving Out* in tackling a genuine problem for many Australian teenagers.

*

Through the films of the past decade or so is a pervasive sense of young people's being subjected to repressive institutions. The latter are usually schools of one kind or other, although it is a hospital for the severely retarded in Gil Brealey's *Annie's Coming Out* (1984) which stands between the physically disabled Annie (Tina Arhondis) and the development of her mental potential. In the three films which have a predominantly school setting — *Picnic at Hanging Rock*, Fred Schepisi's *The Devil's Playground* (1976) and *The Getting of Wisdom* — the *mise-en-scène* works powerfully to create the sense of a heavily authoritarian setting at odds with the impulses of the young inmates in each case. The first and third of these are exclusive independent schools, that in *The Devil's Playground* a Roman Catholic seminary for young boys. In all three are numerous shots of heavy staircases, long corridors, and generally severe interiors, and all three are sombre stone buildings which the cameras render as bulwarks against the alluring freedoms of the world outside: The glimpses of the public private school to which Aunt Vanessa subjects P.S. in *Careful, He Might Hear You* are similarly uninviting; he is humiliated by teachers and bullied by mean rich kids (the film is a little simplistic in its equation of 'rich' and 'bad'). In the films partly set in the government-run schools — Beresford's *Puberty Blues* (1981), Pattinson's *Moving Out* and *Street Hero,* Michael Caulfield's *Fighting Back* (1982) and Ken Cameron's *Fast Talking* (1984) — the *mise-en-scène* oppresses for other reasons. These schools are typically over-crowded, teachers push past jostling students in the corridors, and the rooms are devoid of character and comfort. Whichever kind of institution the adolescents find themselves in, they are not likely to be inspired by what they are taught: the put-upon Sara (Margaret Nelson) in *Picnic at Hanging Rock* is made to memorize a poem by Mrs Felicia Heymans, 'one of our most famous English poets' while her own efforts at writing are dismissed; in *Moving Out,* Gino stumbles through a half-learnt recitation of 'My Country'. In neither posh nor prole school does the student find stimulus for the mind and imagination from the staff who, with the exception of the one resident liberal crusader, are generally cynical, autocratic, lazy, bullying, or a combination of these.

The institutional pressures on youthful growth are not always at the centre of the above films, but they are inevitably negative pressures. Perhaps this is symptomatic of an Australian anti-intellectual approach: formal education is made to look like a set of meaningless rituals compared with street-wisdom or with an empirical testing of one's capacities in 'real-life' situations. On several occasions these films come near to caricature in their presentation of education as a repressive force (for example, the English teacher in *Moving Out*) and in the setting up of too-easy oppositions (caring vs. cynical, etc.). However, the recurrent presence of such forces and oppositions is in itself instructive in the implication that a child's advance towards self-realization is likely to be impeded rather than furthered by the processes of formal education. There is simplism in such a view: the films offer no example of a well-run school which genuinely has its students's interest at heart; the ineffectual staff are men of straw; the crusading types (Lewis Fitz-Gerald in *Fighting Back*, Sandy Gore in *Street Hero*, Ivar Kants in *Moving Out*) are sentimentally conceived; and the kinetic excitement of the streets is too flashily contrasted with the oppressive *milieux* of the schools.

All that conceded, there is still a good deal to admire in these films. At best they find a visual style that renders vividly and accurately the oppositions around which they are structured, and there is a persistent, if not always discriminating, liberalism at work in them. Fred Schepisi's *The Devil's Playground* is the film which most persistently confronts that institutional repressiveness which inhibits the growth of a full sense of identity. Like many Australian films, it is episodically structured but, unlike some

Brothers Sebastian (Charles McCallum), Celian (John Frawley),
Francine (Arthur Dignam), James (Peter Cox), and Victor (Nick Tate)
relax in the seminary staff-room in Fred Schepisi's *The Devil's
Playground* (1976).

(for example, *The Getting of Wisdom*), it achieves coherence by keeping its
young protagonist, Tom Allen (Simon Burke), and his development at the
centre of its narrative, and through a persistently elaborated discourse
about repression and natural impluse.

Brother Francine (Arthur Dignam), whose own repressed desires surface
in furtive visits to the Melbourne City Baths and in erotic fantasies, enun-
ciates the aphorism which gives the film its title: 'An undisciplined mind is
the devil's playground.' It is the work of this rural seminary to keep this
playground free from dangerous equipment, especially from sexual
knowledge and practice. The film's title is ironic since none of the discipline
the school offers is able to subdue the youthful impulses which assert themselves unbidden. The long graceful tracking shot that opens the film on a
scene of boys swimming suggests a freedom at odds with the film's central
concerns. In this place, life is reduced to a series of rituals and rules meant
to act as agents of repression: meals, classroom scenes, the retreat (recalling that in James Joyce's *A Portrait of the Artist as a Young Man*), and the
carefully supervised play, all follow ritualistic patterns which leave little
scope for personal expression. Insofar as the individual imagination is
involved, as it is in the retreat, it is in the interests of ensuring a graphic

140

response to the notions of sin and guilt, and of eternal punishment in the horrors of hell. The celebration following the retreat is a controlled orgy of cakes and soft drinks, hardly enough to dispel the unsettling effect of the preceding scene in which the silent, supposedly contemplative boys dart stones into the stillness of the lake. Such understated images offer perceptive comment on the precarious nature of the control exerted by the institution, more effective than the explicit outburst from Brother Francine about the waste of the body or from Brother Victor (Nick Tate), good-humoured but inwardly deeply divided, about 'too many bloody rules' and how these make for ignorance of the world.[2]

In general, the film eschews this kind of explicitness, preferring to dramatize its criticism of this way of life through the conflicts the institute engenders in Tom Allen. An essentially likeable, outgoing boy, Tom is made to feel that his wholly natural interest in sex is a subject of guilt and embarrassment. His chronic bed-wetting and the daily ritual of washing his sodden sheets (which, in turn, makes him late for mass) is seen as a product of the pervasive repressiveness of this over-disciplined life. On the brief guesthouse holiday with his parents he is attracted to a girl who later writes to him at school, ending her letter with 'love' and kisses. The letter is inevitably opened by one of the brothers who is reproachful at such licentiousness. Tom has enough sense, and enough sense of himself, to resist the perversities of a student gang of sado-masochistic fanatics who engage in 'purification rites' that include the holding of a leg in boiling water. In the end, pushed towards a crisis by the whisking away of his friend Fitz (John Diedrich), who has been restless at the discipline of the school, Tom runs off towards Melbourne, where he is given a lift by Brother Victor and Brother James (Peter Cox) who are on their way to a football match. The film ends on a note of muted applause for this bid for freedom from the confines of the seminary, the influence of which has been largely inimical on both boys and masters. It is a delicately balanced film, subtle in its delineation of the effects of an inhibiting system and ambience on both boys and brothers. The brief escapes into the outside world — Tom's holiday at Mt. Macedon, the brothers' earlier jaunt to the league football match followed by a visit to a pub — suggest an alluring freedom from restraints. Tom has not been seriously warped by his institutional experience but, conscientiously as he tries to maintain his sense of vocation, a stubborn sense of its unnaturalness for *him* finally pushes him out.

*

The education system is not the only institution which provides a target for youthful rebelliousness: the family is habitually presented as non-supportive, imperceptive, and/or repressive. More often than not, youthful identity is achieved in the teeth of family opposition: parents are usually depicted as being as inadequate as teachers in promoting a healthy adult development in their children. Parents are variously unequal to their task: they may be embittered through grinding poverty (as in *My Brilliant Career*), or over-ambitious in ways that make unreasonable demands on their children (as in Igor Auzins' *The Coolangatta Gold*, 1984), or utterly uncomprehending about their children's lives and needs (as in *Puberty Blues*). In other instances, they are dead (the mother in Ross Dimsey's *Blue Fire Lady*, 1977, or both parents in Peter Collinson's *The Earthling*, 1980), or otherwise missing (the father who has shot through in *Fighting Back*, 1982). There are clashes between fathers and sons, where the former want the wrong things for their sons (as in Michael Blakemore's *A Personal History of the Australian Surf*, 1982), and, occasionally, tensions between mothers and daughters (as in *Puberty Blues* and *My Brilliant Career*). However, the chief focus has been on the growth of boys, on their need for adequate father figures, and the difficulty of finding these in what is, ironically, regarded as a man's country.

These male protagonists range from small boys such as P.S. in *Careful, He Might Hear You* to the sons, presumably in their early twenties, in *The Coolangatta Gold.* In the former (based on a novel by Sumner Locke Elliott), P.S. is the subject of a sustained battle for custody between his aunts, Lila from motives of affection, Vanessa more complexly motivated. Their dominant roles are a major exception in these youth-centred films in which men are usually the notable influences on a child's growth. The film's most moving scene, however, is the brief, pivotal meeting between P.S. and his long-absent father, Logan (played by John Hargreaves, with a remarkable awareness of the joy and pain involved in the reunion). Logan is for P.S. a brief incarnation of the *idea* of father, and his importance to P.S.'s growth is symbolized by the child's tenacious grasp of the piece of rock Logan gives him. The film registers Logan's easy charm without suggesting that there is much more to be said for him. Vanessa tells P.S., 'Your father's a bad man. Aren't you glad to have me to protect you from him?', but P.S. is unconvinced. The film may uphold the lower-middle-class warmth of Lila and her Depression-hit husband George (Peter Whitford) against both Vanessa's empty cosmopolitanism and Logan's likeable fecklessness, but Logan matters intensely to the child. As Tom Ryan has noted, 'One of the major strengths of the film [is] a refusal to allow us any simple response to its characters',[3] and, in doing so, *Careful, He Might Hear You* very convincingly moves towards P.S.'s final insistence on knowing who he is. He has been subjected to a range of influences, none of them for unqualified good or bad, and as he walks out the front door of Vanessa's house at the film's end he knows his name and, the film suggests, how to value those influences. He has made enough progress to be able to accept Vanessa's telling him that the piece of rock Logan gave him is not gold. Just before her death in a ferry accident in Sydney Harbour, Vanessa tells P.S., 'Find out who you are and you'll find out how to love someone else'. The inter-connection of these two pieces of knowledge is already making itself felt in P.S. by the end of the film, as he begins to feel for Vanessa, 'all alone' out there, and in the next scene asks his crucial question. *Careful, He Might Hear You* is one of the most striking films of the Australian revival: utterly indigenous in its use of Sydney (the harbour, the quality of light), in its response to the Depression, and in its demotic upholding of unpretentious Australian values (Lila and George, cricket in the streets) against snobbish Anglophile ones (Vanessa, private schools). It is also a powerful piece of melodrama in a tradition which owes much to classic Hollywood. P.S.'s development may be seen largely as a response to those indigenous elements noted above; but the film's lighting, framing, composition, music and use of décor are more resonant of, say, Douglas Sirk or Vincente Minnelli than of other Australian directors. The drama of P.S.'s move towards identity is accomplished in the mode of emotional family melodrama in full cry. Its narrative machinery (the disruptive arrival of an outsider into narrowly circumscribed lives, the convenient disposal of Vanessa, her work for good and ill now done) and its stylistic exploitation of bold contrasts, physical and psychological, earn *Careful, He Might Hear You* a unique place in the often too decorous Australian cinema. Its director, Carl Schultz, exhibits a firm grasp of cinematic conventions and a zest in deploying them which only Richard Franklin has shown in similar measure. As an aside, it is sad that Franklin should have had to go to the US to make *Cloak and Dagger* (1984), one of the best of all films about a child, his fantasy life, and his final acceptance of reality.

Snook (Greg Rowe) tries to repair a damaged motor in Carl Schultz's *Blue Fin* (1978).

Schultz's first feature, *Blue Fin* (1978), also has a young boy as its central figure. The boy, Snook (Greg Rowe), is desperate for the approval of his tuna fisherman father (Hardy Kruger, striking an oddly exotic note) who is having a spell of bad luck, and who vents his anxieties and frustration on his son. When his boat, the 'Blue Fin', is all but wrecked in a cyclone, the rest of the crew lost and the father injured, the boy contrives to bring it back to port by being more resourceful than his father would have believed him. It is essentially a children's film (based on a novel by Colin Thiele, author also of *Storm Boy*) and it does not risk boring its target audience with complex psychologising or the *longueurs* induced by a self-indulgent cameraman. Surprisingly, the film did not do well at Australian box offices, unlike Henri Safran's *Storm Boy* (1977) made the previous year also by the South Australian Film Corporation and with many of the same names involved.

Another children's drama of a young boy's difficult relationship with his father, *Storm Boy* seemed numbingly tedious to the present author who wrote about it as follows in a review of *Blue Fin*:

> At the risk of seeming an insensitive brute, I found most of it [*Storm Boy*] a bore, suffering from a severe attack of Creeping Beauty, that disease endemic in many recent Australian films. I was surprised to find it ran six minutes less than *Blue Fin*; it seemed half an hour longer, lingering over every quivering reed and every exquisite sunset, wearing its poetic intentions on its graceful sleeve.[4]

This sour opinion (still held) was not shared, and the film did well critically, as well as commercially, both here and abroad. Greg Rowe, then eleven years old and in his first film role, played the boy, Mike, who has difficulty in relating to his glum, reclusive father (Peter Cummins) and finds friends in an Aboriginal, Fingerbone (David Gulpilil), and a pelican. What drama there is is apt to be submerged in self-conscious poeticising and the child–father relationship is scarcely explored. However, the *Monthly Film Bulletin* praised it for 'its simple, direct story-line, fine acting and marvellously photographed scenes of natural beauty'.[5] *Blue Fin* retained Rowe, scriptwriter Sonia Borg, cameraman Geoff Burton and music director Michael Carlos, but failed to repeat *Storm Boy's* success. Both directors went on to make other notable films about children: Schultz's *Careful, He Might Hear You* and Safran's *Norman Loves Rose* (1982), which accurately presents the smothering possessiveness of family life as funny to observe but painful to experience.

Norman Loves Rose is something of a maverick among Australian films: it is persistently *funny* about the family whereas most of the other films concerned with young boys on the brink of adulthood play up the frustration and pain involved. Comedies on any theme are rare enough in the Australian cinema for *Norman Loves Rose* to be welcome; but to locate that comedy in middle-class (Jewish) family life was perhaps too unusual for commercial success. Norman (Tony Owen) nurses — and gratifies — an adolescent passion for his sister-in-law Rose (Carol Kane) whom he quickly impregnates whereas his brother Michael (David Downer), engaging in fearsome exercises with bowls of ice cubes, has been humiliatingly unsuccessful. Norman's barmitzvah celebrations present the family in full sail. After the religious ceremony, with the sexes carefully separated, there is a gross, noisy, cheerful party, complete with dripping ice swans and fingers grabbing food, and unconscious *double entendres* from Michael who pompously proposes Norman's health: 'You will assume duties which up to now have been my father's and mine.' Norman, of course, has been assuming such duties with effortless ease for some time. It that sounds tasteless, the film is not.

As much as any Australian film, *Norman Loves Rose* is explicitly focused on family life. If its Jewishness makes it less than typical, it is nevertheless very acute about the fine line between parental love and possessiveness, and about the pressures which family life can exert. The Jewish mother's obsession with progeny is of course a recognizable stereotype, but in the writing (Safran's screenplay) and in the warmth and humorous understanding of Myra deGroot's performance it achieves a subtler delineation. Similarly, Warren Mitchell (a long way from his Alf Garnett *persona*) creates the Jewish dad with prostate trouble and hyper-anxious wife as a whole character. And there is an affecting performance from Downer as Michael, tight-lipped and grim, doggedly and unavailingly coupling with Rose, envious of the apparent sexual triumphs of his randy dental partner Charlie (wittily and painfully understood by Barry Otto). As he recalls bitterly the Gentile girl he loved and let himself be talked out of marrying and despairs over his infertility, Downer cuts through to veins of real frustration. In doing so, he highlights Norman's seemingly effortless — and precocious — adjustment to at least some of the demands of manhood.

The boys in Tim Burstall's *The Child*, an episode of *Libido* (1973), and in *Fighting Back* and *Street Hero* endure rougher rites of passage than Norman, in their dealings with the family. In each case, the father is absent. *The Child*, which contains some of Burstall's most sensitive work and is quite unlike his more commercial projects, hinges on the discovery by the boy, Martin (John Williams), that the governess, Sybil (Judy Morris), to whom he has become attached when his father goes down with the 'Titanic', is having an affaire with his mother's lover, David (Bruce Barry). Written for the screen by Hal Porter, and recalling *The Go-Between* in its glowing evocation of 1912 life in an imposing home and in the child's traumatic discovery, *The Child* offers a tougher treatment of childhood than is usual in Australian films. Through an intelligent use of point-of-view shots, Martin is established as a shrewd watcher of the adult world and the moral shoddiness beneath its elegant surfaces, and this watchfulness reaches an uncompromising climax as he observes David drown, as his father has done. Martin's

Tom (Paul Smith) shapes up for a confrontation in Michael Caulfield's *Fighting Back* (1982).

sexual awakening has been accompanied by disillusion which achieves a black expression in contrast to the film's lovely surface that suggests the paintings of Charles Condor.

Fighting Back and *Street Hero* have been discussed elsewhere, but they should be noted here as representations of teenage maladjustment directly related to an absent father. Tom (Paul Smith) is in fact seriously disturbed, given to outbursts of raging violence at school and at home. The school's remedial teacher (Robyn Nevin) fears that one day 'he might snap completely', and a well-judged crane shot catches the frenzy of his destructive mania as he smashes windows in a locker room while the new teacher, John Embling (Lewis Fitz-Gerald), waits for him to subside. Embling, in his efforts to help Tom, seeks the reasons for his behaviour in his home where he is first seen fighting his sister over a television programme and then kicking and swearing at his mother (Kris McQuade) who ineffectually threatens, 'Don't you ever speak to me like that'. There is a touchingly detailed performance from McQuade as a working-class mum, deserted six years earlier by a brutal husband. She fears that Tom has 'got his father in him, that's his problem'.

The dead father of Vinnie in *Street Hero* is also a major part of his problem. Vinnie loves his mother (Peta Toppano) but reveres the memory of his father. His attraction to boxing and the criminal underworld, which seem to offer him opportunities to emulate this father ('He was the best,' Vinnie idealizes), alienates him from school and from home, where he hates his mother's new boyfriend. Life at home, in a high-rise flat, is cramped and devoid of privacy, and Vinnie is the object of his migrant mother's aspirations about education. For him, trying to live up to a dead father is as inhibiting as Tom's inability to come to terms with his father's desertion. Both are forced to learn that a sense of personal identity lies in directions other than those laid down in their father's behaviour. *Fighting Back* suffers from a certain naïvety in its narrative procedures but, like *Annie's Coming Out*, is transparently well-intentioned; *Street Hero* is a slicker piece of work but is less serious than either of the others. It remains too wedded to its hero's macho view of himself for its own good.

Two Queensland-set films which are structured around father–son relationships are Donald Crombie's *The Irishman* (1978) and Auzins' *The Coolangatta Gold*. Like most of these films about sons establishing themselves in the adult world, typically locked in conflict with fathers and needing to 'prove' or 'find' themselves, these two relegate women (Robyn Nevin in both cases) to the role of observer, minimizing maternal influence on their children's growth. *The Irishman*'s story of teamster Paddy Doolan (Michael Craig) who is unable to meet the challenge of mechanised trans-

Michael Doolan (Simon Burke) leads his father's team as his parents (Michael Craig and Robyn Nevin) watch in Donald Crombie's *The Irishman* (1978).

port is told in its early stages with an attractive narrative sweep, reinforced by cameraman Peter James's splendid tracking shots of the Clydesdale teams at work. Its personal drama is less surely handled and focuses on the younger son, Michael (Simon Burke), who goes searching for his missing father. After their brief reunion, Paddy is killed in an accident and Michael is faced with the responsibilities of manhood. Despite the affectionate observation of family life and the pressures under which it breaks, forcing Michael into premature adulthood, *The Irishman* founders on a too conventional (and, in Australian films of the 1970s, too common) episodic treatment. Susan Dermody writes that: 'Throughout the film, as though sensing the doom laid by stubbornness on his real father, he [Michael] casts about for father-figures'.[6] Such an account imputes a greater structural coherence to the film's episodes than is actually the case.

Few Australian films have received so uniformly poor a press as the much-touted *The Coolangatta Gold*. However, it is ravishing to look at, a marvellous assault on the senses as it records a range of physical activities, such as running, surfing, dancing, hacking away at a banana plantation, motor cycling, all of which are shown to bear on the human drama. Admittedly the latter is not developed in great depth or detail but the film's sheer visual panache distracts attention from a certain cerebral jejeuneness in its plotting. A fiercely competitive father, Joe Lucas (Nick Tate), is determined that his older son, Adam (Colin Friels), will win a Gold Coast triathlon to compensate for his own second place in 1960. His fixation on Adam leads to

Adam (Colin Friels) leads the pack in Igor Auzins' *The Coolangatta Gold* (1984).

his constant depreciation of his younger son, Steve (Joss McWilliam), who, despite his success at karate and as the leader of a profitable rock band, can never gratify his father. As a way of establishing his identity, Steve competes in the triathlon and (in a sequence which owes something to *Chariots of Fire* and *Gallipoli*) deliberately falls and allows Adam to win in the last few yards of the event. Unfortunately, McWilliam, who the plot suggests is the focus of the drama, is the least expressive actor, so that the film's chief interest falls on Tate's obsessive father and Friels' likeable Adam, confused by his father's ambition and by his affection for his brother. Even if the film's psychology is shallow, it has a good deal more vigour and excitement going for it than many more discreetly tasteful Australian films.

There are no more than two or three films which centre on daughter-parent conflict: *My Brilliant Career* does, up to a point, but its real drama is in the growth of Sybylla's determination to pursue the career she wants even if it means irrationally committing herself to an arduous life. Her parents (Julia Blake and Alan Hopgood) are certainly not sympathetic to her aspirations, but by the end of the film she has acquired an inner independence, not only from them but also from the man she loves, which sets her apart from the constraints of everyday poverty. Each successive stage in the film's narrative, whether offering encouragement or hindrance to her, brings her nearer to that sense of self crucial to a writer which, incipiently at least, is what she is in the film's final scenes. It says much for Judy Davis' deeply felt performance that one accepts this potential. *Puberty Blues* is a sharply observant study of two teenage girls at odds with their middle-class parents and the 'good middle-class homes' they come from. Their aim is to be accepted by the surfing jocks of Cronulla Beach, Sydney, and the charm of the film lies in the girls' gradual realization that there is more to life than this. Debbie (Nell Schofield) has constant friction with her parents about the boys she is going out with and when she will be home; her mother tries to include her in the family excitement about a new car; and parental tolerance is almost as irksome as interference. There is very intelligent realization of youthful boredom with parental lives, a sense of the young being utterly at odds with their parents' ideologies — for now, at least. The film has a nicely ironic tone which accurately places both parents and jocks in relation to the girls' development.

The heroine of *Blue Fire Lady* is a nicely-bred, horse-loving girl called Jenny (played by English Cathryn Harrison), whose mother has died from a riding accident and whose father (Lloyd Cunningham) in consequence adopts a firmly repressive line on Jenny's activities. She is to be removed from the prettily photographed rural life to a city boarding school, after which she applies for a job as a groom, establishes her capacities in this role, and is reconciled with her father. This is a film for horsey little girls and on that level it is amiable enough. For adults, there is little compensation: the daughter–father conflict is perfunctorily treated; there is a tepid little feminist touch here and there; and a number of simplistically presented oppositions (Jenny's humane, caring approach to horses versus the assembly-line tactics of the nasty groom; the laughing, happy Australian country family versus mean dad, etc.). It is an unpretentious film and has a good deal to be unpretentious about, including dialogue of unusual banality ('Give old Mother Nature time and she can fix anything', for instance).

*

A not-surprising corollary of all these unsatisfactory, oppressive parental influences and of the recurring pattern of missing parents, is the child's or adolescent's search for appropriate adult models. Conventionally, Jenny, in *Blue Fire Lady*, appreciates the motherly warmth of neighbouring, homely Mrs Bartlett (Anne Sutherland) and the caricatured Italian momma landlady (Marion Edward) she lodges with in the city; Sybylla Melvyn is helped to a firmer sense of her own worth by her graceful Aunt Helen (Wendy Hughes) although the latter's views on the woman's role fall short of Sybylla's own ripening feminism; the girls in *Puberty Blues* find no such model and have to arrive at their sense of self through some bruising experiences; and, most touchingly, Anne (played with real poignancy by Eva Dickinson) in Michael Thornhill's *The FJ Holden* (1977) has already, at seventeen, had to assume her widowed mother's role in the home, with little in the way of adult models to guide her. Her boyfriend's mother (Beryl Marshall) offers only a pretentious guide to table-setting and Mrs Pope (May Howlett), her employer, is merely snootily censorious ('I'd be more careful who I was seen with at lunch-time'). The most appealing aspect of the latter two films is the way in which the girls, with little to inspire them, arrive with some dignity at a sense of their own worth.

As for the boys, it is an encouragingly anti-'ocker' strain to find several looking to women for signs of strength and for constructive sympathy. Martin in *The Child* (*Libido*) turns to his nurse-governess to fill the gap left by his dead father; Vinnie in *Street Hero* and Gino in *Moving Out* both find their most understanding adult acquaintance in a woman teacher (played in both films by Sandy Gore); and whatever Jamie in *The Mango Tree* knows about courage or wisdom (actually not much, but that is because he is a slow learner) he has learnt from his remarkable grandmother, Mrs Carr (Geraldine Fitzgerald). The men under whose influence Jamie falls — boozing remittance man (Robert Helpmann), fanatical Preacher Jones (Gerard Kennedy), and ineffectual teachers (Terry McDermott, Ben Gabriel) — are in their various ways unsuitable as surrogate father figures. The most glamorous possibility for the role is Bundaberg's celebrated flying ace, Bert Hinkler (Tony Bonner), who visits the Queensland town fleetingly, and takes Jamie for a flight, his grandmother reluctantly freeing him from his promise not to fly. A thematic point is made here: that Jamie is poised for

150

independence and Mrs Carr's relenting is a recognition of this. But Bert Hinkler is on his way next day. It is Mrs Carr who best equips Jamie for manhood and, in a better, more rigorously structured film, the viewer might have been left at the film's end with a stronger sense of how this has been achieved.

Elsewhere, Mike in *Storm Boy* finds education for heart and imagination, not from his taciturn father but from his Aboriginal friend, Fingerbone; P.S. has, in *Careful, He Might Hear You*, two versions of maleness — his briefly glimpsed father and dim but kind Uncle George — as part of the pattern of influences at work on him; and young Jim (Tom Burlinson), eponymous hero of George Miller's *The Man from Snowy River* (1982), following the death of his father, casts about for someone to admire. On hand, and no help to Jim or the audience, are a tiresomely aphoristic old-timer, Spur (Kirk Douglas, appalling in one of the two roles he plays), and Clancy of the Overflow (a role in which Jack Thompson is defeated by lines like: 'I wouldn't swap the sunlit plains for all the tea in China. It's a vision splendid'). By the end of the film, he's done what he's gotta do — he has found the colt that killed his father — and Spur solemnly pronounces: 'He's not a lad, brother; he's a man.' 'The Man from Snowy River', intones Clancy, as the soundtrack strikes up 'Waltzing Matilda'.

If *The Man from Snowy River* strikes one as a witless extravaganza, it is still a good deal preferable to *The Earthling*, as mawkish and ludicrous a piece of father-searching as the Australian — perhaps any — cinema has offered. As David Stratton has reported, with proper asperity, a Sydney lawyer, Andrew Martin

> ... brought together American producer Elliot Schick and Stephen Sharmat, who then imported American stars William Holden and Ricky Schroeder [the lachrymose kid from *The Champ*] while a British director of no great distinction, Peter Collinson, was brought in to direct ... Apart from the scenery there would, of course, be nothing Australian about *The Earthling* which could just as well have been made in Arizona.[7]

Despite these precautions, the film has failed dismally wherever it has been shown, and rightly so. When the parents of Sean (Schroeder) are killed as their campervan hurtles over a cliff, he heads off into the central Australian bush where he meets up with embittered Foley (Holden), who is not interested in taking on a companion. Nevertheless, the two reach a final understanding, symbolized by the meeting of outstretched hands and, when Foley dies, one assumes that Sean, catapulted into precocious manhood, will make his own way back to civilization. It is difficult to give a full sense of the awfulness of the whole enterprise without quoting extensively. Foley has an inexhaustible fund of philosophic claptrap ('Some day you're gonna die, but until then you fight like mad to stay alive. You're on your own', and 'You're deaf [to everything including] your own heartbeat. There's a whole symphony going on and you don't hear a thing') which, one also assumes, makes a man of Sean. Visually, too, the film is dire: that is to say, its preposterous story is punctuated by images of monotonously majestic scenery and improbably 'planted' wild-life, all at the service of Sean's education.

Much more modest and effective is the use made of Redback (Steve Bisley) who runs the bike-wrecking yard in *Fast Talking* and acts as a sort of father figure to Steve (Rod Zuanic), whose actual father is a drunken bully. There is a welcome lack of sentimentality in the way Ken Cameron's screenplay and Bisley's performance present Redback. On the one hand, he warns Steve, 'Don't bring smack into my yard'; on the other, he does not set out to be a consciously moral influence and, at the end, as Steve flees from the law, Redback just says, 'Your choice, pal . . . you can take off. At least you can say you gave them a run for your money.' Bisley plays with a casual authority that gives the role its proper status in the drama and he avoids the clichés that dog the presentation of the surrogate fathers in these films.

*

In more than half of the films discussed in this chapter, the issue of adolescent sexuality is a key element in the search for identity. Australian films of the 1970s and 1980s, taking advantage of the greater candour in sexual matters permitted by censorship in those decades, have generally eschewed the more conventional romantic approach that characterized, say, Hollywood films of earlier decades. As a result, films such as *Blue Fire Lady* and *The Man from Snowy River* seem curiously old-fashioned in their representation of sexual feeling between teenagers when compared with that in most recent Australian films. The chaste kisses of these two films contrast with the more realistic approach of the urban teenage film such as *The FJ Holden* or *Puberty Blues*, in which youthful ignorance and insecurity make sexual fumblings as painful as they are exciting — and inevitable. The two films which offer the most intelligent discourse on teenage sexuality are Nicolas Roeg's *Walkabout* (1971) and *Picnic at Hanging Rock* in both of which (despite Weir's disclaimer of interest in this aspect of this film[8]) inexactly apprehended sexual longings are integrated into the texture of the film.

The girl (Jenny Agutter) in *Walkabout* is pushed by crisis into assuming an adult role to ensure the survival of her young brother and herself in the Australian desert. One aspect of her adult role is a more sensitive awareness of the possibilities of a seemingly hostile landscape; another is her sense of herself as a young woman, suddenly aware of her sexuality and of its effect on the young Aboriginal (Gulpilil) who helps them. He, on the brink of tribal manhood, is destroyed by her disingenuous refusal to understand this effect. The film's final scene of washed-out sunlight in a Sydney flat suggests that the dramatic convergence of cultural and sexual oppositions some years before has left her unsettled but not enriched. The girls in *Picnic* are, with the exception of fat Edith (Christine Schuller) who is first glimpsed counting her St Valentine's day cards as possessions, their romance lost on her, ripe for sexual awakening. Weir may well be more interested in 'other areas: sounds, smells, the way hair fell on the shoulder, images — just plain pictures.'[9] On the basis of the film itself, the sexual motif works controllingly in making those images *mean*. What we have seen at the College — St Valentine's Day; Sara's crush on Miranda (Anne Lambert), exquisite and swan-like, in an image the film repeats; the girls in their virginal white, who are like sympathetic Mlle de Poitiers (Helen Morse) and unlike the other teachers — has encouraged the reading of a sexual sub-text. The Rock, on the other hand, is presented as alluring as well as ominous, as inviting a release from sexual inhibition. The three girls who disappear, leaving Edith behind to run screaming back to the rest of the school party, seem almost to float through the trees as if to the embrace of a lover. The young English aristocrat, Michael Fitzhubert (Dominic Guard), and the Australian groom, Albert Crundall (John Jarratt), who observe them, respond — the one with quivering sensitivity, the other with crude realism — to the sexual challenge of the fleeting image. The climax to the film's persistent use of the sexual motif as a link between Rock and College comes in the scene in which Irma (Karen Robson), restored from the Rock and recovered from her ordeal, visits the school gym to say goodbye to her fellow pupils. Into the oppressive scene comes Irma, clad in a long crimson cloak and crimson hat, a striking figure as she appears in the doorway, flanked in the frame by the two rows of girls doing posture exercises. Whatever has happened to Irma on the Rock — and she has refused, or been unable, to tell — it has changed her from romantic schoolgirl to assured woman. The girls sense a new — sexual? — knowledge about her and crowd round hysterically demanding explanations.

This romanticized, if still sharply erotic, representation of teenage sexuality is a long way from the back-seat couplings of *The FJ Holden*. In these, Anne (Eva Dickinson) submits to the unwelcome attentions of Bob (Carl Stever) as a preliminary to a more protracted session with his mate Kevin (Paul Couzens), whom she does fancy and might even love if he gave her a chance. But like the girls in *Puberty Blues*, Anne is subject to what Meaghan Morris has described as 'the mechanism of conformity to group norms which dictates down to the last detail the acceptable forms of taking freedom'.[10] There is both resignation and pleasure in Anne's submitting to Kevin — and submitting is what it usually amounts to for the girls in these films. Whatever their social class, their sexual conditioning negates the possibility of their being the instigator. Insofar as sexual experience is a key element in their adult identities, it will be as passive receiver. 'What's it like "screwin"?...What do I do?' asks one of the girls in *Puberty Blues*. 'Nothing ... just lie there', is the answer she gets. These girls have been indoctrinated, overtly by their peers, implicitly by their mothers, with the idea of its being for boys' pleasure. 'You're so lucky', one says, 'if a boy doesn't insist on sex', but there is no question of saying no if he does. They will do what is expected of them, partly for conformity's sake, partly because they also see sexual activity as a rite of passage.

The wry realism of these two films and of *Mouth to Mouth* contrasts with the more conventionally lyrical approach adopted by Kevin Dobson to the scene of Jamie's sexual initiation in *The Mango Tree*. Although Christopher Pate is too limited an actor, and too old, for the role of Jamie, the scene does suggest an authentically adolescent clumsy gentleness, and he is considerably helped by Diane Craig's touchingly willing French teacher. In the following scene, his grandmother is aware of what has happened ('I've seen rut before') and accepts it as a necessary stage in his growth. The trouble with this often attractive and ultimately ramshackle film is that it signally lacks a sense of *pressure* on Jamie, the pressure of a range of events (including sexual blooding) internalised so as to lead to tension, anxiety, and growth. There is a contrast, too, between Bruce Beresford's ironic realism in his representation of teenage female sexuality in *Puberty Blues* and the tactful warmth with which, in *The Getting of Wisdom*, he realizes the feeling between Laura and the beautiful older girl, Evelyn (Hilary Ryan). Laura is possessively jealous of Evelyn's male admirer, glimpsed at the opera to which Evelyn has taken her. Eventually, Evelyn invites Laura to her bed to comfort her. There is sensuousness, but not sensuality, in the way the film handles this scene with Evelyn beckoning from the lower right of the frame, the shot angled in such a way as to stress the distance Laura must traverse to accept the invitation. The importance of the scene is that it draws from Laura a capacity to receive affection as well as to smother an adored object with it; in this respect it is a key stage in her growth.

Although this book is essentially concerned with the Australian feature film, mention should be made here of Michael Blakemore's irresistibly attractive *A Personal History of the Australian Surf*, a dramatized documentary of his own childhood and adolescence. It draws on most of the aspects of growing up considered in this chapter — father–son conflict, European influences ('My thoughts were a childish attempt to mythologize the landscape', with piratical imaginings on Sydney beaches), school and university which offered little stimulus to an imagination saturated with the movies, and sexual frustration — and does so with grace and wit. His doctor father wants him to follow in his footsteps and to conform to an image of manly, outdoor Australian boyhood. He is not impressed with young Michael's theatrical leanings and it is only the boy's surfing skill that saves him from ignominy. The beach and the theatre are the two chief magnets of his boyhood and teens, joined by a third as he watches girls cavort on the

154

beach. When visiting English actor Robert Morley offers him his chance in the theatre, he decides that: 'It was time for the straight poofter to come out of the closet', and engages in his last battle with his father, 'without whose opposition', Morley says, 'you would undoubtedly have become a lifeguard'. Few of the fiction films about adolescence have been so perceptive or worn their wisdom so lightly.

The kinds of emotional pressures exerted upon children and adolescents outlined above have been represented in films in ways that make growing up seem a difficult and sometimes dangerous process. Although most of these films conscientiously depict forces and individuals that help to promote a healthy sense of youthful identity, the overriding impression is one of the obstacles and constraints that impede such a growth. Tom Allen may escape the strictures of the seminary at the end of *The Devil's Playground* and Sybylla Melvyn may seem to await a new life with optimism at the end of *My Brilliant Career*, but one is left wondering if the repressions and inhibitions of the life leading up to this point can be so easily eradicated. Australian films have rarely shown children at the centre of a sustaining family life (an Australian *Meet Me In St Louis* is all-but-unthinkable) or as subject to benevolent institutional concern. It is more usual to find children in danger, as in *Careful, He Might Hear You* or *Fast Talking*, or adolescents adrift in an unheeding, materialistic society, as in *Mouth to Mouth* or *The FJ Holden*. The resilience some of these films suggest at the end is more likely to be the result of pragmatic individual adjustment than of benign influences at work.

[1]   Geoffrey Gardner, 'Moving Out', *Cinema Papers*, No.42, March 1983, p.63.

[2]   Schepisi has claimed: 'I wasn't trying to paint the Brothers black. They are products of a system and were trying to do the best they could, believing they were doing the right things while maybe doubting some things. They taught obedience which is one of the vows, so it's pretty tough.' Quoted in Sue Mathews, *35mm Dreams*, Melbourne: Penguin Books, 1984, p.37.

[3]   Tom Ryan, '*Careful, He Might Hear You*' in Al Clark (ed.), *The Film Yearbook 1985*, Melbourne: Curry O'Neil Ross, 1984, p.196.

[4]   Brian McFarlane, '*Blue Fin*', *Cinema Papers*, No.19, Jan.-Feb. 1979, p.221.

[5]   David Badden, '*Storm Boy*', *Monthly Film Bulletin*, British Film Institute, London, Vol.45, No.529, Feb. 1978, p.31.

[6]   Susan Dermody, 'Action and Adventure', in Scott Murray (ed.), *The New Australian Cinema*, Melbourne: Thomas Nelson, 1980, p.87.

[7]   David Stratton, *The Last New Wave*, Melbourne: Angus & Robertson, 1980, p.291.

[8]   'Peter Weir: Towards the Centre', interviewed by Brian McFarlane and Tom Ryan, *Cinema Papers*, No.34, September-October 1981, p.325.

[9]   *Ibid.*

[10] Meaghan Morris, 'Personal Relationships and Sexuality' in Scott Murray, (ed.), p.142.

9 History Lessons: Then and Now

> The 'lessons of history' are not inscribed in the simple existence of a past; they are the product of the construction of a history which can be deployed in contemporary arguments.[1]

In the late 1970s it became almost a cliché among reviewers to draw attention to the number of new Australian films set in the past; implying an evasion of the present-day realities of Australian society. It is true that many of the most successful films of the recent revival — Peter Weir's *Picnic at Hanging Rock* (1975), Ken Hannam's *Sunday Too Far Away* (1975), Fred Schepisi's *The Devil's Playground* (1976), Phil Noyce's *Newsfront* (1977), Gillian Armstrong's *My Brilliant Career* (1979), among others — were set in periods between twenty and eighty years before their time of production. However, too little consideration has been given to what constitutes 'historical films' and to ways in which such films might be seen to offer pertinent commentaries on contemporary life as well as explorations of aspects of the country's past. In fact, among the films set in the past (and they are numerically fewer than their success rate might suggest), there are scarcely any which belong simply to the 'costume melodrama' genre. There are Terry Bourke's idiotic piece of *petit guignol, Inn of the Damned* (1975); Donald Crombie's engaging, but unambitious *Kitty and the Bagman* (1982) and Kevin Dobson's *Squizzy Taylor* (1982), which remain resolutely period pieces; and George Miller's *The Man from Snowy River* (1982), which affects to be more than a period piece and is uninteresting even on that undemanding level.

Before considering in any detail the kinds of historical films which the Australian cinema revival has thrown up, it is worth considering what the term may imply.

1 Most obviously, a historical film is one set in a time recognizably past, and an inescapable requirement for such a film will be at least minimal accuracy in matters of setting and costume, and in relation to the way the characters speak and behave. Bill Gammage, credited as 'Military Adviser' to *Gallipoli* (1981), says that:

> ... I got the impression, and accepted the view, that historians were there basically to make sure that a lack of authenticity would not turn people off the film.[2]

Without making a god of literal realism, one does not usually want to be distracted in viewing a re-creation of the past by a merely careless error, like the vulgar joke (about a new bull's making a lot of cows happy) improbably given to Sybylla (Judy Davis) in *My Brilliant Career*. Australian period films have generally got right the look and sound of times past; in fact, have lavished a great deal of loving care on doing so.

2 There is a distinction to be drawn between those films which set out to re-enact and interpret historical events and those which merely locate their narratives in the past. Among the former are such films as Richard Lowenstein's *Strikebound* (1984) which offers a sympathetic exploration of the Gippsland miners' strike of the 1930s; among the latter, which may be revealing about the periods in which they are set but are not subject to the constraints of authenticity enjoined on the former group, are Carl Schultz's *Careful, He Might Hear You* (1983) and *Picnic at Hanging Rock*. It is not that one group is more or less 'historical' than the others: what distinguishes them is the nature of their interest in the past. In the latter group, the emphasis is on the personal drama; in the former, the personal dramas are seen as directly connected with and influenced by the specific historical events that provide the impulse for the films.

3 In their representations of earlier periods, films (whether fictionally-based or otherwise) provide a valuable source for historical study. They become, in effect, documents relevant both to the times in which they are set and to those in which they are made. Their interest is not limited to their representation of actual historical events such as those portrayed in Peter Weir's *Gallipoli, Strikebound,* or David Bradbury's documentary, *Nicaragua no pasaran* (1984); it is as likely to be found in the narration of fictional events set in a reconstructed past, as in the small-town provincialism in Ken Hannam's *Break of Day* (1976) or in the attitudes embodied in a fictional character such as Len Maguire (Bill Hunter) in *Newsfront*.

4 Historical representations are inevitably selective and subjective. There is no question of a mirror relationship between film and historical reality: the latter must always be mediated by the film-maker who, whatever degree of objectivity he may aim at, structures and composes and edits his material in such a way as to provide a particular view of the period or events, or both, involved. Bruce Beresford's re-enactment of a 'true' episode in the Boer War, *Breaker Morant* (1980), whatever its objective authenticity, is eloquently imbued with an anti-British, anti-authoritarian attitude that is characteristic of other such diverse films by the same director as *The Adventures of Barry McKenzie* (1972) and *The Getting of Wisdom* (1977). Further, there is frequently an element of nostalgia in the diligence that goes into reproducing the physical attributes of an earlier period, as in Kevin Dobson's *The Mango Tree* (1977), or for what may seem the simpler values of such times, as enshrined in Grandma Carr's humane dignity in the same film. In any case, the audience is being offered, in Keith Tribe's term, 'the construction of a history', not a text innocently reflecting the past.

5   Given that all historical films involve the construction of narratives (and, it may be added, that all narratives are at least vestigially concerned with the creation of histories[3]), it may be seen that such constructions serve diverse functions. A film set in the past may provide, without loss of period authenticity, a context for understanding the present. *My Brilliant Career*, set eighty years earlier, and Tom Cowan's *Journey Among Women* (1977), set about a hundred and eighty years earlier, both contribute to the feminist debates of the 1970s. It may be that the lines of debate emerge more clearly for being freed from the distractions of contemporary familiarity. Other films, in examining the past, may throw valuable light on the present and how it has come to be as it is. The changing relations between Australia and Europe (Britain in particular) provide a sub-text in such films as *Breaker Morant, Gallipoli*, and Sophia Turkiewicz's *Silver City* (1984). The historical films of the 1970s and 1980s have been notably concerned with exploring motifs, themes, structures, and oppositions which have been — and are — elements in the national mythology. The 'mateship' motif, for example, so central to male-dominated Australian mythology, is scrutinized in films as disparate as *Gallipoli*, Richard Franklin's *The True Story of Eskimo Nell* (1975), *Newsfront*, and Michael Thornhill's *The FJ Holden* (1977). (The latter, set in then-contemporary Sydney, has already acquired the historical value that so quickly and tenaciously attaches itself to film through the power of *mise-en-scène*.)

6   The approach to character varies sharply in the historical films. Some have dramatized the lives of people who actually existed, relying to greater or lesser degree on existing records, such as Mrs Aeneas Gunn's autobiography for Igor Auzins' *We of the Never Never* (1982), or the public knowledge and sporting records of swimmer Dawn Fraser's life in Ken Hannam's *Dawn!* (1979). Some have placed fictional characters in a dramatization of historical events — for example, Guy Hamilton, the journalist in Indonesia at the time of an actual military coup, in Peter Weir's *The Year of Living Dangerously* (1982) — whereas a film such as *Strikebound* dramatizes true events and the actual historical figures involved. There is, too, a group of films which appears to be offering fragments of biography, not of historically important or even actual people, but as a means of giving order to the incidents which comprise the narrative. *The Mango Tree, The Devil's Playground, The Getting of Wisdom*, and *Newsfront* fall into this category: some of these have *auto*biographical resonances, but the protagonists are not important, except emblematically, in the construction of Australian history. Their function in these films is to concentrate certain influences at

158

work on individual lives at various points in Australian history. And there is at least one further, admittedly minor, sub-category in which actual historical figures are represented in films by themselves: three Prime Ministers, Ben Chifley, Robert Menzies (both via newsreel footage in *Newsfront*) and John Gorton (in a 'cameo' appearance in Bruce Beresford's *Don's Party*, 1976); Aggie and Wattie Doig in documentary interviews in *Strikebound*; and singer Slim Dusty as himself in Rob Stewart's *The Slim Dusty Movie* (1984) are examples. In general, whether a character is created for a film or is based on an actual person the details of whose life are known, the filmmaker must try to balance the claims of two sorts of allegiance: that to historical authenticity and that to dramatic truth and coherence. For most film audiences, one suspects the latter is more important: that is, it will matter more in relating to *We of the Never Never* whether Angela Punch-McGregor's embodiment of certain character traits is dramatically absorbing than whether it is a 'true' representation of the historical figure of Mrs Aeneas Gunn.

7 Finally, it may be said that, if all films come to acquire historical significance through the perceptual immediacy of their *mise-en-scène*, then Australian films of the 1970s and 1980s have created a fascinating record of aspects of contemporary life. Tim Burstall's *Petersen* (1974), John Duigan's *Mouth to Mouth* (1978) and Michael Pattinson's *Moving Out* (1982) are examples of films which may well come to assume the status of historical documents. In their portrayal of oppositions such as youth and age, working

Former Prime Minister John Gorton, in a 'cameo' appearance in Bruce Beresford's *Don's Party* (1976).

and middle classes, poverty and affluence, they become repositories of the social history of their times, no less so because they reflect, like all the films discussed in this chapter, their makers' attitudes and selectivity.

These comments are not intended as exhaustive in relation to the representations of the past to be found in recent Australian films. They merely suggest the variety of approach which the film-makers have adopted in imposing narrative order on the past so as to make it accessible and/or palatable to present-day audiences. Most of the forty-odd films of the last fifteen years which may be loosely characterized as historical films (with rare exceptions: for examples, *The True Story of Eskimo Nell* with its fantasy elements) have been in the realist mode. They have eschewed the stylization practised by Paul Cox, for instance, in his contemporary romances or Russell Mulcahy in the outback thriller *Razorback* (1984). Most have adopted a straightforward linear approach to narrative, paying a good deal of attention to slice-of-life verisimilitude. Their chief interest has lain in the uses to which narrative manipulation and *mise-en-scène* have been put in exploring and exploiting the past. They will be considered here in relation to the four main periods which have attracted film-makers.

Colonial Days

Less than a quarter of the forty historical films have been set in the remoter past — that is, before the period of the 1890s when it may be suggested the nation's myths began to assume shapes still recognizable today. This may be the result of greater production expenses in re-creating the more distant past; or it may reflect a more pressing interest in times and episodes of which the influence is more clearly apparent in the present. There are in fact scarcely a half-dozen films firmly set in colonial Australia: *Inn of the Damned, The True Story of Eskimo Nell,* Tim Burstall's *Eliza Fraser* (1975), Philippe Mora's *Mad Dog Morgan* (1976), *Journey Among Women,* John Honey's *Manganinnie* (1980), and Tom Haydon's documentary *The Last Tasmanian* (1978), the latter not so much *set in* as interpreting the records relating to an episode of this period.

The fiction films set in this period are all characterized by themes of flight and pursuit and most often with the setting up of a community/wilderness opposition. The communities depicted are essentially British in their orientation — in their administration and their authority structures — and the films' sympathies are directed towards protagonists who have either not found a place in the communities or have been established as outsiders in relation to them. The anti-British, anti-authoritarian stances they exhibit recur in the films set in later periods; the films under discussion here suggest that such stances have always been part of the national texture.

The most interesting of these films is Tom Cowan's *Journey Among Women* which was made for a tiny budget ($170,000) and in difficult cir-

Jane (Helenka Fink), one of the convict women, in Tom Cowan's
Journey Among Women (1977).

cumstances (cast and crew lived together in the Hawkesbury River forests
of New South Wales for six weeks, in conditions resembling those in the
film). The film was a modest commercial success, in spite of having no
'names' and little in common with the other period films which did well at
that time. Further, it is clearly as much interested in its feminist theme as in
the more obviously commercial prospects of the pursuit of a group of convict women into the Australian bush in the very early days of European
settlement. Cowan himself has said:

> I think the film is pretty clearly about the present, and one of the ways I
> look at the film is that it is a sort of journey through time; one of its themes
> the struggle for emotional liberation. Perhaps it's a bit obscure.[4]

In the event, its weakness is not so much obscurity as a failure quite to meld
its more conventional narrative elements with its ideological concerns;
however, in its use of an historical setting to point up contemporary issues,
it remains one of the most provocative and intellectually ambitious films of
recent years. Co-written by Cowan, producer John Weiley, and poet-
dramatist Dorothy Hewett (with other contributions from the cast), it posits
the idea of women's capacity to establish a less aggressive, less hierarchical
community than the oppressive, male-ordered society from which they
escape. The central character is Elizabeth (Jeune Pritchard), daughter of a
colonial judge, who helps the women to escape. Initially, she is seen as both

exploited (as a woman, she can have no serious role in the colony) and unthinking exploiter of her maid, Meg (Nell Campbell). Finally, however, as a result of her experiences with the convict women, she arrives at a more clear-eyed awareness of the wrongs of the society she has left and to which she returns. The women's bush idyll has been brief and its end swift, bloody, and inevitable, but Elizabeth's previous vaguely humane orientation has been stiffened.

It may be, as Susan Dermody claims, that 'the over-riding myth of the film is the frequently reactionary one that sees women as mysterious creatures who are close to nature, ... more intuitive than logical ...'.[5] Nevertheless, *Journey Among Women* is unique among Australian feature films in its determined focussing upon women's roles in the country's history. There is minimal (but sufficient) concern for period authenticity, but the film's real interest is in exploring certain contemporary issues. It is a film of rough edges and undigested elements, but it is formally striking in its highly conscious use of the past as an arena for the display of these issues. Stylistically, it creates oppositions of nature and civilization, freedom and oppression, tenderness and brutality, all in the images which remain in the mind after its flaws are forgotten.

What *Mad Dog Morgan*, set in the mid-nineteenth century, shares with *Journey Among Women* are a persistently anti-authority stance and the sense of a release which the bush offers from the brutalities of a corrupt society. Morgan (played by American actor Dennis Hopper, his anti-establishment *persona* aptly feeding into the role) is introduced as an outsider to white society: he is smoking opium with Chinese friends on the gold diggings when the Chinese camp is attacked by police. The massacre of the Chinese is an early and powerful signifier of a brutally chauvinistic society (fear of migrant workers has been a continuing element in Australian history) and his brutality is further evidenced in the twelve years' hard labour to which Morgan is sentenced for stealing a man's clothes and in the treatment meted out to him in prison. Released after six years, Morgan 'disappears like a bloody black', learns to use the often-threatening landscape, and is befriended by an Aboriginal, Billy (David Gulpilil), who joins him in his bushranging activities. Gradually the aura of folk-hero attaches itself to him; less true, historically, of Morgan than of Ned Kelly, but another sort of historical truth is inscribed here: the characteristic Australian sympathy for one who leads authority a dance and, in so doing, aligns himself with those classes traditionally at odds with that authority.

Although the film begins and ends with a claim by Victorian Detective Police Officer Mainwaring (Jack Thompson) that he is presenting the true story of Morgan, in fact the history which the film offers is not so much that of actual events and characters as that of a dramatized, more generalized sense of historical issues. For instance, its picture of a callous authority (embodied in excellent performances from Frank Thring as Superintendent

162

Cobham and John Hargreaves as a stiff, upper-class-speaking magistrate) suggests a British, class-based oppressiveness; and the film's network of sympathies includes Irish, Chinese, Italian and Aboriginal men, all of whom may be seen as at odds with — indeed, as the natural objects of — that oppressiveness. Representatives of British rule do not emerge with credit in films such as this (or *Journey Among Women* or *Eliza Fraser*): they are seen essentially as imposing an administration on a community they do not understand and on a landscape unlike any they have known. The former inadequacy promotes dissidence, the latter offers retreat if not, in the end, protection for outsiders from society.

Whereas *Mad Dog Morgan* generally received enthusiastic local reviews but performed poorly at the box-office, the reverse was true of *Eliza Fraser*, released a few months later. Like *Morgan*, its title character is based on an actual historical figure, whose story coincidentally received another airing in the same year (1976) in Patrick White's novel *A Fringe of Leaves*, although the names were changed there and the whole tone was decidedly more serious than in Burstall's film and David Williamson's screenplay. In the film, set in 1836, Eliza (Susannah York) is fitted out with a portly, suspicious husband (amusingly and touchingly played by Noel Ferrier) and two lovers, McBryde (John Castle), a womanizing sea-captain, and Bracefell (John Waters), a convict whom the Frasers meet at the Moreton Bay penal settlement run by a sadistic commandant, Fyans (Trevor Howard). On leaving Moreton Bay, the Frasers' ship is wrecked and they embark on a journey of survival, involving Aboriginals, convicts, and the reappearance of Bracefell. Finally, Eliza, now a widow, tells her sensational

Captain Fyans (Trevor Howard, right) farewells Captain Fraser (Noel Ferrier) and his wife Eliza (Susannah York) in Tim Burstall's *Eliza Fraser* (1975).

tale at fairgrounds and heads for England to make her fortune there.

The film is not seriously interested in the history of Mrs Eliza Fraser, but settles, in picaresque style, for an entertaining amalgam of adventure melodrama and sexual comedy. Nevertheless, it is more interesting as history than this description would suggest. In its depiction of British attitudes as embodied in Fyans, Fraser, and McBryde — respectively brutal (in carrying out British-imposed laws), pompous ('I'm a British sea-captain, I'm damned if I'll be ordered around by a savage'), and exploitative (selling a lurid account of Eliza's ordeal, abetted by her) — *Eliza Fraser* is explicitly bent on exposing the follies, and worse, of the British in the colony's early days. There is a further dig at the British at the very end when the final caption records that 'it took eight months for Eliza to make her fortune' in Britain — that is, at the expense of British gullibility. The characterization of Eliza herself, as a woman of some pluck and resource, is in itself historically interesting: in the society from which she is accidentally separated, her particular qualities would have found no place. In surviving the wreck, her period with the Aboriginals, the loss of her husband, and her career as *raconteuse*, she assumes a stature that would otherwise have been denied her.

The last point is true of the escaped convicts of *Journey Among Women* and of Mad Dog Morgan, who also acquire qualities the colonial community would have suppressed when they are forced to seek survival in the natural world. In each of these films the opposition of society and the bush is structurally important; each is structured around a fugitive theme, with the fugitives coming to terms with an alien setting, with the pursuers and/or rescuers representing an unprepossessing authority, whereas those they seek are at odds with that authority. All three are characterized by violence, imbued in *Journey Among Women* and *Mad Dog Morgan* with a stronger sense of ideological responsibility than in *Eliza Fraser* where it is deployed in the interests of melodramatic *frissons*. They are distinguished from each other, however, by their approaches to their historical content: *Journey Among Women* uses the historical setting to reflect on a contemporary issue; *Mad Dog Morgan* purports to present an historical document; *Eliza Fraser* exploits the picaresque mode in the interest of parody and melodrama.

In the matter of characters, Mad Dog Morgan and Eliza Fraser are both, with some distortion, based on actual historical figures whereas the characters in *Journey Among Women* are wholly fictitious, embodying certain classes and attitudes of the times. The only other two films of this earlier period which need to be mentioned here — *Manganinnie* and *The True Story of Eskimo Nell* — feature fictional characters but to different purposes. Manganinnie (Mawuyal Yarthalawuy) is a created character set in the context of a true event: she is a lone Aboriginal who is separated from her tribe during the notorious 'black drive' in Tasmania of the 1830s. That

Two lost ones: Joanna (Anna Ralph) and Manganinnie (Mawuyal
Yanthalawuy) in John Honey's *Manganinnie* (1980).

is, although fictional, she represents a set of possibilities for women caught
up in a particular historical event. The film is a modest and touching account
of her journey with another lost child: Joanna (Anna Ralph), the daughter of
a white settler. The actual 'black drive' is, in effect, no more than the film's
narrative starting point. *The True Story of Eskimo Nell*'s protagonist, Dead
Eye Dick (Max Gillies), is less a character than the deflation of a myth. Dick,
claiming to have lost an eye in a Yukon bar-room brawl, has come to the
Australian goldfields to pursue the legendary beauty of the title. Trying to
establish himself as a great roisterer and womanizer, Dick constantly fails to
live up to his image of himself and in dramatizing this failure Franklin tilts at
the myth of the Australian frontiersman — and at the contemporary films
like Tim Burstall's *Alvin Purple* (1973) and Bruce Beresford's *Barry
McKenzie* which had exploited a crude 'ockerish' sexuality. The real interest of *Eskimo Nell* is in its exploration, ribald and affecting, of the Australian
mateship myth, entangled as it is with unexpressed sexual elements. Dick,
when he finally meets Nell (a plump whore, rather than, say, the Lily
Langtry ideal of William Wyler's *The Westerner*, 1940), is too ill to perform,
and can only know her sexual charms vicariously through the account of his
mate Pete (Serge Lazareff).

These latter two films — *Manganinnie* and *Eskimo Nell* — share with
the other three discussed, the narrative structure of a journey and/or pursuit which virtually disappears in those films set in the post-1890 period.

Elements of this structure do appear in *The Chant of Jimmie Blacksmith* (1978), for instance, but in these films in which the colony becomes a nation the drama tends to be centred on communities. However, some of the other structuring motifs and oppositions found in the films set in the last century recur frequently in films set in later periods: notably, the outsider(s)/authority and exploiter/exploited binarisms; and the particular manifestations of both of these in regard to the role of women in Australian society, to the country's treatment of its Aboriginals (and other non-Anglo-Saxon races), and to the deeply ambivalent attitudes to the idea of Britain as both formative and oppressive in Australian growth.

Towards Nationhood

The batch of films which explore aspects of the period in which Australia may be said to have achieved nationhood (that is, roughly from the 1890s to just after the First World War) may be subdivided into:

1   Those which deal with actual historical events (*Breaker Morant, Gallipoli*);

2   Those which tell fictionalized stories of actual lives (*The Chant of Jimmie Blacksmith, My Brilliant Career, The Getting of Wisdom*, and, with a slight difference, *We of the Never Never*); and

3   Those which locate wholly fictional narratives in this key period of Australian history (*Picnic at Hanging Rock, Break of Day, The Mango Tree, The Man from Snowy River*).

These include some of the most critically and commercially successful films of the new Australian cinema and it is interesting to speculate on the reasons for their success. Some of them are clearly very good films, the work of the ablest film-makers of the revival: directors such as Peter Weir, Bruce Beresford, Fred Schepisi, and Gillian Armstrong; cameramen, such as Russell Boyd, Ian Baker, and Don McAlpine; actors who have become major stars, such as Jack Thompson and Judy Davis. However, part of their appeal, at least locally, surely lies in their explorations of a period in which Australia was becoming distinctively Australian. A group of scattered colonies had been federated to form a nation in 1901; Australians had fought in an international war in South Africa at the turn of the century and, most memorably, at Gallipoli in 1915; and popular poets, such as A.B. Paterson and Henry Lawson, and a popular journal, *The Bulletin*, had enshrined a peculiarly Australian response to people and events. The three decades which comprise this period may be seen as the crucible in which the national myths have been distilled. These may have been subsequently submitted to critical scrutiny but in the popular imagination they are still seen as the

166

repository of the elements which make 'Australia' a concept to be grappled with, not just an antipodean curiosity.

What this concept of Australia embodies, as it is presented in the films set in this period, is a complex and in some ways contradictory amalgam of liberating and repressive forces at work in the national life. On the one hand, they offer a real, sometimes exhilarating sense of individuals whose histories represent a break with constricting traditions. Even when the outcome is tragic, as in *Breaker Morant*, one senses director Bruce Beresford's response to an emergent national spirit which refuses to concur with an imperialist credo which has come to seem merely exploitative. On the other hand, these films also focus attention on those aspects of the national life which the official histories of the time have tended to marginalize: the treatment of the Aboriginals, at worst brutal, at best paternalistic, or of women, for instance. Some of the films set in these decades may be seen as tentative steps towards a rewriting of the history of the period from the point of view of such repressed groups.

Most of the films set in this period are discussed elsewhere because they touch on commonly recurring themes. However, in aggregate they build up a quite comprehensive picture of attitudes and events across three decades, viewed not with affectless objectivity but from clearly identifiable vantage points. Bruce Beresford's excellent *Breaker Morant* is based on the Boer War court-martial of three officers of the Bushveldt Carbineers who are sacrificed to British imperalism and to fear of Germany's entering the war on the side of the Boers. It is safe to say that such a film would not have been made, let alone enjoyed such a success, in the late 1930s when films on the theme of Empire, from either Britain (*The Four Feathers*, 1939) or Hollywood (*Gunga Din*, 1939), focused on the heroism involved in imperial enterprises. In the early 1940s, Hollywood made a number of commercially profitable films extolling the traditions and virtues of British life (for example, *Random Harvest*, 1942, *The White Cliffs of Dover*, 1944). These, like *Breaker Morant*, were also products of *their* period when the concept of 'Britain' was regarded as an ideal worth fighting for or as a justifiable imperialist motive. A 1980 Australian film of a British imperialist adventure was extremely unlikely to espouse such attitudes, even if its victims had not also been Australians.

The film begins with 'Soldiers of the Queen' being played by a brass band in a rotunda, in Pietersburg, Transvaal, in 1901. From this brief shot, the camera cuts to a courtroom around which it prowls before moving in to a close-up of Morant (Edward Woodward). The rest of the film cuts between the court-martial and enactment of the events, which have given rise to it: the shooting of Boers who have killed and mutilated British Captain Hunt (Terence Donovan), and the killing of a German missionary before he could spread word about the Carbineers holding a group of Boer prisoners. Whereas, the film implies, the latter charge was the result of a decision

Defence counsel, Major Thomas (Jack Thompson) and the three court-martialled officers — Morant (Edward Woodward), Handcock (Bryan Brown), and Witton (Lewis Fitz-Gerald) — in Bruce Beresford's *Breaker Morant* (1980).

taken between Morant and Handcock (Bryan Brown), in the case of the former they were acting under orders from Kitchener (Alan Cassell) himself. Morant and Handcock are executed in a very movingly staged sequence: at dawn, they join hands as they walk up the hill to the chairs in which they receive the firing squad's bullets. The third officer, Witton (Lewis Fitz-Gerald), is sentenced to life imprisonment, commuted to three years, after which, a caption informs us, he wrote a book called *Scapegoats of Empire*, the title of which comes close to encapsulating the film's drama. Ironically, too, Witton is the only one of the three on trial who has enlisted for the glory of the Empire.

However, *Breaker Morant* is not a simple-minded anti-British tirade. Certainly, it deplores imperialism and the brutalities practised in its name; but more complexly it offers a subtle and absorbing examination of a hierarchy of loyalties and orders. (In this respect, it resembles Beresford's *The Club*, 1980.) If Kitchener is discharging responsibilities, as he sees them, to the British government, Morant, Handcock, and Witton justifiably claim loyalty to Hunt as their commanding officer, through whom, in turn, they receive Kitchener's orders. In the courtroom itself, the tension is sustained, not just through the intrinsic interest of the trial, but partly through the relationship of trust which develops between Australian defence counsel, Thomas (a detailed, atypical performance from Jack Thompson) and the three defendants, and that between Thomas and his English counterpart,

168

Major Bolton (Rod Mullinar), whose respect for Thomas grows as the trial proceeds. As well, Beresford and his cameraman, Don McAlpine (one of Australia's two or three best), maintain such a skilfully unfussy deployment of the camera, which tracks and pans and cranes in ways that underline the drama, highlighting both the stiff formality of the court and the relationships and tensions between the personnel involved, that there is nothing theatrically constraining in this setting.

Beresford's film presents the facts of the case with considerable regard for authenticity. In terms of attitude, it reflects that questioning of blind allegiance to a British cause which surfaced tentatively in Australian parliamentary debates of the time, and more vehemently in the influential journal *The Bulletin*. The textbook formalities of the prosecution (and the cynicism of the Establishment which promotes it) throw into relief the informality, with its provision for human warmth, which characterizes those on trial and the man who defends them. Such a constrast reflects 1980 thinking even more forcefully than 1901 facts.

The British are more directly criticized in Peter Weir's *Gallipoli* although it is a less obviously polemical film than *Breaker Morant*. Despite its title, it is less a film about a place and a war than one about Australia, taking as its focus what it meant to be Australian in 1915. In relation to Gallipoli and the First World War, Weir and scriptwriter David Williamson present and dramatize two contrasting attitudes: patriotism, not so much for Australia as for England and Empire, and the isolationism of Australia in relation to world events. Representing the former, Archy (Mark Lee) has only a vague and emotional idea of what the war is about, but he is in no doubt that he must go. The early reading from Kipling, the great author of Empire, indicates the sense in which 1915 Australia was still part of the imperial family, and is echoed in the challenge of the slogan, 'The Empire Needs You'. That Archy is one of the Australians sacrificed to protect the British is just the final stage of his incomprehension — and a slap in the eye for patriotism. In Frank (Mel Gibson), one aspect of isolationist Australia is seen. For him it is 'not our bloody war. It's an English war', and he finally joins up because he feels a little out of things. The meeting with the camel driver (Harold Baigent) reinforces the sheer physical isolation of Australia. The old man has not heard of the war, has not even been to Perth; he once knew a German, he says, but he is essentially incurious about the war. In the end, it is mateship, not patriotism, that leads Frank to the war.

The film is aware that between these two attitudes is a kind of muddled middle ground. In a marvellously-lit (by cameraman Russell Boyd) scene of night farewell as a troopship leaves Fremantle, the soundtrack offers a medley of popular tunes, including not just 'Australia Will Be There', but 'England, Home, and Beauty', and a few scraps of 'Auld Lang Syne'. What is being registered here is not merely mixed motives but a farewell to the kind of isolationism that would never again be possible for Australians. Once the

169

English come to be represented by actual physical presences (the 'silly ass' officers in Cairo, the coldly exploitative officers at Gallipoli, historically 'unfair' but ideologically significant in terms of the film) instead of slogans, the criticism assumes a sharper edge.

The protagonists of *The Chant of Jimmie Blacksmith, My Brilliant Career*, and *The Getting of Wisdom* have their sources in actual lives and in notable Australian novels. Thomas Keneally's Jimmie Blacksmith is based on a New South Wales Aboriginal, Jimmie Governor, who in 1900 exacted a bloody revenge on the white employers who had exploited him and insulted his (white) wife. The film, like the 1972 novel, fictionalizes Jimmie Governor's tragedy but retains its horrific truths. Miles Franklin wrote *My Brilliant Career* when she was sixteen and it was first published by Blackwood's, Edinburgh, in 1901. Its heroine, Sybylla Melvyn, is semi-autobiographical: an outback girl who rebels against the sterility of life on her father's poverty-stricken farm, longs for the life of the arts, resists the offer of a rich marriage, and finally comes to terms with rigours of the life she had so gratefully fled. Laura Ramsbottom, the heroine of *The Getting of Wisdom* (1910), is essentially a portrait of the artist — Henry Handel (née Ethel Lindesay) Richardson — as a young girl. Richardson herself has written that the book was intended as:

> ... a more or less subtle story of a young girl's growth ... [Laura is] a girl with a difference. For this particular one was a writer in the making; and, even thus early, the taint of her calling was in her, marking her off from the rest of her schoolmates.[6]

In each case, the directors (respectively Fred Schepisi, Gillian Armstrong, and Bruce Beresford) and their collaborators have respected their sources and gone to considerable pains to reproduce the period. As films, *Jimmie Blacksmith* and *My Brilliant Career* are more successful than *The Getting of Wisdom* which does not, in the end, trust the idea of 'a writer in the making' as being sufficiently cinematic.

As historical films, they share the fictional representation of actual lives and, as well, offer insights into the periods in which they are set, a period remote from each of the film-makers as it was not for Franklin or Richardson at the time of writing, but as it was for Keneally in 1972. Both *My Brilliant Career* and *The Getting of Wisdom* reflect something of the position of women in Australian society at the turn of the century. However, Armstrong's film takes a much more firmly feminist line in relation to Franklin's text than Beresford does to Richardson's, although both have the same scriptwriter, Eleanor Witcombe.[7] *My Brilliant Career* is a tougher, less compromising film than *The Getting of Wisdom*: both acknowledge the difficulties confronting a girl of unusual intelligence and aspiration in the Australia of the 1890s, but Beresford's film sacrifices the seriousness of the novel by opting for a more glamorous outcome for its heroine. In its suggestion of a sexual relationship between Laura (Susannah Fowle) and the older girl, Evelyn (Hilary Ryan), it is both direct and discreet; in its presentation of the clashes between Laura's imaginative capacity and the stultifying effect of the Ladies' College's conventional, fact-based education system, heavily European in its orientation, it finds comedy and a clear historical perspective. It is in its failure to follow through the implications for Laura — in that time and place, the opportunities open to one of her proclivities *were* severely limited — that the film loses its nerve. In doing so, whatever its incidental felicities of *mise-en-scène* and acting, it diminishes its importance as an historical reconstruction or as a commentary on the contemporary scene.

Part of the strength of Armstrong's film is that, as well as beautifully reproducing the physical aspects of the 1890s (a triumph for production designer Luciana Arrighi), it also provides a late 1970s commentary on Miles Franklin's novel. And, in so doing, it uses its narrative set in the 1890s to explore and comment on late 1970s feminist issues. Whereas Franklin's heroine remains somewhat confused about her reasons for refusing Harry Beecham, perhaps partly a matter of reticence about Sybylla's distaste for men, partly of the period's less focused resentment of male oppression of women, the film makes it quite clear that Sybylla (Judy Davis) loves Harry (Sam Neill) but knows that in marrying him she will be crucially submerging aspects of her identity. Without undermining the film's feminist sympathies, the generous treatment of the character of Harry (he is considerably more attractive than Miles Franklin's character) makes his love worth having and Sybylla's rejection of it more moving and impressive. A late 1970s perspective has produced not just a faithful adaptation of a period piece — it was not a period piece for Miles Franklin — but, rather, a critical commentary on the novel's thinking. Armstrong apparently considered updating the film by a decade or so, but claims that:

> . . . the more I read the clearer it became to me that for her [Franklin] that was always the greatest period of her life. It was the period of the first birth of Australian nationalism and she was very much a part of it and very proud of being a part of it.[8]

In fact, the film's connection with 'Australian nationalism' is not explicitly stated though it is pervasively felt in Sybylla's attempt to come to terms with herself as an Australian woman in an arduous situation. In accepting her situation she is also accepting this country at a particular time in its history as the setting for and pressure upon her own aspirations. The parallels with Australian women in the 1970s working out the terms of their own lives are as apparent as they are unforced.

The Chant of Jimmie Blacksmith is concerned with the plight of an individual outsider rebuffed by the white society he tries to enter, and is in this sense a critique of Australian racism. Again and again in the film Jimmie

(Tommy Lewis) is isolated in the frame, whether at a cricket match at which he is given afternoon tea at a remove from the white players and their women or against a potentially hostile landscape of rocky outcrops. Further, the film, like the novel, is set at the time of Federation, the formal declaration of Australian nationhood, and one of its bitterest ironies is that this nation is so unsure of its identity that it cannot admit a hybrid like Jimmie to its citizenship. There is talk of Federation and the Boer War and anti-British sentiments, and the film very acutely catches the insecurity underlying such talk, an insecurity that flares in the treatment meted out to Jimmie and to which he ultimately responds with appalling bursts of violence. But it is essentially one man's 'declaration of war'. Schepisi himself claims that: 'It was never meant to be the definitive Aboriginal picture, as everybody seemed to expect'.[9] As the dramatization of one individual's clash with the uneasily dominant, not to say brutal, culture, it is a powerful piece of filmmaking, no less so for 'its failure to make concrete an analysis of the social formation in the period, and to place these in relation to historical forces', as Annette Van den Bosch[10] has sententiously observed. Schepisi has made a film, not a treatise. However, in focusing on his individual outsider protagonist and through a passionate arrangement of images, he has made painfully clear that Jimmie — jaw half-shot away, caught asleep in a convent bed, ignominiously bundled into the back of a police van — remains to the end the victim of 'historical forces' that have, for good and bad, helped to shape Australia.

Igor Auzins' *We of the Never Never* is based on the true story of Mrs Aeneas Gunn whose marriage takes her to the outback of Australia where she must learn to cope, both as a white among Aboriginals and as a woman among men. Mrs Gunn's autobiographical book is a well-loved Australian classic and the film retains its main historical figures; unfortunately, as a film it fails on all counts. As a narrative of outback tribulation it is slack and episodic; as the story of one woman's courageous fight against a variety of daunting challenges it suffers from a lustreless star (Angela Punch-McGregor) in a vaguely-written role; and it signally fails to explore, from a 1980s point of view, any of the historically significant issues it raises. The opportunity to examine male/female, white/black, city/outback oppositions as they obtained at the turn of the century is frittered away, when not in fact bypassed. There is no sense of Auzins' or scriptwriter Peter Schreck's having considered using the white city woman's situation in a male-dominated outback world as an organizing narrative principle. What is left is an achingly slow, boringly high-minded account of minor incidents set against Gary Hansen's impressive wide-screen photography of the Northern Territory.

The other films set in this crucial period of national myth-making are *Picnic at Hanging Rock, Break of Day, The Mango Tree,* and *The Man from Snowy River.* The box-office success of the last commands the atten-

Mrs Aeneas Gunn (Angela Punch-McGregor), flanked by publican
(Tex Morton) and stockman (Tony Barry) in Igor Auzins' *We of the
Never Never* (1982).

tion which its dramatic merits would not. Based on A. B. Paterson's famous
bush ballad, the film presumably presents Australians with a picture of
themselves which they want to endorse and one which tallies with the
images the rest of the world has of Australia. The legendary Australian
affection for the underdog (a powerful element in such historical landmarks
as the Eureka Stockade's battle for miners' rights and Gallipoli), especially
when, against odds, he eventually acquires a hero's status, undoubtedly
explains part of the film's appeal. *The Man from Snowy River* is an historical film only in the sense that it is set in the past: its reproduction of the
surface of the period is undermined by spurious gestures of contemporary
relevance ('Would you condemn her to domesticity?' the heroine's aunt asks
a bullying father). Paterson's poem (published in 1895) and Miller's film
nearly ninety years later both found an immediate public: the former has
'gleams of authentic poetry',[11] whereas the film is unrelievedly banal in all
its human dealings, interesting neither as period melodrama nor as a mod-
ern-day commentary on a minor phenomenon of Australian literary — and
social — history.

   Break of Day and *Picnic at Hanging Rock* share the same producer (Pat
Lovell), scriptwriter (Cliff Green), and cameraman (Russell Boyd), and both

set fictional stories in the early years of this century. The historical interest of *Picnic and Hanging Rock* is in its representation of a pervasive European influence incongruously at work in the Australian bush. The College run by Mrs Appleyard (Rachel Roberts) is clearly organized on English middle-class lines as indicated earlier. Elsewhere, in the scene of a lakeside garden party attended by the State Governor, the occasion is characterized by the playing of 'God Save the Queen' as the Governor leaves, and of Mozart's 'Eine kleine Nachtmusik', and by the upper-class English demeanour of the guests, contrasted with the relaxed Australian-ness of the groom (John Jarratt) who sits drinking beer at a remove from them. Only the menials in the film are presented as unequivocally Australian. Green's screenplay described the College as 'An island of hard stone and English garden, marooned in the bush, dreaming of Europe. Hopelessly'.[12] This description encapsulates nicely the historical interest of the film: a newly transplanted, intrusive culture is ultimately swallowed up by the pre-history of its setting; and one of the film's fascinations is its representation of an historical phenomenon — the Anglo-Australian motif — which has been powerfully felt in the life and arts of this country.

Despite the somewhat plodding treatment of its central drama of Tom, a young Gallipoli veteran (Andrew McFarlane), caught between pregnant wife, Beth (Ingrid Mason), and arty city lady, Alice (Sara Kestelman), *Break of Day* is not without interest as an historical film. Unlike *Picnic at Hanging Rock*, it is connected to a specific historical event: the hero has wounded himself to get invalided home from Gallipoli, and this works towards some demystification of a central national myth. However, the implications of this are not carefully enough worked through, despite the heavily underscored parallels with his failures to observe the rules professionally (with regard to the country newspaper he has inherited) or personally (with regard to his marriage). The notion of a Gallipoli veteran who has shown cowardice is an audacious one for an Australian film but, apart from the irony of the city lady's wanting to paint him as 'the true spirit of Anzac' and some boorish pub talk about Australians at war, it is not explored in close enough relation to Tom's emotional conflict. The film shares with *Picnic at Hanging Rock* an insight into the parochial, anti-stranger feeling of small Australian towns in the early part of the century (and perhaps even now). Although this feeling is much nearer to the centre of *Break of Day* as Tom's liaison with Alice draws the smirking innuendoes of the locals, it recalls the attitude of the neighbouring town towards the girls who come from remote places to be students of Appleyard College. What the two films share is the depiction of a suspicious curiosity, mingled with social prejudice, in ways that provide a commentary on the traditional friendliness of Australian small-town life. In *Break of Day*, this prejudice is exacerbated by Alice's being both a city woman and an artist — on both counts an object of suspicion.

The last of the films set in this period, *The Mango Tree*, is one of a number of Australian *bildungsfilms*, and one of the least. Set during the The First World War in Bundaberg, Queensland, it foregrounds the growth of teenager Jamie Carr (Christopher Pate) in a context of local bigotry and the echoes of world affairs. Like too many Australian films, *The Mango Tree* is very loosely constructed, mistaking a series of events for a coherent narrative, but it does convey a sense of the leisurely life of a remote town. Such life is as much the stuff of history as the ads for Mary Pickford and Your Country Needs YOU, the arrival of air ace Bert Hinkler, a real-life hero, or the lethal influenza epidemic of 1919. What might have created a powerful sense of historical continuity — the coming-of-age of Jamie and the death of his remarkable grandmother (Geraldine Fitzgerald), with her sense of roots in a once-dangerous country — is vitiated by the uneveness of the playing. Whereas Pate is unequal to the demands of his role (and too old for it), Fitzgerald plays with a warmth, dignity and style that threaten to unbalance the film, with the suggestion that what was important about it dies with her.

Between Wars

There is a less distinctive flavour about the films set in the between-wars period. However, structurally they are apt to be looser than those set in the two previous periods; they grow out of tensions more pervasive than particular (with the notable exception of *Strikebound*, though even there the conflict is representative of a larger and longer-lasting social divisiveness than its actual historical referent might suggest); and they reflect a restless, transitional period in which independence and conservatism jostle somewhat uneasily for places both on the national level and in the individual lives the films present. The films set in the 1920s and 1930s exhibit the same patterns as those of the two periods previously considered. Some purport to present actual lives, as in Kevin Dobson's *Squizzy Taylor*, or events, as in Richard Lowenstein's *Strikebound*, whereas others evoke past times through the lives of fictional characters, as in John Power's *The Picture Show Man* (1977) or Michael Thornhill's *Between Wars* (1974).

In terms of what these films add to the cinematic representation of Australian history, the Great Depression of the 1930s is, unsurprisingly, a recurring influence. Curiously, however, there is no film that addresses itself head-on to this key source of Australian mythology. Like *The Chant of Jimmie Blacksmith* in relation to the Aboriginal question, films such as Donald Crombie's *Caddie* (1976) and Carl Schultz's *Careful, He Might Hear You* use the Depression as a motivating factor in the lives of their central characters. Caddie's (Helen Morse) struggle to raise her children after desertion by an unfaithful husband is presented, like the book on which it is based, as a personal history. It is warm-hearted, eliciting sympathy for its heroine as she braves the swill of the Sydney pub where she works as barmaid and the rigours of Depression poverty, but it offers personal resilience rather than political action as the response to problems deriving from economic recession. In *Careful, He Might Hear You*, a small boy, P. S. (Nicholas Gledhill), is torn between two ways of life: that represented by his rich Anglophile aunt, Vanessa (Wendy Hughes), and his homely aunt, Lila (Robyn Nevin), and her Depression-victim husband, George (Peter Whitford). Vanessa opens the child's eyes to a pretentious, English-derived culture which only increases his longing for the warmth of affection in which Lila and George have raised him. In this response, the film makes its contribution to the notion of the Depression as a time not only of bitterness and poverty but also of conditions favouring mutual support and the enshrinement of the 'Aussie battler' image. In this way it uses the historical situation as *Caddie* does: as an element of plot design, rather than as a subject in itself.

In these films, history is seen as what happens to individual, insignificant lives which have little effect on the major currents of political, social, and economic change. In this sense, *Strikebound* is again an exception. The film is dedicated to 'the men and women of the Australian Labor Movement and the strength they found ...'. It is a reconstruction of the events that occurred in the South Gippsland coalfields in the 1930s. Although changes have been made for dramatic reasons, the film confronts a major political issue — labour versus capital — directly, rather than through dramatizing fictional lives. In the manner of Warren Beatty's *Reds* (1981), it interviews the actual historical figures of Agnes and Wattie Doig whose comments on the events of forty-five years ago are heard before their younger selves (expertly played by Carol Burns and Chris Haywood) appear in acted incarnations. The strike is in no sense a plot device: it is what the plot is *about*; and Lowenstein has side-stepped more conventional narrative suspense in the interests of keeping his eye on the historical struggle. The Doigs' personal story is presented as part of the record of historical events. That is, the film is aware that those engaged in serious political matters also lead individual domestic lives and those lives are importantly affected by the nature of their public involvement. Nevertheless, their personal story is subordinated in the screenplay to the historical struggle; and the film ends with the now elderly Mrs Doig saying on the soundtrack: 'I'm proud to be a member of the working class. They've done heroic things and they'll do more.' It is an appropriate note because it reinforces one's sense that this has been a film about a whole class and a cause: Aggie and Wattie Doig matter chiefly because of their commitment to that cause. *Strikebound* is not without flaws (the management figures are rather crudely written and played) but to date it is the best Australian film about working-class lives, seriously interested in their daily hardships, the meagreness and the warmth, the ideological pressures and the need for unity — and unionism. As such it is more than a record of a 1930s event; it invites contemporary reconsideration of class struggles through its reconstruction of the past.

Of the other films set in this between-wars period, two deal with underworld violence in the big cities, *Squizzy Taylor* and *Kitty and the Bagman*, both effective in physical re-creation of the 1920s but not of much historical interest otherwise. More interesing are *Between Wars*, which charts the clashes of a former army doctor (Corin Redgrave) with reactionary authorities over two decades; David Stevens' *Undercover* (1983), an amiable account of the growth of the Berlei corset firm with its 'Australian-made is well-made' slogan; *The Picture Show Man*, a good-natured but too leisurely tale of a travelling cinema operator (John Meillon) in rural New South Wales in the 1920s, whose business is threatened by a go-getting American rival (played by expatriate Australian Rod Taylor); Donald Crombie's *The Irishman* (1978), which traces the efforts of Clydesdale teamster Paddy Doolan (Michael Craig) to fly in the face of progress in mechanized transport in 1920s Queensland; and Simon Wincer's *Phar Lap* (1983), celebrating Australia's most famous race-horse (born in New Zealand) which died in America in 1932 after acquiring a legendary name as underdog-turned-hero in Australian sporting annals. Only *The Picture Show Man* and *The Irishman* have so far attracted much overseas attention, notably at festivals, but they all offer some interest as histories. They reflect, for example, an Australian resistance to change and a suspicion of American brashness and high-pressure business methods. Conservatism, except as depicted in the snooty Victorian Racing Club in *Phar Lap* or in the Royal Commission in *Between Wars*, is viewed sympathetically, progress warily (*The Picture Show Man, The Irishman*) or comically (*Undercover*). In all but *Undercover*, women are marginalized and this is no doubt an accurate reflection of the times portrayed. These are all likeable films, perhaps (with the exception of *Phar Lap*) too low-key for major success. The mystique surrounding Phar Lap is perhaps too intransigently Australian for the film to repeat its local success overseas.

The films of this period suggest a country somewhat unwillingly coming to terms with change. The Second World War obviously hastened this process, notably in the shifting relationships with Europe and America; but to date the new Australian cinema has produced no serious film about the war. *Attack Force Z* (1982), a disaster-prone production, originally to be directed by Phil Noyce and finally salvaged by Tim Burstall, is set in the West Pacific in the last year of the war, and, despite the 'futility of war' theme in its final image, it is not a film of ideas. It is, in fact, a negligible and incoherent film which wastes a strong cast (Mel Gibson, John Waters, Sam Neill and Chris Haywood) on a dim story of Australian buddies involved with the Chinese resistance against the Japanese.

Newsreel cameraman Len Maguire (Bill Hunter) and his soundman
Chris Hewitt (Chris Haywood) in Phil Noyce's *Newsfront* (1978).

Post-War Change

Following the Second World War, the composition of Australian society
changed radically as immigration policy encouraged large numbers of Europeans to settle here at a time when Australia was in the grip of a very
conservative Liberal government. The films set in this period register some
of the tensions arising from these two factors; from, that is, a country irrevocably changing in the face of an administration, and perhaps even of a
national attitude, which was resistant to change. Films such as *Newsfront*
and *Silver City*, in dramatizing such tensions, offer sharp insights into
national prejudices.

Phil Noyce's *Newsfront* (1978) is the one remarkable film set in this
period. In it, changes in the Australian political and social scene are
interwoven with and reflected by the contrasting careers of the Maguire
brothers, Len (Bill Hunter) and Frank (Gerard Kennedy). Len is top
cameraman for Cinetone News, an all-Australian newsreel company; Frank
works for Newsco, the rival firm which is American-owned. Frank seeks a
career in Hollywood; Len remains in Australia, an old-fashioned, Labor-
voting patriot, stubbornly clinging to integrity even as his marriage to the

thin-lipped Fay (Angela Punch-McGregor's[13] best performance) fails and as television threatens the newsreel industry. A skimpy synopsis cannot do justice to the richness of *Newsfront*. Through its brilliant wedding of black-and-white newsreel footage with (mainly) coloured 'live' action, it records:

1   Actual historical information relating to the period: the arrival of post-war European immigrants, the growth of anti-Communist feeling leading to Prime Minister Menzies' failed attempt to abolish the Australian Communist Party (1951), the change from Ben Chifley's Labor Government to Menzies' Liberal regime, the Redex cross-country motor trial, the visit of Amercian Vice-President Nixon (1953), the disastrous Maitland floods of 1954, the Melbourne Olympic Games (1956) in which the Russia-Hungary water-polo clash is recorded by the television cameras;

2   The more diffusely felt changes in moral and sexual mores, in relation to extramarital affairs, abortion and conservative Catholicism, as explored through the lives of the film's fictional characters;

3   The relation between the fictional characters and the actual historical events, and how, in some cases, they influenced those events through their professional involvement with the media; and

4   How, first through the rivalry of the two newsreel companies and then through the coming of television, the construction of twentieth-century history has been profoundly affected by the growth of visual media.

Although covering a wide panorama of events, the film never falls into the trap of being merely episodic as so many recent Australian films have done. Noyce (as director and co-author of the screenplay) never loses his grip on the interaction of the public and personal, on the connection between large historical events and private lives. The latter are observed with enough subtlety and sympathy not to be dwarfed by the drama of the newsreel footage; and, above all, Bill Hunter's superb performance, as Len, recorder, maker, and victim of a decade's history, gives the film a steely coherence. Like the heroes of *The Irishman* and *The Picture Show Man*, he is 'just a bit old-fashioned' as one character says of him, but he is more interesting than either of the others because at his core is a thinking man's integrity rather than mere stubbornness. The film as a whole is comic, touching, socially incisive and politically intelligent. David Stratton, describing it as 'one of the best and certainly one of the most likeable new Australian films', claims that:

> The awesomely skilful juggling of the live action with the newsreel footage sometimes takes the breath away, but the film is peopled with such rich, human characters that every movement is cherishable.[14]

Few would want to quarrel with this assessment, and it gathers together several aspects of the film's importance as an historical document.

The migrant arrivals glimpsed at the start of *Newsfront* are moved centre stage in Sophia Turkiewicz's *Silver City* (1984). The latter is an historical film concerned with a 'true' aspect of Australian post-war life: the European migrant influx which gave rise to the 'New Australian' idea, now replaced by more sophisticated notions of multiculturalism. Some real-life figures are represented (for example, Arthur Calwell, Labor Minister for Immigration), but the real historical importance of the film is in its depiction of Australian attitudes towards foreigners. These attitudes reflect a xenophobia born of an insecure sense of superiority and that deep-rooted suspicion of strangers glimpsed earlier in *Break of Day*. These unattractive aspects of Australia are dramatized in a customs officer's seizure of an eiderdown, in the bullying approach of the migrant camp director, in the use of a loud hailer for barking out orders in largely uncomprehended English to the new arrivals, in the surly reaction of a country barman (sharply sketched by Ian Gilmour) to the request of the heroine, Nina (Gosia Dobrowolska), for a vodka or cognac, and in the small-town confrontation between Nina and some local yobbos, who talk of 'bloody refos' and 'one of the nuts and bolts'. Some of these incidents are perceptively observed (for example, the scene in the country pub), others are crudely written, so as to underline the nastiness. However, *Silver City* works best as a sociological study of cultural clash, with very exact attention to the decor of migrant camps, trains, and shops, an acute ear on occasions for dialogue which nails the period, and a sympathetic

The migrant camp in Sophia Turkiewicz's *Silver City* (1984).

sense of the difficulties of being a migrant in the face of the blank incomprehension and hostility Australia frequently offered to 'displaced persons'. Where it fails is in the pallid romance between Nina and Julian (Ivar Kants), a fellow migrant who is married to her friend Anna (Anna Jemison). Unlike *Newsfront, Silver City* does not successfully integrate its individual drama with the circumambient historical processes.

Silver City is the most ambitious of the films which touch on the migrant situation in Australia. Others include Tom Cowan's *Promised Woman* (1975), about a proxy bride rejected on arrival in Australia; Paul Cox's *Kostas* (1979) with its romance between a Greek taxi driver (Takis Emmanuel) and a middle-class Australian divorcee (Wendy Hughes); and *Cathy's Child* (1979), directed by Donald Crombie and based on an actual *cause célèbre*. Cathy Baikis (Michele Fawdon), whose child is abducted by her Greek husband, is finally reunited with her child as a result of the efforts of a journalist, Dick Wordly (Alan Cassell), on whose book the screenplay is based. It is a minor film but it does highlight the problems faced in this country by migrants unsure of legalities and confronted by unsympathetic officialdom. The latter is often signified by a notably English accent, as in the case of Arthur Dignam's Minister for Immigration.

Like *Cathy's Child* in that they present actual lives involved in struggles of various kinds are Gil Brealey's *Annie's Coming Out* (1984), in which a physically disabled girl has been wrongly diagnosed as mentally defective, and Ken Hannam's *Dawn!*, in which swimming star Dawn Fraser kicks against discipline and official strictures. The chief interest in these films, and of Fred Schepisi's loosely autobiographical *The Devil's Playground* (1976), the chronicle of a teenage boy's sojourn in a Catholic seminary, lies elsewhere, but in their reconstruction of individual lives they inevitably touch on aspects of Australian history: on ways of thinking, on official attitudes and the failure of these adequately to allow for individual difference. To conclude this survey, there are two films which construct fictional narratives against the background of historical events: Ken Hannam's *Sunday Too Far Away* (1975) and Tom Jeffrey's *The Odd Angry Shot* (1979). The former, a realistic account of shearers on an outback sheep station in 1955, observant, unsentimental, episodic, is suddenly given a different narrative status near the end when the shearers strike because their prosperity bonus is to be withdrawn. What has been presented as 'historical', in a generalized way, is now given a last-minute authentication which sunders its dramatic structure. The film has *not* been about the shearers' strike of 1955 but about the pressures of lives lived in remote places. *The Odd Angry Shot* does not pretend to be *about* Australian involvement in the Vietnam war on a level of formal history; its concern is to distil a certain kind of Australian humour and camaraderie among 'characters who are governed by forces beyond their control, and who are shown in a position of defeat at the close of the film.[15]

'Characters who are governed by forces beyond their control ...': considering the aggressive element that looms so largely in Australia's images of itself, it is perhaps surprising that so many of the films considered in this chapter are centred on such characters. Against the resilience of, say, Laura in *The Getting of Wisdom*, or Eliza Fraser, or P. S. in *Careful, He Might Hear You*, one is struck by the predominance of protagonists who are caught up by history, but with little capacity for altering its course. This is as true of actual historical figures such as Breaker Morant as of fictional creations such as Paddy Doolan. Further, those who may be seen as victors (for example, Wattie Doig in *Strikebound*) are outnumbered by those 'shown in a position of defeat' (for example, Mad Dog Morgan, Jimmie Blacksmith, Tom in *Break of Day*). If one accepts the notion that the lessons of history are 'the product of the construction of a history which can be employed in contemporary arguments', it is interesting to ponder what such representations of Australian history reflect of present-day perceptions of the country's past.

[1]   Keith Tribe, 'History and the Production of Memories', *Screen*, Winter 1977–78, Vol.18, No.4, p.10.

[2]   Bill Gammage, 'Working on *Gallipoli*', in Anne Hutton (ed.), *The First Australian History and Film Conference Papers*, Sydney: Australian Film and Television School, 1982, p.86.

[3]   This point is more amply explored by Tom Ryan, 'Historical Films', in Scott Murray (ed.), *The New Australian Cinema*, Melbourne: Thomas Nelson, 1980, p.114.

[4]   'Tom Cowan', Interview with Tom Ryan and Nadya Anderson in *Cinema Papers*, No.15, January 1978, p.204.

[5]   Susan Dermody, 'Action and Adventure', in Scott Murray (ed.), p.84.

[6]   Henry Handel Richardson, 'Some Notes on My Books', *Virginia Quarterly Review*, 1940, reprinted in *Southerly*, Vol.23, No.1, 1963, p.13.

[7]   In fact, according to Armstrong, Witcombe's screenplay had finally to be 're-worked' by a script editor. See Sue Mathews, *35mm Dreams*, Ringwood: Penguin, 1984, p.142.

[8]   Quoted in Mathews, p.142.

[9]   *Ibid.*, p.42.

[10]   Annette Van den Bosch, 'Australian History and Its Reconstruction in Australian Film', in Anne Hutton (ed.), p.244.

[11]   Frederick T. Macartney, Introduction to *The Collected Verse of A. B. Paterson*, Sydney: Angus & Robertson, 1951, p.viii.

[12]   Cliff Green, *Picnic at Hanging Rock. A Film*, Melbourne: Cheshire, 1975, p.4.

[13]   She was at this time known as Angela Punch.

[14]   David Stratton, *The Last New Wave*, Sydney: Angus & Robertson, 1980, p.212.

[15]   Tom Ryan, 'Historical Films', in Scott Murray (ed.) p.120.

Part Three: TAKING STOCK

10 Major Contributors: Here Today ...?

Behind the Australian film revival of the 1970s and 1980s there are clearly many individuals, companies, and government instrumentalities that have earned their place in the story. A good number of these have been referred to in passing, some at greater length, in the earlier chapters of this book, but, given the largely thematic organization employed there, it is perhaps useful to look a little more closely at some of the key contributions. Rightly or wrongly, fairly or unfairly, it is actors and directors who have received the most publicity and it is they who, in the public perception of the new Australian cinema, have been the most influential in creating a sense of what that cinema is like. Such a perception no doubt undervalues the role of producers above all, but as well the work of other major collaborators impinges less than it ought. One thinks particularly of scriptwriters, directors of photography, production designers and art directors, and music directors. There are reference books[1] which comprehensively list the credits of those involved in the Australian film-making industry, but these of their nature do not give much sense of the kinds of contribution made. Inevitably in a male-dominated industry (and country), women, except as actresses, are notably few on the ground, at least in the mainstream cinema with which this book is concerned. Curiously, then, four of the most notable producers of the revival have been women.

The Producers

In delivering the John Grierson Memorial Lecture for 1984,[2] Joan Long (one of the four) claimed that: 'The producer makes it happen and the director puts it on the screen.' She further subdivided producers into (a) the 'entrepreneurial' producer who works closely with the money brokers *and* on the making of the film, and (b) those who supervise without their reputations as artists being on the line. Most films of the Australian renaissance, she claimed, were initiated by producers, citing *Picnic at Hanging Rock* (1974), *Caddie* (1976), *My Brilliant Career* (1979), and *Puberty Blues* (1981) as examples. On the last named, which she co-produced with Margaret Kelly, the director, Bruce Beresford, was not involved until six weeks before starting, by which time the screenplay was solidly developed.

Long's background includes directing for the Commonwealth Film Unit in the 1950s and screenwriting for such films as *Caddie* and *The Picture*

Show Man (1977). She also produced the latter, as well as *Puberty Blues* and *Silver City* (1984). *Caddie, Puberty Blues,* and *Silver City* reveal a marked concern for the difficult role of women in Australian society, and a sharply critical response to repressive forces within that society, whether bureaucratic or merely male. Margaret Fink, producer (and designer) of *The Removalists* (1975) and, most notably, of *My Brilliant Career,* reveals in the latter, in her choice of Miles Franklin's novel and of Gillian Armstrong as director, Eleanor Witcombe as scriptwriter, and several other women in important positions, a more obviously feminist line than Long. Indeed, she is on record as having 'responded to the book', because 'Obviously Miles is a proto-typical feminist, and I think I have always been one . . .'[3] Like Joan Long she has successfully broached the male world of financing: for *My Brilliant Career,* she secured investments from Greater Union Organization (one of the major Australian distributors), the Victorian Film Commission and the New South Wales Film Corporation. It was not easy, even believing in her subject as she did, and she has not made another film until her current project, an adaptation of Christina Stead's *For Love Alone.* Directed by Stephen Wallace, this is the story of a young girl's search for sexual love in Sydney and London: it sounds a very Fink-like enterprise.

The third in this distinguished quartet of women producers is Patricia Lovell who has acted as producer or executive producer on two films with director Peter Weir, *Picnic at Hanging Rock* and *Gallipoli* (1981), on two with Ken Hannam, *Break of Day* (1976) and *Summerfield* (1977), and on Ken Cameron's *Monkey Grip* (1982). There is less obvious thematic coherence here, but three of the films are among the most impressive of the revival. It may be, as Joan Long claims, that women producers are no more than ten per cent of the total in Australia; it may also be true that it is still easier for a woman to set up as a producer than as a director; the record of these three is nevertheless significant in terms of the *quality* of their achievement if not yet in terms of numbers of films. The fourth, Jill Robb, with a long career in television and in documentary, has staked a claim on critical attention with her first feature production, *Careful, He Might Hear You* (1983). In her new venture, *The More Things Change . . .*, again (like *Careful*) adapted from a novel by Sumner Locke Elliott, she has chosen as director Robyn Nevin, long one of the best actresses in Australia but with hitherto no directing experience. In the precarious state of the Australian film scene at present, this seems a daring if heartening piece of risk-taking.

At the time of writing, several other women's names occupy the producer's credit on films in production: Jane Scott (associate producer on *My Brilliant Career*) on *Top Kid* (directed by Carl Schultz) and *On Loan* (directed by Geoff Bennett); Sandra Levy and Julia Overton on *The Other Facts of Life* (directed by Esben Storm) and Overton (with Richard Mason) on *Room to Move* (directed by John Duigan); Clytie Jessop, producer *and* director (and Andrena Finlay, co-producer) of *Emma's War*, starring Lee Remick; Jane Ballantyne, co-producer with director Michael Pattinson of *Moving Out* (1982) and with director Paul Cox of *Man of Flowers* (1983), on *Cactus* (directed by Cox); and Barbi Taylor, co-producer with Richard Franklin of *Roadgames* (1981), on *Frog Dreaming* (directed by Brian Trenchard-Smith).

Less than ten per cent they may be, but the first four names at least have so far made a more distinctive contribution than most of their male counterparts, though this perception may be the result of their having received more publicity *because* of their sex. Among the men, Byron Kennedy's sudden death when his helicopter crashed in the Blue Mountains robbed the industry of one of its most exciting creative talents. Associate producer on Tim Burstall's *The Last of the Knucklemen* (1979), he then formed Kennedy Miller Pty Ltd, with director George Miller, and went on to produce *Mad Max* (1979), *Mad Max 2* (1982) and the absorbing television mini-series, *The Dismissal* (1983). Not many Australian films have evinced the sort of energy and flair displayed in these films. No-one could accuse producer Antony I. Ginnane of lacking energy or consistency, but it is the consistency of the truly awful. Apart from his co-production of *Patrick* (1978, with director Richard Franklin), the names of his films resonate with exploitative shoddiness of one kind or other. They include *Fantasm* (1976, money-making soft-porn, directed by Franklin), *Blue Fire Lady* (1977, Mills and Boone on horseback, directed by Ross Dimsey), *Thirst* (1979, directed by Rod Hardy), *Harlequin* (1980, directed by its star, David Hemmings) and *The Survivor* (1981, Hemmings again), three abortive attempts to capture the international market with varieties of supernatural hocus-pocus, and, worst of all, *Turkey Shoot* (1982, directed by Brian Trenchard-Smith) in which a series of mutilations provides a challenge to the stomach while the mind is left undisturbed. It may be true, as David Stratton says, that: 'Tony Ginnane is the only film producer in Australia who behaves like everyone's idea of an American film producer';[4] my idea of an American film producer is someone like David Selznick or Hal Wallis who may have *behaved* like a producer but also made memorable films.

There are other much more reputable names of course — Phillip Adams, Richard Brennan, Gil Brealey, Richard Mason, Anthony Buckley, John B. Murray, and Hal and James McElroy, for example — though it is doubtful if any of them, apart from Adams, means much outside the industry or implies the sort of personal imprint which *auteurists* find in their director heroes. Adams, of course, is a well-known public figure, but more so as a columnist and spokesman for various aspects of the film industry than as producer of particular films. In fact, he was producer on three of Bruce Beresford's early films — *The Adventures of Barry McKenzie* (1972), *Don's Party* (1976), and *The Getting of Wisdom* (1977) — and in the 1980s has been executive producer of films such as *Lonely Hearts* (1982) and *Fighting*

Back (1982). Brennan has worked twice with the as-yet under-valued Stephen Wallace, on *Love Letters from Teralba Road* (1980) and *Stir* (1981), and with Gillian Armstrong on *Starstruck* (1982), also under-valued; Buckley has made four films with director Donald Crombie — *Caddie, The Irishman* (1978), *The Killing of Angel Street* (1981) and *Kitty and the Bagman* (1982) — but what thematic and stylistic consistency they reveal appears to belong to Crombie since his *Cathy's Child* (1979), pro-duced by Pom Oliver and Errol Sullivan, exhibits a similar range of interest and sympathies; Mason has worked twice with John Duigan — on *Winter of our Dreams* (1981) and *Far East* (1982) — and on the children's film *Let the Balloon Go* (1976, directed by Oliver Howes); John B. Murray, with a background in documentary as producer-director-writer, has produced and directed *The Naked Bunyip* (1970), produced *Lonely Hearts* (1982, directed by Paul Cox) and *Devil in the Flesh* (1985, directed by his son, Scott Murray), and co-produced *We of the Never Never* (1982, directed by Igor Auzins); Gil Brealey, while head of the South Australian Film Cor-poration, produced *Sunday Too Far Away* (1975, directed by Ken Hannam) and the endearing outback man-and-his-dingo story, *Dusty* (1982, directed by John Richardson); and the McElroy brothers together produced three Peter Weir films (*The Cars that Ate Paris*, 1974, *Picnic at Hanging Rock*, 1975, and *The Last Wave*, 1977) as well as several other features and television series.

In writing about the producers, I find I still keep naming the directors after the film titles, perhaps because they have often been more articulate than other contributors, perhaps because in Joan Long's words they 'put it on the screen'. This is not a situation peculiar to Australia: apart from the likes of Selznick or Val Lewton or Alexander Korda or George Lucas, there are not many producers anywhere whose names on the credits set up expectations of a particular kind. However, it would be wrong to undervalue their essential, often initiatory role in any appraisal of the new Australian cinema.

The Directors

After just over a decade of this revival, it is already possible to speak of a 'first generation' of directors, implying those whose reputations were firmly made in the 1970s and those in large part responsible for the repu-tation of the revival itself. They are, above all, Peter Weir, Bruce Beresford, and Fred Schepisi, all of whom are now at least temporarily lost to Australia. Weir is the nearest Australian approach to an old-fashioned *auteur*, not that he makes old-fashioned films or that he would relish the *auteur* label. (In fact, he has specifically repudiated it.) However, certain recurring preoccu-pations — the awareness of the extraordinary hovering at the edges of the ordinary, the limits of rational understanding, the hostile potential of the natural world — are present in the first three features (*The Cars that Ate Paris, Picnic at Hanging Rock, The Last Wave*). In the latter two, the distinctive visual appearance, conniving at the conflation of the real and the fantastic, is the work of cameraman Russell Boyd, who also shot Weir's next two, *Gallipoli* and *The Year of Living Dangerously* (1982). *Gallipoli* marked a change of pace for Weir but in it, *The Year of Living Dangerously* and his first American film, *Witness* (1985), his interest has been engaged by heroes at large in a hostile world, whether of war, political turmoil, or urban violence. His collaboration with David Williamson, author of the screenplays for *Gallipoli* and *The Year of Living Dangerously*, has been salutory for him. Weir's own intuitive, professedly non-cerebral approach to film-making may in time have led him into the sorts of dissatisfying obscurities that threaten the last third of *The Last Wave*. Williamson's firm grasp of social and political elements has provided him with a reliable narrative framework on which to display his perceptual strengths and his sensitive alertness to atmosphere.

Whereas Weir's *Witness* has been critically well-received and commercially successful, Beresford's American biblical epic *King David* (1985) has been greeted unequivocally as a disaster. Beresford responded expansively to the conditions of production in the US when he made his first film there, *Tender Mercies* (1982), which was nominated for Best Picture and Best Screenplay Oscars; at $7m the film cost more than seven times the budget of any of his eight Australian features. However, within the financial constraints imposed on him at home, he established an enviable track record as

Peter Weir directing *The Cars That Ate Paris* (1974).

a prolific and popular film-maker. If his films lack the strong personal qualities of Peter Weir's, they reveal an admirable control over pacing, *mise-en-scène*, and editing. He is in fact a compleat craftsman. After the money-making successes of the Barry McKenzie films, he made *Don's Party, The Getting of Wisdom, Money Movers* (1979), *Breaker Morant* (1980), *The Club* (1980), and *Puberty Blues* (1981). Those are all interesting films; they have recurring interests in the structure of hierarchies (*Money Movers, Breaker Morant, The Club, Puberty Blues*), in resistance to authorities of various kinds (*The Getting of Wisdom, Breaker Morant, The Club, Puberty Blues*); the social observation of particular *milieux* is acute, whether of the ageing radicals of *Don's Party*, the military prison and court martial of *Breaker Morant*, the League football committee machinations of *The Club*, or the teenage surf-and-sex world of *Puberty Blues*. Not one of these is dull; Beresford elicits excellent performances from a range of actors (from Graham Kennedy in *Don's Party* to Nell Schofield and Jad Capelja as the restless teenagers in *Puberty Blues*); and he has unobtrusive skill in keeping a confined scene (for example, *The Club* or *Don's Party*) from seeming static. Beresford's films may lack the intensity and the mysteriousness of Weir's but, until the apparent evidence of *King David*, one would have trusted him to make modestly enjoyable films — not especially personal, but with an edge to them. As I write, he has returned to Australia (1985) to direct *The Fringe Dwellers*, based on the novel by Nene Gare.

'Personal' *is* the word for Fred Schepisi's Australian films, particularly for *The Devil's Playground* (1975), a loosely autobiographical story of a teenage boy who leaves a Catholic junior seminary after finding that he has no vocation. It is a touching and charming film, sharpened by some abrasive insights into the effects of a repressive system of education (he is much more tough-minded about this than Beresford is in *The Getting of Wisdom*). Financially, it did reasonable business, without actually making a profit; critically, it was very well-received and it won the Best Film award at the 1976 Australian Film Awards. It was this success, presumably, that enabled Schepisi to raise the $1.2m for his next film, *The Chant of Jimmie Blacksmith* (1978), the investors including the Australian Film Commission, the Victorian Film Corporation (now Film Victoria), and Hoyts cinema chain. The film marked Schepisi's third collaboration with author Thomas Keneally who had written the screenplay for 'The Priest', Schepisi's episode in the portmanteau film, *Libido* (1973), played Father Marshall in *The Devil's Playground*, and provided the source novel as well as playing the cook in *Jimmie Blacksmith*. Although a film of undeniable power in its treatment of a half-caste Aboriginal cut off from his tribal life and denied access to white society, and despite its haunting images of constriction and alienation, *Jimmie Blacksmith* was a bitter disappointment financially to Schepisi. David Stratton has observed that 'Schepisi's films are concerned with people trapped in a situation and trying to get out';[5] perhaps Jimmie's failure to do so helps to account for the failure of this film — often remarkable, occasionally over-explicit in relation to its serious theme — to find a satisfactory audience. Schepisi's first two American films, the ambitious Western *Barbarosa* (1981), which has acquired a minor cult status, and *Iceman* (1984), a $10m film about the resuscitation of a prehistoric man by a team of scientists, have both done poorly at the box-office, though *Barbarosa* received some critical praise for the visualization of its mythic aspirations. Perhaps his film version of David Hare's play, *Plenty*, will allow this unusually gifted and individual film-maker a chance for critical *and* commercial success.

Of the 'first generation', Tim Burstall's is the longest if not the most distinguished record, his most recent film being an adaptation of Morris West's novel, *The Naked Country*. He won an award at the Venice Film Festival in 1960 for his short film, *The Prize*, worked throughout the 1960s on documentaries and children's films, made the disastrous feature film, *2000 Weeks* in 1968, and in 1971 scored a box office success with *Stork*, based on a play by David Williamson, first performed at the experimental La Mama Theatre in Melbourne. *Stork's* success derived no doubt partly from its bawdy treatment of male sexuality, partly from Burstall's skilful handling of players (Bruce Spence, Jacki Weaver particularly) and situations. His next film, 'The Child' episode of *Libido*, a sensitive study of youthful disillusion, is in a quite different vein and, although it contains some of his best work, he has never returned to this kind of quiet intimacy. Throughout the 1970s, he persistently ruffled critical feathers with films such as the vastly

Director Tim Burstall (centre), with actors Mike Preston and Gary Day, on the set of *Duet for Four* (1982).

popular *Alvin Purple* (1973), *Petersen* (1974) and *Eliza Fraser* (1976). *Petersen*, which he rightly described as being about 'the collision of working-class values with those of the contemporary, university-educated middle classes',[6] received a critical mauling, especially for its sexual candour, but ten years later it looks like a key film of the revival. Burstall's energy and his determination to entertain make him a necessary corrective to the more decorous line of Australian film-making. There has long been talk of his filming D.H. Lawrence's *Kangaroo* and his abrasive willingness to offend might make him just the man for the job; the film will star Judy Davis and Colin Friels.

Among the others who got started in the 1970s, Gillian Armstrong, after her *succès d'estime* with *My Brilliant Career* and the charming musical *Starstruck* (1982), indifferently received in Australia despite its wit and verve, has had mixed success with her first American film, *Mrs Soffel* (1985), a sombre romantic drama starring Diane Keaton and Mel Gibson; and Richard Franklin, notoriously under-valued in Australia despite the real proficiency of *Patrick* and *Roadgames*, has been better appreciated abroad. An ardent admirer of Hitchcock (as a student of the University of Southern California, he was invited as an observer on the set of *Topaz*, 1969), he has directed a quartet of witty, inventive thrillers, none of which has succeeded in Australia. Perhaps it is his unashamed commercialism; perhaps it is his failure to address Major Australian Themes; perhaps it is his sheer technical impudence: for whatever reason, *Patrick* and *Roadgames* (the latter is one of the most exhilarating of all Australian films) have been well-liked in the US and his two American-made films, *Psycho II* (1983) and *Cloak and Dagger* (1984), both considerably more than *hommages* to the master, failed to find audiences here, despite enthusiastic American reviews. He is now filming *Link* in England after which he is returning to Australia to film *Drums of Mer* from Ion Idriess's novel.

Australia *needs* the liveliness of Franklin at least as much as it needs careful but less exciting directors such as Donald Crombie and Ken Hannam who, having deserted the quiet humanism of, say, *Caddie* or *Sunday Too Far Away* respectively, reveal themselves stylistically at sea in the big-budget spectacle of *Robbery Under Arms* (1985). It needs also the kind of liveliness and daring one applauded in Phil Noyce's *Newsfront* (1978), with its brilliant juxtaposing of newsreels and staged action, and in his big-city thriller, *Heatwave* (1982), in which an often dazzling technique subserves a serious theme. An Australian suspicion of the arty or pretentious, a suspicion that sometimes works in a wholesome cutting-down-to-size way, sometimes towards a boorish anti-culturism, may make Paul Cox's future dubious. However, no other Australian films so unevasively confront the inner life and the life that goes on between two people as his three films of the 1980s — *Lonely Hearts, Man of Flowers* (1983), and *My First Wife* (1984). The latter two are both flawed, sometimes florid films, but they point to a quirky, disquieting talent, and they derive from a man who *wants* to make 'small' films, believing that 'no film of lasting importance was ever made on a fat bank account'.[7] Ian Pringle, whose haunting study of two men coping with solitude, *The Plains of Heaven* (1982), was coolly received in Australia although it won a minor prize at Mannheim in 1983, is another who believes that the future of the local industry lies with 'smaller, tighter budgets'.[8] His newest film, *Wrong World* (1985), which has won an overseas award for its star, Jo (*Starstruck*) Kennedy, awaits release in Australia.

Apart from those already named, the directors who offer most promise for the 1980s are the likes of Carl Schultz who, in *Careful He Might Hear You*, has beautifully exploited the structures of melodrama; the John Duigan of *Mouth to Mouth* (1978) and *Winter of Our Dreams*, with their feeling for precarious urban life, rather than of the flashy exoticism of *Far East* (1982); Richard Lowenstein whose *Strikebound* (1984) is the best film about Australian working-class life and politics; Stephen Wallace, director of *Love Letters from Teralba Road*, the prison drama, *Stir, The Boy Who Had Everything* (1985), which won an award at Moscow, and now getting a big chance with *For Love Alone*; David Stevens, whose humane touch made kindly comedy from an unlikely subject in *The Clinic* (1982); and George Miller, whose success with the *Mad Max* films has taken him to America (to direct a segment of Steven Spielberg's four-part *Twilight Zone — the Movie*) and back again for *Mad Max: Beyond Thunderdome*.

Miller has said he finds the Hollywood experience 'immensely interesting' but not 'as a permanent way to work, because it is less organic — more specialized and compartmentalized — than our present approach to the work here. I am interested in examining the entire craft of film-making'.[9] However, directors who have felt hamstrung by inadequate budgets or frustrated by lacklustre promotion will continue to be attracted by the Hollywood approach. There is no point in taking a high moral stand in relation to this: film-makers want to make films, and one can only hope that enough of the talents referred to above will find the encouragement they need to keep working here.

The Players

Traditionally, mainstream Western cinema has been dominated by those actors who, sometimes mysteriously, have acquired the status of stars. Stars, not by any means necessarily the 'best' actors, have exerted extraordinary pull at the world's box offices. Even though the phenomenon was past its palmiest days by the 1970s, a star 'name' and the image it conjured up was far from harmful to a film's financial prospects. Without the backing of a studio system and perhaps even without much other conscious attention to star-building, the new Australian cinema has yielded a small but imposing cluster of players who, by virtue of their special rapport with camera and audiences, look like certifiable stars. In being so, they must be said to have made a significant contribution to the revival.

Some have already attracted international attention. Jack Thompson, Bryan Brown, Mel Gibson, Sam Neill, Judy Davis, Angela Punch-McGregor, Helen Morse have all appeared in one or more British or American productions, although at this stage it is probably true to say that only Gibson (born in the US) has commanded a star following outside Australia. This may be because he is the only one whose screen *personae* have typically exhibited heroic traits — as street-wise Frank sobered into manhood at Gallipoli, or as Mad Max out there doing battle with the forces of anarchy, or as Guy Hamilton arriving at political and romantic commitment in the strife-torn Indonesia of *The Year of Living Dangerously*. Even the soppy fatuities of *Tim* (1979) did him no harm, in fact established his romantic potential and won him an Australian Film Award as Best Actor. Although none of his overseas films — Roger Donaldson's *The Bounty* (1984), Mark Rydell's *The River* (1985), or *Mrs Soffel* — has been a palpable hit, few actors anywhere have enjoyed that kind of exposure in recent years.

If Gibson is now the best-known actor of the Australian revival, it may be partly because he is the one who seems to belong most securely in a male star tradition stretching back to Clark Gable and it may be also because he does not seem distinctively Australian as, say, Thompson and Brown do. Sam Neill (actually a New Zealander), with his cultivated tones and an un-Australian elegance, made his name as a thinking girl's romantic lead in *My*

Sam Neill as Captain Starlight in Donald Crombie and Ken Hannam's *Robbery Under Arms* (1985).

John Hargreaves as the prisoner faking blindness in Claude Whatham's *Hoodwink* (1981).

Brilliant Career and was snatched up almost at once to star in two international films (Graham Baker's *The Final Conflict*, 1981, and Jeannot Szwarc's *Enigma*, 1982). Several others followed before his return to Australia to star in *Robbery Under Arms*. The gallant bushranging hero, Captain Starlight, complete with English aristocratic connections subdued to the demands of Australian bush camaraderie, ought to have clinched his stardom, but the film bungles its chances and Neill is left stylishly at the centre of a film that does not deserve him. Working at a pace that matches Gibson's, his next two films are Fred Schepisi's *Plenty*, made in England, co-starring Meryl Streep, and Stephen Wallace's *For Love Alone*, currently in production in Sydney.

Gibson and Neill have had most international experience at this stage, but Thompson and Brown and several others such as John Hargreaves and Bill Hunter offer more readily identifiable readings of Australian experience. Thompson's 'ockerish' characters, in films such as *Wake in Fright* (1970), *Sunday Too Far Away*, *Petersen*, Terry Ohlsson's *Scobie Malone* (1975), Michael Thornhill's *The Journalist* (1979), and *The Club* are much less homogeneous than they might suggest at first glance. At their most interesting, in, say, *Sunday Too Far Away* and *Petersen*, there is a touching vulnerability, a capacity for wonder at what may be out of reach. Even the apparently mindless yahoo of *Wake in Fright* has flashes of real good nature that catch our censoriousness off-guard. His more obvious 'hero' roles have been in atrocious films such as *Scobie Malone* and *The Journalist*, and some of his most effective work has been in character roles, such as the somewhat bumbling outback lawyer who grows in moral stature in *Breaker Morant* as the court martial proceeds, and the conscientious, limited parson in *The Chant of Jimmie Blacksmith*. He has not worked, it seems, at developing a star image: he has the presence for it, a presence compounded of bronzed digger looks, a relaxed, quizzical good humour with a touch of the 'lair', a suggestion of strong, instinctual reaction to situations; but he has opted more for the actor's stature than the star's aura, so that he is wasted in the empty mythicizing gestures of his role of Clancy in *The Man from Snowy River* (1982).

Bryan Brown's screen *persona* is characteristically more aggressive than Thompson's. The larrikin element, the quick disrespect for authority, and the sexual assertiveness equip him well for star roles such as that of Morgan O'Keefe in *Far East* and, again opposite Helen Morse, in the television mini-series, *A Town Like Alice* (1981). However, less obviously leading-man roles in the two Stephen Wallace films, the inarticulate husband in *Love Letters from Teralba Road* and the 'crim' in *Stir*, and the softening ex-radical in *Winter of Our Dreams* have made better use of his abilities, suggesting respectively the dangerous potential beneath the tough surface and the insubstantiality of that toughness. He has not yet been lucky with his overseas work (for example, Jim Goddard's *Parker*, 1985); perhaps, like Hargreaves and Hunter who have not yet filmed overseas, he is too indigenously Australian for major international success. Hargreaves has simply got better and better since his first film, Tom Jeffrey's *The Removalists* (1975), in which he played a callow young policeman succumbing to the authority of his position. He was dead right as the giver of *Don's Party*, trading on fading sexual charm and clinging to an outworn radicalism, brilliantly inventive as the devious 'con' in Claude Whatham's *Hoodwink* (1981), very moving as the scapegrace father in *Careful, He Might Hear You* and as the distraught husband in *My First Wife*, and magisterial as Jim Cairns, defeated politician of the Whitlam years in television's *The Dismissal*. There is a knowingness about the larrikin streak in some of his characters — he knows, that is, to what uses he is putting it — and a sudden capacity for emotional capitulation that make him arguably the most interesting actor in Australian films.

It is Hunter, however, who has so far given the best performance in an Australian film. His newsreel cameraman in *Newsfront* suggests a lifetime of taking things as they come, learning what to value and holding on to it and sloughing off the dross; loyal, liberal, conservative, married to a nag for longer than most would bear it, and finally leaving her without losing integrity. It is a richly written role and Hunter invests it with the subtlety and humanity that too few of his roles have drawn on. Only *The Dismissal*, in which he plays Rex Connor on a losing wicket, has given him an opportunity comparable to the one he had in *Newsfront*, and he took it with both hands. He seems born to play Chifley-nurtured Labor men, sticking to ideals in a messy, increasingly internationalized Australia.

These six are, to be Irish about it, the first eleven of Australian actors. They have had more chances than some others, but there is a group of young men who seem poised to challenge their supremacy. Most notable among these are Colin Friels, fecklessly charming as Noni Hazlehurst's junkie lover in Ken Cameron's *Monkey Grip* (1982) and imbuing a skimpily-written role in Igor Auzins' *The Coolangatta Gold* (1984) with a complexity that makes him the film's dramatic centre; Richard Moir as the troubled young architect, pulled between ambition and commitment, in Phil Noyce's *Heatwave* and the loner shaken out of complacency in Ian Pringle's *The Plains of Heaven*; Tom Burlinson, who made valuable use of boyish determination as *The Man from Snowy River* and as Tommy Woodcock, the legendary strapper, in Simon Wincer's *Phar Lap* (1983); and Lewis Fitz-Gerald projecting an uncloying sincerity as the crusading young student counsellor in Michael Caulfield's *Fighting Back*. The latter two have yet to try something more demanding than innocence at bay, but all four, still barely thirty, look set to fill leading roles for the next decade and to provide some re-workings of the male images in Australian films.

There is an extraordinary rich vein of character players among Australian actors at present working in films, and no space here to do more than list some of those whose names on a cast list is a guarantee of that sharpness of felt life, that sense of a role that is lived in rather merely inhabited. Some such as Bill Kerr (Uncle Jack in *Gallipoli*, the dingo-owner in *Dusty*), the absurdly under-used John Stanton whose commanding presence almost pulled Donald Crombie's *Kitty and the Bagman* (1982) together, and Norman Kaye who played two eccentrics for Paul Cox, one endearing in *Lonely Hearts* and one dangerous in *Man of Flowers*, can, and sometimes do, carry whole films. Others, by filling in the spaces round the films' protagonists, contribute that sense of textural abundance so crucial to what is essentially

Tom Burlinson as Jim Craig with Sigrid Thornton as Jessica in George Miller's *The Man from Snowy River* (1982).

a realist cinema. They provide the *behaviour* that can sometimes make a film look like a transparent window on the world. Some of these are: the ubiquitous Chris Haywood, with his suggestion of East End-boy-on-the-make (sometimes cheery as in *Newsfront*, sometimes treacherous as in Esben Storm's *In Search of Anna*, 1979, sometimes lethal as in Russell Mulcahy's black horror-comedy, *Razorback*, 1983); Ray Marshall, whose wry, weary father in Michael Thornhill's *The FJ Holden* (1977), country town mayor in *Newsfront*, and wily Labor back-bencher in *The Dismissal*, are just three of a dozen or more perfectly realized sketches; the chubby, bumptious go-getters John Ewart has honed so variously in *Petersen, Newsfront*, and (comically) in Henri Safran's *Bush Christmas* (1983), as an inept horse thief; the charismatic Aboriginal actor Gulpilil, a striking image of organic belonging in the outback vistas of Nicolas Roeg's *Walkabout* (1970), equivocally seedy and threatening at Sydney's urban edges in *The Last Wave*; Tony Barry whose weather-worn, laconic Australian-ness gives shots of truth to films as tedious as *We of the Never Never* and Quentin Masters' *Midnite Spares* (1982); and Ray Barratt, Noel Ferrier, Frank Wilson, Barry Otto, Nick Tate, John Clayton and . . . The list is an impressively long one; the faces are all well-known in Australian films even when the names are not, and, as in the days of classic Hollywood, these character players, mapping little bits of a variegated Australian male image, are among the constant pleasures of the new Australian cinema.

The men have been treated first because, perhaps inevitably in this country and indeed in the present-day film situation internationally, they

Ray Marshall, versatile character player in numerous films, such as Michael Thornhill's *The FJ Holden* (1978).

have dominated the scene. Not only have more films focused on male actors and activities but there is a much less pervasive sense of a corporate female image's having been built up, or even of individuals' having established the recognizable *personae* that characterize some of the men. This is true even of the busiest — of Wendy Hughes or Judy Morris, for instance, with, to this point, twelve films each to their credit. Of them all, only Judy Davis is on the way to international renown, largely as a result of her Oscar-nominated performance in David Lean's *A Passage to India* (1985) in which her way of projecting an unsettling intelligence happily served the needs of the role. Instantly a figure to reckon with after her second film, *My Brilliant Career*, she gave two more carefully thought-out, emotionally detailed perform-ances in roles as different as the defensive, vulnerable hooker in *Winter of Our Dreams* and the trimly repressed preacher's wife in *Hoodwink*. However, by the time she played the militant greenie in *Heatwave* some of the mannerisms (the suspicious glance, the mocking smile) were beginning to look like an actress's equipment rather than a character's attributes. There is, nevertheless, an emotional power, so far largely held in restraint but at least glimpsed in all her films, that calls out for a role she can really make a meal of.

The Australian-ness of her characters lies in their quickness to detect and undercut pomposity and pretension; the other two best-known women stars, Wendy Hughes and Helen Morse are, like Mel Gibson among the men, cast in a more traditional star's mould. To say this is not to depreciate their intelligence or their versatility but to infer that they give off a star gloss in whatever roles they play. Hughes has played a range of glamorous, independent women (for example, Amy in *Newsfront*, the gallery-owner in Paul Cox's *Kostas*, 1979, one of the three socialite Robin Hoods in Peter Maxwell's caper comedy, *Touch and Go*, 1980) but, at her very best, as in *Careful, He Might Hear You* or *My Brilliant Career*, she can suggest the neurotic tensions held barely in check beneath an elegant surface. And when the neuroses are foregrounded, as in the role of the inhibited Patricia in *Lonely Hearts*, she can be very affecting, subduing her beauty in a way that suggests turning in on the character rather than a triumph of make-up and coiffure. Helen Morse's range has exhibited itself in fewer films: the deli-cately lovely, sympathetic Ma'mselle in *Picnic at Hanging Rock*, the Aussie battler of *Caddie*, and the sexually sophisticated cosmopolitan of *Far East* offer three distinct images of women. The last perhaps suits her best and offers the most likely pointer to her development: as heroine of roman-tic melodrama (she confirmed this again in the television mini-series, *A Town Like Alice*), if the Australian cinema would throw off decorum long enough to develop this genre. The sort of films notoriously known as 'women's pictures', which made stars of everyone from Constance Bennett through Merle Oberon to Eleanor Parker, might have been invented for Hughes and Morse.

Judy Davis as Kate Dean with Tui Bow as Annie in Phil Noyce's
Heatwave (1982).

Helen Morse in the title role of Donald Crombie's *Caddie* (1976).

Morse's overseas venture, Michael Apted's *Agatha* (1979), based on Mrs Christie's famous disappearance in 1926, offered her no more than a likeable cameo, but it was well-received, whereas Angela Punch-McGregor's American film, Michael Ritchie's unanimously panned *The Island* (1980), did nothing for her. Tom Ryan makes a case for the way 'her characters manage to maintain an appealing self-assurance in the face of hardship',[10] but on the evidence so far she seems to me a fine character actress (*vide Newsfront* and *The Chant of Jimmie Blacksmith*) but lacking the warmth and amplitude for star roles. She is charmless in Michael Robertson's *The Best of Friends* (1982) and Brian Kavanagh's witless comedy thriller, *Double Deal* (1982), and her *persona* is too undeveloped to carry *We of the Never Never* or Gil Brealey's *Annie's Coming Out* (1984). The two earlier films, by limiting the emotional demands they made on her, enabled her to etch very incisive impressions — of aggrieved conventionality and dim promiscuity respectively.

Potentially more exciting than any of these women is Noni Hazlehurst, whose one major role to date, as the vulnerable but resilient Nora in Ken Cameron's *Monkey Grip* displayed at once generous reserves of feeling and intelligence. One hopes that her new film, *Fran* (produced and directed by Glenda Hambly), will exercise these qualities fully; it gives her a role to which she is committed: that of a young welfare mother embittered by childhood as a ward of state, now coping with her own children.[11] There are 'Aussie battler' elements in these roles, but the concept has become more sophisticated than it is in those roles played by, for instance, Carol Burns as the Union wife in *Strikebound* or Robyn Nevin as the homely, working-class aunt in *Careful, He Might Hear You*. Nevin is forever looking worried at the edges of films (as in *The Irishman* or *The Coolangatta Gold*) instead of dominating them as she could if someone would write her the role she

Wendy Hughes as Vanessa in Carl Schultz's *Careful, He Might Hear You* (1983).

deserves. She is too young and, as Carl Schultz's *Goodbye Paradise* (1982) has shown, too witty to be trapped in maternal brow-furrowing. Elizabeth Alexander (of *Summerfield*) and Olivia Hamnett (of *The Last Wave*) both suggest elegant leading lady potential in spite of underwritten roles, and Judy Morris has made a dozen features of which only Peter Weir's tele-feature, *The Plumber* (1979) and Chris McGill's romantic drama, *Maybe This Time* (1980), actually focused on her and *used* her nervy delicacy. If scripts have been the weakest element in Australian films, it is the women stars who have suffered most from this.

As with the men, there is a rich resource in the ranks of the character actresses and, again, there is not space to do more than pick out a few of the most notable. Carole Skinner's laconic short-order cook in *Monkey Grip* and her slatternly mum of a filthy litter in *My Brilliant Career* are only two from her gallery of marvellously recognizable types; Sandy Gore, with a strong theatrical background, steals films such as Henri Safran's *Norman Loves Rose* (1982) and David Stevens' *Undercover* (1983) from under the noses of their ostensible stars, with, respectively, an abrasive display as a soured-off suburban divorcée and a stylish caricature of *soignée* sophistication; Kris McQuade is very moving as two different kinds of care-worn wives and mothers in *Love Letters from Teralba Road* and *Fighting Back*; and Pat Bishop, in her one feature film, *Don's Party*, was voted Best Actress in the 1977 Australian Film Awards for her disaffected wife. Many of these women, like the character players of British films in the 1940s and 1950s, have distinguished stage reputations. Marion Edward (very funny in *Road-games* and *Strikebound*), Patricia Kennedy, Monica Maughan (both in *The*

Carole Skinner as Mrs McSwat, protecting her brood from their governess, Sybylla (Judy Davis), in Gillian Armstrong's *My Brilliant Career* (1979).

Julia Blake as the Matron in Richard Franklin's *Patrick* (1978).

Getting of Wisdom), Bunney Brooke (in Ken Hannam's *Dawn!*, 1979), Pat Evison (kindly maternal figures in *Tim* and *The Clinic*) and Julia Blake (mad-eyed Matron in *Patrick*, worn-out mum in *My Brilliant Career*) are others in a long list of such stage-trained actresses who have successfully negotiated terms with the camera.

With women's roles in Australian films, too often one has to be grateful for bits and pieces. Few films are built around them: more often than not they are relegated to anxious wives and mothers, defined in terms not of their individuality but of their relationship to men. Insofar as women figure in the national mythologies it is in the subsidiary roles in which the new Australian cinema has most typically represented them.

The Look of the Films

This chapter has concentrated on those who make the showiest contribution but it is clear that there is a slew of other collaborators who have had a major role in lifting Australian cinema in the 1970s and 1980s to a level of professionalism that can bear comparison with films made anywhere. Those opening shots in *Picnic at Hanging Rock*, before any actor appears, in which the rocky outcrop gradually defines itself behind a water-colour mist, owe their shimmering quality to cameraman Russell Boyd. Boyd was director of photography for four Peter Weir films — *Picnic at Hanging Rock, The Last Wave, Gallipoli,* and *The Year of Living Dangerously* — giving to each a distinctively appropriate visual sheen. The sheer beauty of *Picnic at Hanging Rock* is not achieved at the expense of the sinister suggestiveness of many of the images, and its contrast with the desert glare of *Gallipoli* or the sodden urban streets and skyscapes of *The Last Wave* or the sweltering tropicality of *The Year of Living Dangerously* is as much Boyd's achievement as Weir's. Most recently, he has photographed Gillian Armstrong's first American film, *Mrs Soffel* (1985).

From the start of the revival, it was apparent that, whatever else might be said of the films, they would all *look* as good as outstanding cameramen could make them. Don McAlpine lit the interiors of *My Brilliant Career* with a soft radiance which evoked the period as surely as Luciana Arrighi's immaculate production design, but his virtuosity was as dramatically apt in the way his camera tracked and panned about the suburban house in *Don's Party* or the committee rooms in *The Club*. Even a soft-centre, rickety film such as Kevin Dobson's *The Mango Tree* (1977) is easy to look at throughout because of Brian Probyn's lustrous images of Bundaberg and canefields, of early morning riverscapes and the mellow beauty of old weatherboard houses; and, in still worse films, *We of the Never Never* and *The Man from Snowy River*, the wide-screen compositions, the work of Gary Hansen and David Eggby respectively, almost divert attention from the tiresome humans who will keep cluttering up the frame. In fact, it could be argued that these superb cameramen, along with, say, Ian Baker (*The Devil's Playground, The Chant of Jimmie Blacksmith*), Geoff Burton (*Sunday Too Far Away, The Picture Show Man*), and Peter James (*Caddie, The Irishman*) were key figures in the nostalgia boom which threatened to dominate the re-emergent industry. They made the past look so inviting, abetted as they were by production designers and/or art directors such as Arrighi, Leslie Binns (*The Mango Tree*), David Copping (*Picnic at Hanging Rock, The Picture Show Man*), and Richard Kent (*The Getting of Wisdom*), that it is no wonder producers and directors were inclined to linger there.

However, the harsher outlines of modern Australian life, especially of urban life, were just as eloquently imaged in films such as *The FJ Holden* (cameraman David Gribble, art directors Lissa Coote and Monte Fieguth), *Mouth to Mouth* (cameraman David Gribble, production design Clark Munro), and *Moving Out* (cameraman Vincent Monton, production design Neil Angwin). These three films have an utterly convincing look of outer suburban sprawl or inner suburban desuetude (coffee bars, shopping malls, factories, crummy backyards), illuminated occasionally by intimations from nature that it was not always, and does not always have to be, like this.

Production design in Australian films has often been superlatively right in conjuring up the past. Whatever else films such as *My Brilliant Career, The Mango Tree, Newsfront*, and Sophia Turkiewicz's *Silver City* had going for them, their control of the material aspects of *mise-en-scène* (sets, furnishings, costumes) was unerring. In a lesser film such as *The Mango Tree*, there is a suggestion of the camera's lingering over the authenticating *bric-à-brac* when the director should have been concentrating on other kinds of authenticity. In a film as good as *Newsfront,* much of its ideological potency derives from the unobtrusive exactness with which it renders, say, a suburban barbecue or an outback country dance, let alone its brilliant blending of newsreel and staged drama to provide macro- and micro-versions of the life of the times. And in modest modern-set films such as *The FJ Holden* and *Moving Out,* the interiors of houses at subtly different social levels, or of shops and schools, are realized with such quiet accuracy as to be all but taken for granted until one begins to see how much they contribute to the films' impact.

The Sound of Music

Writing as one on whom the musical soundtrack impinges only if it is striking in a rather showy, obvious way, I can do no more than refer to those scores which have stayed in the mind for that sort of reason. The two most prolific film composers to date have been Bruce Smeaton and Brian May, each of whom has about twenty films to his credit. Smeaton is responsible for the co-ordination of Beethoven, Mozart, and Gheorghe Zamphir's pan pipes in the interests of establishing some potent dramatic effects in *Picnic at Hanging Rock*: for example, the use of 'Eine Kleine Nachtmusik' as an accompaniment to the European-style garden party contrasts vividly with the haunting notes of the pan pipes which elsewhere speak of more sinister goings-on. And his full-blooded score for *The Chant of Jimmie Blacksmith* (he worked with Schepisi on *The Devil's Playground* and the American *Barbarosa* as well) is a fitting reinforcement of the film's passionate imagery. May, who has scored some truly terrible films (*Thirst, Breakfast in Paris,* 1982, *Turkey Shoot*) has risen brilliantly to the occasion for Richard Franklin on *Roadgames,* Peter Weir on *Gallipoli* (drawing on Albinoni, Bizet and others), and George Miller on *Mad Max* and *Mad Max 2,* suggesting a versatility that has too often been wasted on trash. However, the score that stays most resonantly in my mind is Max Cook's lushly romantic contribution to *Careful, He Might Hear You.* Cook seems to have understood perfectly the melodramatic power of Carl Schultz's direction and Michael Jenkins' screenplay and to reinforce the tensions surrounding the struggle for identity at the film's heart. Among others who have made memorable contributions to the soundtracks of Australian films are Bill Conti, whose score fed into the exuberance of *The Coolangatta Gold*; Charles Marawood who, with cameraman Peter James, gave the first half-hour of *The Irishman* a romantic sweep that John Ford might not have disdained; Cameron Allen whose scores added an edge of threat to *The Night the Prowler* (1978), *Stir, Hoodwink,* and *Heatwave*; internationally famous music director, Maurice Jarre, whose inspired arrangements for *The Year of Living Dangerously* considerably enhanced the film's stirring melodramatic power; Nathan Waks, whose work on *My Brilliant Career* (and using Schumann's 'Scenes from Childhood') helped to create that tone of blended poignancy and resilience which is part of the film's meaning; and Bruce Rowland's popular, if somewhat overwrought, work for *Phar Lap* and *The Man from Snowy River*. Finally, there should be mention of the role of music in the Paul Cox films: Norman Kaye, the music director on *Lonely Hearts*, plays a character who is a piano tuner by profession and who plays the accompaniment to an elderly citizens' sing-along; in *Man of Flowers*, Kaye's character plays the local church organ in moments of high emotional excitement and the soundtrack is dominated by Donizetti; and, in *My First Wife*, the hero (John Hargreaves) runs a classical music radio programme, and the film persistently uses a musical high culture (Haydn, Gluck, etc.) in counterpoint to the uncivilized passions which take up its foreground.

The Writers

It has become a cliché to say that the recurring weakness of the new Australian cinema is in its screenplays, but, as with most clichés, there is an element of truth in it. Apart from David Williamson, whose reputation as a playwright preceded and still outstrips that as a screenwriter, no one else has yet emerged as a major figure, and it may be that he is the only one powerful enough to exert a real influence on the final products. For a while it seemed that Everett de Roche, who wrote the screenplays for Richard Franklin's *Patrick* and *Roadgames* (and for his latest film *Link*) might be a significant name, but his non-Franklin films, with the exception of Colin Eggleston's *Long Weekend* (1978), have lacked the teasing wit that made the thrillers so enjoyable. Apart from the directors who have written or co-written their own screenplays, there is no more than a handful of writers who require to be mentioned here: Sonia Borg, Bob Ellis, Cliff Green, Alan Hopgood, and Eleanor Witcombe.

There are some general dissatisfactions with the screenplays that should be noted because they bear importantly on certain weakenesses in Australian films. To begin with, too few of the films exhibit any architectural approach to narrative, opting instead for episodic procedures. The result is that the films fail to *build*; they appear constructed on the string of beads principle, some of the individual beads attractive in themselves but precariously threaded together. This is sometimes due to the absence of a controlling theme, sometimes to the failure of the screenplay to suggest a convincing inter-relation of character and action. The 'growing up' films (for example, *The Mango Tree, The Getting of Wisdom, The Devil's Playground*) offer considerable evidence for this failure of sturdy structuring principles. As a result, one is often left with the pleasure of savouring incidental insights in the way of character observation, for instance, rather than the sense of a fully developed or developing character. This means that the burden of fleshing out a sketchily written role often falls on the actors who must fill out the wispy suggestions in the screenplay with aspects of their own *personae*. Excellent actors such as Wendy Hughes and John Hargreaves almost manage, in *My First Wife*, to distract attention from the lacunae in Bob Ellis and Paul Cox's screenplay, whereas Angela Punch-McGregor in *We of the Never Never* and Christopher Pate in *The Mango Tree* are defeated by the ramshackle, episodic nature of Peter Schreck's and Michael Pate's screenplays respectively. Further, and this may have something to do with the large number of adaptations as opposed to original screenplays, the dialogue often has a literary as opposed to *literate* quality. By literate I mean here a truth to the letter of the way people speak, a conversational authenticity which one finds in such disparate films as *Stir* (written by Bob Jewson) and *Newsfront* (written by Bob Ellis and Phil Noyce). Given the overwhelmingly realist thrust of Australian films, this is an important element in the creation of their illusions of reality. Films as important to the revival as *Picnic at Hanging Rock* (Cliff Green's screenplay) and *My Brilliant Career* (Eleanor Witcombe's screenplay) do not always achieve this kind of verisimilitude and such criticism is only partly answered by adverting to their period setting. What may *read* satisfactorily on the novel's page can *sound* stilted when spoken on-screen.

What is to be said for the screenwriters in the face of these endemic weaknesses? Williamson, a master of the abrasive exchange, of the dialogue of discord and vituperation, has written very lively scripts for *Petersen*, accurately rendering distinctions of class and educational levels, for *Gallipoli* and *The Year of Living Dangerously* in which the structure is firmly lashed to a shaping idea (the ties of friendship and competition in the former, the movement towards commitment in the latter), and for *Phar Lap*, which creates recognizable types in a pre-ordained narrative line. He has also adapted several of his own plays, with most notable success in *Don's Party* which very acutely catches the evening's verbal decline from various kinds of witty attack to various kinds of semi-drunken self-revelation. *Don's Party* offers a wholly literate display of literate people behaving with boorish self-indulgence.

'I won it in a card game', snaps Dr Robert Helpmann when Matron Julia Blake asks where he got his complex new piece of medical machinery in *Patrick*. Everett de Roche's best screenplays keep the verbal jokes coming in ways that nicely complement Richard Franklin's visual wit. De Roche also knows how to suggest just enough about his characters for the audience to place them as types (for example, Susan Penhaligon's plucky nurse in *Patrick*, Marion Edward's garrulous, enigmatic holiday-maker in *Roadgames*); and in the bickering, selfish young couple (John Hargreaves and Briony Behets in *Long Weekend*) he has drawn two full-length studies of egoistic self-indulgence. There is a dark wit, too, in the dialogue, characterization, and bizarre situations (the wild pig pulling away half a room while

Don Lane's inane variety show goes on yabbering on the television set) in *Razorback* in which the surreal effect is reinforced by Dean Semmler's garish cinematography.

But none of the de Roche-scripted films has won popular acceptance which is more likely to be accorded to the fruits of gentler — more *genteel* — talents, such as Sonia Borg's adaptations of Colin Thiele's children's novels, *Storm Boy* (1976), and the crisper but less well-liked *Blue Fin* (1978), or the fancy aphoristic touches of Cliff Green's *Picnic at Hanging Rock* script ('What we see, and what we seem, are but a dream, a dream within a dream', etc.). At the other end of the taste spectrum, Alan Hopgood's screenplays for *Alvin Purple* and its sequel *Alvin Rides Again* (1974), the dire *Pacific Banana* (1981), directed by John Lamond with whom Hopgood collaborated again on *A Slice of Life* (1982), mistake smut for ribaldry, and reveal little of the wit and good humour that made his 1960s' play, *And the Big Men Fly*, such a success. At Alvin's twenty-first birthday, his father intones: 'There are openings everywhere for the right man. Find out what you want to do and then extend yourself. In this world there is no one who can afford to be slack.' Only in the screenplay for *The True Story of Eskimo Nell* (1975), which he co-wrote with director Richard Franklin, is there any real warmth or pathos in his treatment of the comedy of the sexual life.

Among the directors who are also the authors or co-authors of their own screenplays, the most notable include John Duigan, Fred Schepisi, Tim Burstall, Phil Noyce, and George Miller. Duigan has had a hand in the script for all his features (except the *Dimboola* aberration of 1978) and the edgy urban realism of *Mouth to Mouth* and *Winter of Our Dreams* is as much the product of an ear for speech rhythms as of an eye for ambience. Schepisi's romanticism, intense and austere, is in the scripts as well as the images of those loners in a hostile world, in *The Devil's Playground* and *The Chant of Jimmie Blacksmith*. Burstall is included here for his tightly scripted adaptation of John Power's play, *The Last of the Knucklemen*, in which a fine regard for differences in diction colludes with agile camera work to keep a claustrophically set piece moving and varied. Phil Noyce worked with Bob Ellis on the marvellously right-sounding *Newsfront*: Ray Marshall at the country dance talks of 'the do or die spirit that gave us this great land of ours', utterly sincere in the blandness of the sentiments, and Angela Punch-McGregor's Fay, the rigidly conventional wife, puts a life-time of disapproval into the lines she is given: 'I wish you wouldn't talk like that, Len', and to Len, when the anti-Communist referendum has been defeated, 'I hope you're satisfied'. It is not that there is anything remarkable about such dialogue in a literary way, but, in the mouths of two expert character players, its literacy becomes apparent.

There is not yet a great Australian screenplay. The few that have been published (*Picnic at Hanging Rock, Sunday Too Far Away, The Getting of*

Wisdom) certainly do not read well on the page, and are all structurally faulty. One is often struck by the sudden aptness of a phrase which seems to cut through to the bedrock of Australian-ness, but one does not often register the power or coherence of the screenplay as a whole, and this is not just because its separate identity is lost in the finished film. Few Australian films keep one riveted with narrative suspense; few even seem to be interested in anything as vulgar as making the audience frantic to know what-happens-next. If there is not yet a great Australian film, despite remarkably gifted directors, cameramen, composers, production designers *et al.*, the chief cause may be the deficiency of the blueprint.

[1]   For example, *Australian Motion Picture Year Book 1983* (eds Peter Beilby and Ross Lansell), Four Seasons in association with *Cinema Papers*, 1982, and John Stewart's *An Encyclopaedia of Australian Film*, New South Wales: Reed Books, 1984.

[2]   Joan Long, 'A View from the Inside', the 8th John Grierson Memorial Lecture, State Film Centre, Melbourne, 19 November 1984.

[3]   'Margaret Fink, Producer', interviewed by Peter Beilby and Scott Murray, *Cinema Papers*, March–April 1979, p.285.

[4]   David Stratton, *The Last New Wave*, Sydney: Angus & Robertson, 1980, .248.

[5]   *Ibid.*, p.139.

[6]   Tim Burstall, 'What's it like on the receiving end of Australian film criticism', *Cinema Papers*, November–December 1975, p.214.

[7]   Peter Ellingsen, 'Man of Films', an interview with Paul Cox, *The Age*, Melbourne, 3 May 1985, p.11.

[8]   *Ibid.*

[9]   Quoted in Sue Mathews, *35mm Dreams*, Ringwood: Penguin, 1984, p.276.

[10]   Tom Ryan, 'Faces of Australia', in Al Clark (ed.) *The Film Year Book, Volume Two*, Currey O'Neil Ross, Melbourne: 1984, Australia Supplement, p.12.

[11]   Since I wrote this, she has won the 1985 Australian Film Institute Best Actress Award for this performance.

11 Progress and Prospects

At the time of writing this, August 1985, the Australian film industry is waiting to hear the announcement of the annual Australian Film Institute Awards and, even more breathlessly, the Labor Government's determinations on the fate of the tax concessions relating to film-making in this country. As to the former, all four of the finalists in the Best Film category are low-budget films and none has so far been picked up by major distributors, although one, Glenda Hambly's *Fran*, has been sold to the Channel 7 television network. There can be little cause for optimism if the year's 'best' films (and they dominate most of the Award categories) are likely to be hard to see in the cinemas. However, issues relating to actual films, and to their artistic quality, take up nothing like the newspaper space accorded to the jittery financial climate currently prevailing in the industry. 'Anguish in film industry as tax breaks face axe'[1] runs a recent and typical headline in the financial pages of a national weekly. These two apparently unrelated topics — the Awards and the possible withdrawal of tax shelters for investors — are in fact both intimately related to the future of the Australian cinema, raising as they do two critically important questions: what sort of films are likely to be made here in the future? and what economic stability can an Australian film industry expect to find? The answers to these questions are anybody's guess, although there are plenty of people — in and out of the industry — who are prepared to make bold statements about what the

Noni Hazlehurst in her AFI-award winning title role in Glenda Hambly's *Fran* (1985).

209

answers should be. In concluding this book, it is perhaps worth attempting some assessment of what the new Australian cinema has achieved to date and of what some of its possibilities may be in the light of the present situation.

So Far

Whatever crisis the Australian industry is now passing through (and it usually *is* passing through one), there is no gainsaying the fact that there have been fifteen years of continuous film-making in a country where, in the preceding twenty-five years, there was virtual drought. In those years, as discussed in Chapter 1, a trickle of American and British companies used Australia as a colourful backlot for films which, in the main, might have been made anywhere and which did nothing for the indigenous industry. To all intents and purposes, there was *no* indigenous industry. Wildly variable in quality they may have been, but the films of the latest revival have provided scope for local film-makers on a scale unknown since the silent days. Further, they have allowed audiences at home and abroad to see and hear Australians on their screens with a frequency and naturalness unimaginable even twenty years ago. The number of directors, actors, cameramen, musical directors and others who have been steadily employed — who have made *careers* — in the Australian film revival would constitute a real achievement even if the films were a good deal less attractive than they are. Life may feel precarious within the industry; to an outsider, there is at least an industry to contemplate and that seems like something to be grateful for. And this book scarcely even touches on the independent and documentary film-making which some commentators would certainly find more interesting than the feature film industry with which I am concerned. One can — and should — be critical of what is going on, of the films that have brought about the revival: the point is that there is at least a product to be critical about and, before 1970, this was scarcely the case.

If Australian films are no longer — to use the journalists' cliché — the flavour of the month either here or elsewhere, it is certainly true that, perhaps for the first time, they have acquired a world-wide reputation. Perhaps they never will capture mainstream international markets (that is, essentially the US market), but on more modest levels they have been greeted with surprised pleasure. Some crucial successes at Cannes (see Chapter 2) suddenly alerted the international film community to a new and distinctive voice. A film such as Ken Hannam's *Sunday Too Far Away* (1975) could not have come from anywhere else; despite some structural faults, it was a film distinguished by a remarkable freshness of observation in regard to lives both ordinary and, to most people, exotic. The 'Mad Max' films and, to a lesser extent, George Miller's *The Man from Snowy River* (1982), have cracked the US distributional big-time, but it may be dangerous for all Australian film-makers to set their sights on this kind of commercial success. Phillip Adams may be right when he says: 'In my view, our natural market is not the US but Europe',[2] even if his reason ('I suggest it is because we make films for grown-ups') is suspect. He may be right in the sense that the best Australian films to date have tended to be too quiet for the vast mass-market, tapped in any case only by the occasioal blockbuster and certainly not by every or even most American films. The kind of success Australian films have enjoyed has generally stopped short of that mass-market but should not be discounted for that reason. There are *other* kinds of success: films as diverse as Bruce Beresford's *Don's Party* (1976) and Paul Cox's *Lonely Hearts* (1982) have won widespread critical acclaim in Britain and the US and appreciative audiences in what are somewhat dismissively known as 'art houses'. Such success seems infinitely preferable to the easy distribution ride of the Fox-backed mutant, Ken Annakin's *The Pirate Movie* (1982): perhaps there is a real place, modest but reliable, for art-house movies that do not need subtitles in the English-speaking world.

'Film culture' is an amorphous and overused term but if it can be said to refer to a climate of informed opinion about film, a climate in which issues relating to film as an art form and as an industry are debated, then it is true to say that the years since 1970 have seen a remarkable development in Australia. It is not that there was no critical interest in film before then but that now the proponents of such a culture have something local to chew on. The by-now-annual conferences on film or on the relations between film and history have substantial Australian content, not all of it flattering to local achievements but a least finding it worth debate. There are several well-established film journals (for example, *Cinema Papers*, now twelve years old in its present form; *Filmviews*, which is subtitled 'The Film Users' Quarterly'; and *Filmnews*, which is published by the Sydney Filmmakers Co-operative) and articles on the Australian cinema are also found in journals with a broader cultural base. There is a heartening growth in book-length studies of the Australian cinema, including critical studies, reference books, and works of pioneering research such as Andrew Pike and Ross Cooper's indispensable *Australian Film 1900–1977* which describes every feature film made during those eight decades. Several documentary films have been made, exploring various aspects of the new Australian industry, the best known being Scott Murray and Gordon Glenn's *Australian Movies to the World* (1983). And throughout the 1970s and 1980s there has been a proliferation of screen studies courses in secondary and tertiary educational institutions, as well as the film schools which provide practical training. All of these may be seen as by-products of that increasing awareness of film which the existence of a local industry has done so much to stimulate. It is not that books, journals, courses, and conferences are wholly or even primarily given over the contemplation of the Australian scene, but that the development of indigenous production provides a valuable first-hand context for such activity.

None of this brief summarizing account of the real achievement of the past decade or so is intended to suggest that the new Australian film industry is now so firmly established that its future is secure. The opening remarks of this chapter indicate that this is not the case, but fifteen years of continuing production in a country whose previous film history was fitful, to say the least, is worth recording. It is worth recording even as one acknowledges that, beneath the elegant, lively, intelligent surface created by critical successes such as Peter Weir's *Picnic at Hanging Rock* (1975), Gillian Armstrong's *My Brilliant Career* (1979), and *Lonely Hearts*, there is the repellingly flabby underbelly that any film industry might develop. In this respect I mean not just vulgar box-office successes from Tim Burstall's *Alvin Purple* (1973) to *The Man from Snowy River*, but a slew of truly dreadful films many of which may never be seen outside this country and are, indeed, only fleetingly seen in Australia itself. There is neither space nor inclination to do 'justice' to, say, the puerile smut of John Lamond's *Pacific Banana* (1981) or the sadism of Brian Trenchard-Smith's *Turkey Shoot* (1982). They will no doubt find their way on to cable television or video, at home and abroad, and they are no doubt no worse than their trans-Pacific counterparts. Australia, however, can scarcely afford them. One wonders how they raised the production money when more worthwhile projects have problems in doing so; given their here-today-gone-tomorrow release patterns, it seems unlikely they can ever offer a return on the investor's outlay. And from the aesthetic point of view, the industry cannot afford them: if they are, generally, so little known as not to diminish widely the credibility of the emergent Australian cinema, they certainly contribute nothing to it. It may be said that such films at least provide work for members of the film professions, but their level of ineptitude is so abysmal that they demean those who take part in them. It would perhaps be worth investigating the *kinds* of awfulness these films exhibit; very often they are failed attempts at genre film-making (thrillers, sex films, romantic melodramas, etc.), throwing into relief again the fact that the major achievements of the period have not easily lent themselves to genre classification. They are characteristically *not* films aimed at exploring aspects of Australian-ness and, while to do so is no criterion of worth, the films which have built a reputation for Australian cinema in 1970s and 1980s have tended to be those which look and sound as if they could not have been made anywhere else.

Australian Films at Home

If merely being Australian is no guarantee of a film's commercial success in local cinemas, it is also true that the revival of the past decade or so has found receptive audiences for most of its best films — and for not a few others. It is true, too, that Australian audiences have taken pleasure in seeing Australian places and faces and hearing Australian voices in their cinemas, and that the industry's complaint that exhibitors and distributors shied away from the local product in favour of overseas films no longer holds good as it did in the earlier decades of this century. However, it is still hard to discern reliable patterns of audience response. In the past twelve months, two very expensive films (by local standards), Ken Hannam and Donald Crombie's *Robbery Under Arms* (1985) and Igor Auzins' *The Coolangatta Gold* (1984), opened to largely unfavourable notices and both failed to find satisfactory audiences. Equally, though, Richard Lowenstein's excellent, more modestly-budgeted *Strikebound* (1984) was also a box-office failure whereas *The Man from Snowy River* is one of the all-time commercial successes in this country. That is, there is no more reliable connection between quality and commercial success here than anywhere else. Similarly, there is no reliable connection between kinds of films and commercial success: 'period' films such as Bruce Beresford's *The Getting of Wisdom* (1977) and *My Brilliant Career* succeeded where Kevin Dobson's *The Mango Tree* (1977) and Igor Auzins' *We of the Never Never* (1982) failed; George Miller's *Mad Max* (1979) was a box-office hit while Richard Franklin's teasing thriller-cum-road movie, *Roadgames* (1981), was little liked; Beresford's *Puberty Blues* was a major success of the 1981–82 holiday period whereas no subsequent 'youth' movie has been popular. All one can say with certainty is that it is now possible to see most Australian movies, that they are there to be seen as they were not before 1970, and that in some cases a great many people do see them.

The Managing Director of the Greater Union Organization, David Williams, believes that too many Australian films are being made (often before their screenplays have been sufficiently refined): 'We shouldn't try to put more than twelve Australian films in the marketplace in any given year, because each is a difficult sale. The whole campaign has to be designed here.'[3] To an outside observer there appears to be some truth in the idea that more films are being made than, given the limited resources (with regard to both production and audiences), this country can support. With the stimulus of the tax concessions, too many ill-conceived projects have found funding. However, Michael Thornhill, producer-director of Edgecliff Films, dismisses such a notion on the grounds that it is impossible to monitor which films will or will not be made, claiming that not enough films are made to catch the public interest, the only valid criticism being that the great increase in production since 1982 has grossly inflated the cost of film-making here.[4] As to Williams' argument that each Australian film is 'a difficult sale', Alan Finney, National Director (Marketing and Distribution) for Village Roadshow, believes that: 'We overestimate the number of American films that arrive pre-sold. There are not more than perhaps four a year like this, and these are not the films that distributors spend their time on.'[5] In Finney's view, it is not intrinsically more difficult to market Australian films than the vast majority of overseas films arriving here.

Finney is also adamant that Australian film-makers have no responsibility for projecting the national life, whereas many commentators on film have argued that an indigenous cinema can have the highest profile of any art form in promoting and defining a culture. The distinguished film critic, Sylvia Lawson wrote as long ago as 1965:

> When the people of our 1920s saw them [the films of Raymond Longford, Tal Ordell's *The Kid Stakes*, etc.] they must have emerged with a freshened sense of where and who they were.
>
> It is this sense of identity which a community's own film-making confers upon it as nothing else can.[6]

Whether or not film-makers should *want* to engage with issues of national identity, many of the most important films of the Australian revival have indeed done so, as I have argued in the central chapters of this book. This has not always worked in their favour: they have too often uncritically reflected certain national myths; the large number of 'growing up' films, for example, tends to perpetuate the idea of Australia as a Peter Pan country, hovering forever on the brink of maturity. However, a lot of the pleasure that Australian audiences have taken in the films of the revival has undoubtedly derived from seeing the physically and psychically familiar on their screens, presented lovingly or, less often, with degrees of critical scrutiny. This is by now less true than it was in the later 1970s; there are by now too many Australian films for the pleasures of mere recognition to be sufficient to sustain interest. This in itself may be a sign of the maturing of Australian audiences in their reception of local films.

Australian Films and Overseas Connections

After claiming that: 'Australian films in the US have done just about as well as it is possible for foreign films to do', Sue Mathews ends by warning that: '. . . the Australian cinema needs to keep a close watch on just whose dreams it is we are dreaming'.[7] She echoes here a not uncommon apprehension about the dangers of pursuing international success: that it may be at the cost of what has made Australian films seem distinctive overseas. *Mad Max 2* (1981) and *Mad Max: Beyond Thunderdome* (1985) have definitively broken into mainstream American distribution but, the argument sometimes run, they are not the sort of films which made the revival news at home and abroad. The need for overseas — and especially American — markets may lead to attempts, as likely as not doomed, to move away from the very qualities that have won critical support for Australian films. So far, with no more than two or three exceptions, they have found their support

Aunty Entity (Tina Turner) in George Miller's *Max Max: Beyond Thunderdome* (1985).

with critics and the art-house audiences who are more likely to be influenced by critical opinion into seeking out such films. As Mathews goes on to say, '. . . the qualities for which films are appreciated by the art-house audiences are not the same qualities that produce a blockbuster'. The real fear may be that, in desperate pursuit of the blockbuster's audience, Australian film-makers may both fail in the attempt and lose the more modest but enthusiastic audiences they have found in less commercially ambitious exhibition situations.

What are the qualities, then, that have attracted a certain kind of overseas audience? Tim Pulleine, writing in the BBC *Radio Times* in 1984, begins an article on a BBC-2 season of Australian films like this: 'For a decade now, the Australian film industry has been the toast of the world', and goes on to speak of *Picnic at Hanging Rock* which, 'with its meticulous period reconstruction and its refinement of visual atmosphere, has come to be seen as the 'typical' product of the Australian new wave'.[8] He identifies the 'high standards of craftsmanship' that have come to be associated with Australian films; Pauline Kael, ageing *enfant terrible* of American reviewers, on the other hand finds that: 'There's no essential excitement in them',[9] meaning by 'them', the 'well-crafted' film category to which she would confine most of the new Australian cinema. Both writers, that is, are recognizing similar qualities in Australian films, one to praise and the other to berate. The sorts of 'period reconstruction' and 'refinement' Pulleine praises are seen by Kael as 'terribly well done' but timid and academic, lacking (with the exception of Fred Schepisi's films) 'that sense of personality' and 'crude vitality' she finds in the American films she prefers. Kael in fact discerns many of the reasons why overseas people find Australian films attractive (the beautifully shot landscapes, a certain gentility) but chides them for doing so. And Sue Mathews detects a nostalgic element at work in the US art-house enthusiasm for Australian films: 'Many American observers remark how the films echo British and American styles of the 1940s and 1950s, with their straightforward narratives and lack of cinematic self-consciousness', their praise for the 'freshness' of Australian films 'reflecting a longing for past films and for an idea of a past reality in which things were simpler and better'.[10]

Up to a point the foregoing is a recognizable account of what has made Australian films modestly popular overseas, in the two biggest English-speaking markets at least. When Americans or Britishers tell one how much they like Australian films, they tend to refer to *Picnic at Hanging Rock, My Brilliant Career, Breaker Morant* (1980) or (not always noticing the difference) *The Man from Snowy River*. They certainly do not mean and do not talk about the 'Mad Max' films or Richard Franklin's thrillers, as if, perhaps, there were no point in seeking out Australian films for what the Americans can do 'better'. However, Paul Cox's films — *Lonely Hearts, Man of Flowers* (1983), and *My First Wife* (1984) — have won critical acclaim and audience enthusiasm overseas, without their belonging either to the 'decorous, well-crafted' school of Australian film-making or to the recognizable genres of *The Man from Snowy River* or *Mad Max*. They are a particularly interesting case in considering the phenomenon of Australian-films-abroad: their Melbourne suburban settings may be unobtrusively exotic, but their focus is one the inner lives of their protagonists (not common in Australian films); they seem obdurately 'art-house' in their orientation, especially in the context of world cinema, but the fact that they are English-speaking perhaps gives them the edge of accessibility over the European films they resemble; and they are symptomatic of the importance of critical approval for Australian films when competing overseas with the massive campaigns of the major American studio products. Cox himself is more cynical than many about the success of Australian films abroad: he believes that they 'have not really influenced people like [*sic*] the German new wave cinema has', he argues: 'It was just a very cute thing that was happening at the time [that is, the 1970s] and it was done with great dedication'.[11] He may well be right about Australian films not having influenced film-making elsewhere; equally, however, it is true that the new Australian cinema has scored a measure of dignified success overseas, perhaps by answering a need at a particular time.

Another — and from time to time controversial — aspect of the Australian-overseas connection is that of Australian artists (directors and actors principally) at work overseas and of their overseas counterparts working here. The latter has been a continuing element in Australian film history and is briefly referred to in Chapters 1 and 3. There used to be a certain glamour attaching to overseas stars' coming to film here — from Eva Novak to Helen Twelvetrees, Maureen O'Hara, Robert Mitchum and others over five decades — and in the 1970s there were notable perform-

216

ances from Richard Chamberlain in Peter Weir's *The Last Wave* (1977), from Geraldine Fitzgerald in Kevin Dobson's *The Mango Tree*, still perhaps the most wholly achieved performance by an actress in an Australian film, and from Edward Woodward in Bruce Beresford's *Breaker Morant.* However, the climate has changed and Actors' Equity has now built up a complex set of conditions which make it very difficult for a producer to import an overseas star. One sympathizes with Equity's urge to protect the local performers, but the presence of an overseas 'name' is sometimes necessary to ensure distribution beyond Australia, even if it is no guarantee of bringing customers into the cinemas of Milwaukee or Manchester. In a *Cinema Papers* interview, actress Angela Punch-McGregor, who has worked in the US (in Michael Ritchie's bizarre disaster, *The Island*, 1980), opposes the idea of overseas actors' working in this country. Defensively, she claims that: 'it must be impressed upon investors that Vanessa Redgrave in an Australian film will not sell it overseas: it will sell because of its content and Australian style'.[12] (Equity had vetoed Redgrave for the role played by McGregor in Gil Brealey's *Annie's Coming Out*, 1984.) However, in the same interview she says: 'I don't think the Australian contingent overseas is really any threat to the American or British film industries. If we import a lot of overseas actors into our country it is a threat because of numbers more than anything.' There may be some truth, if little generosity, in such a view.

The 'Australian contingent overseas' is so far scarcely an invasion. Peter Weir, Fred Schepisi, Bruce Beresford, Richard Franklin, and Gillian Armstrong, among directors, have all filmed in the US and/or Britain with results varying commercially and critically from Weir's box-office hit, the stylish thriller *Witness* (1985) to Beresford's Biblical epic, *King David* (1985), a failure with audiences and critics alike. Some of these directors are on record as still wanting to work in Australia: Beresford, Franklin and Armstrong's next films are indeed Australian and are in each case based on Australian novels, respectively Nene Gare's *The Fringe Dwellers*, Ion L. Idriess's *Drums of Mer*, and George Johnston's *Clean Straw for Nothing* (the latter to be partly shot in Greece). One can at this stage only speculate on how overseas experience may have refined their techniques or how far their American-made films (Beresford's *Tender Mercies*, 1983, as well as *King David*, Franklin's *Psycho II*, 1982, and *Cloak and Dagger*, 1984, Armstrong's *Mrs Soffel*, 1985) have established reputations that might pave the way overseas for the films they make in Australia. At this point, their skills (and those of actors such as Judy Davis and Jack Thompson and of cameramen such as Russell Boyd who co-shot *Mrs Soffel* and John Seale who shot *Witness*) have gained international recognition and a wider exposure than would have been the case if they had restricted themselves to local production. While there is still some inevitable talk of 'brain drain',[13] more positively one would like to think there might be benefits for

Australian films, both at home and abroad, to be had from such overseas involvement.

Sylvia Lawson wrote in 1965 that: 'No film that ever mattered was made by a casual visitor to the country or city in which his story was set.'[14] The films made in Australia by Werner Herzog (*Where the Green Ants Dream*, 1983) and by Dusan Makavejev (*The Coca Cola Kid*, 1985), not without interest and a certain random, eccentric vitality, might seem to support her view. However, it is at least arguable that the two most perceptive accounts of certain aspects of Australian life are to be found in Canadian Ted Kotcheff's *Wake in Fright* and British Nicolas Roeg's *Walkabout* (both 1971). Kotcheff's exploration of the myths of mateship and Australian macho camaraderie has not been surpassed by any of the native forays into this field; and Roeg's poetic response to the landscape (and urban man's alienation from it) has an interpretive freshness denied to all but two or three other films of the revival. It would be a pity if protectionism or chauvinism discouraged such ventures.

In 1984, Scott Murray wrote that: 'For almost all Australian films, it is now no longer possible to break even in the local market. Overseas audiences must be found.'[15] With the increased budgets of most Australian films in the 1980s, this is probably true, and the situation inevitably raises questions such as: Will 'Australian' films be replaced by films simply 'made in Australia'? Will they lose those qualities of Australian-ness that have made them attractive to certain overseas audiences? Will producers become obsessed with the search for recipes for 'successful' films? Will there be an increased tendency towards co-productions and, if so, is Australia likely to retain that elusive 'creative control'? A recent report writes of those Australian producers who 'are sceptical of co-productions, particularly with the United States. They say we risk the possibility of losing our integrity and becoming a cheap production house making films for Americans'.[16] Suzanne Wagner, producer and marketing executive, disagrees: 'Collaboration does not entail a loss of identity. One has to think in terms of pooling expertise, of global talent.'[17] Whoever is right, the results are likely to become apparent in the latter half of the 1980s, especially if the withdrawal of tax concesssions make it increasingly difficult for Australian producers to fund their projects locally.

Money

Currently the financial situation of the Australian film industry is very precarious, even more so than it has characteristically been throughout the revival, and for the reason suggested at the start of this chapter. There is an immense amount of writing in newspapers and journals about finance in the Australian film industry, with headlines in 1985 such as: 'You too can be in the movie business'[18] (February); 'Big budgets can distort a picture, says director'[19] (March); 'Anguish in film industry as tax breaks face axe'[20] (June); 'Producers battle for filmland's tax bonus'[21] (July); and 'Film villain a threat to a national dream'[22] (August), in which the 'villain' is the Australian Film Commission, which is described as Labor Treasurer Paul Keating's 'own regulatory body'. The climate, that is, has become distinctly threatening as the fate of 'Section 10BA', the industry's tax relief scheme under the Income Tax Assessment Act, hangs in the balance. There are those who believe that, without the tax concession offered since 1980 by 10BA, the Australian film industry will be unable to find investors. At present, under 10BA, a 133 per cent deduction is available for approved investment in Australian film, with net income from the film exempt from tax for up to 33 per cent of the amount of the original investment.[23] It is now feared that this concession will be withdrawn because of the losses the Treasury has sustained as a result. It is also feared that it will be replaced by a fund to be distributed by the AFC, amounting (John Dingwall claims) 'to virtual nationalisation of film',[24] a not unlikely possibility for a Labor Government to contemplate. Others have argued that the very existence of 10BA has encouraged the wrong kind of investor and has led to films being made as a tax haven rather than for their intrinsic merit.

Whatever the outcome of this bitterly contentious issue — and it is difficult for an outsider to sift the often contradictory and violently held opinions of those in the industry — it does seem certain that there is government 'recognition that there needs to be a film industry'.[25] Further, there is some consensus that Australia will not have a film industry without a form of government subsidization. Michael Thornhill claims that the real issue is whether this support will be 'direct through subsidy or indirect through tax', adding that he does not believe 'the industry will ever be able to stand commercially on its own two feet in the marketplace'.[26] Alan Finney, of Village Roadshow, commenting on the subsidy situation in the Australian industry, believes that film-makers here have been insufficiently daring: 'The people who make the movies and the money men are at one — they don't want what's daring.'[27] Most would agree that, with the comparative availability of funds (under 10BA and with the subsidy of the AFC and the State corporations), too many trashy and/or ill-prepared films have got off the ground in the last few years. And a good many would feel a sympathetic alignment with Phillip Adams when he wrote:

> I also make no apology for the fact that the film industry will stay subsidized. Whether the government does it through taxation incentives or through direct grants is almost irrelevant. All art is subsidized. If we had the free market applying in Australia, you could close the art galleries, you could close the opera, the ballet, the theatre, the lot. It is all subsidized. You either want it or you don't. If you want it, you have to pay for it.[28]

Adams, wary of the 'international' approach, is here speaking, with characteristic rhetorical flourish, for a protected industry as the only one which can survive in a country with a limited market and uncertain access to world markets. He concludes his essay (based on a paper given to a seminar in Perth, 1983) in the same uncompromising tone:

> We got into this industry for one reason: to give ourselves a national voice, to give ourselves a sense of national purpose and a national identity, and to throw that away would be a disaster and a fiasco.[29]

One does not have to be a super-patriot to agree that if Australian films are to find audiences they had better have something distinctive about them. As there is not much evidence so far of Australia's capacity to beat the Americans at their own game, it may be wise as well as desirable to aim in different directions.

American mainstream distribution should not be seen as the only grail worth pursuing. There are other, admittedly more modest, markets — the art-houses, cable and network television, video — that could supplement local returns on worthwhile local films. Funding availability has in some cases led to productions' beginning too quickly, before screenplays (the great Australian weakness) are really ready. And, too often, the urge to make films that people everywhere will want to see has resulted in productions that no one has wanted to see anywhere. If the tax concession goes, one salutory effect might be some radical re-thinking about the sort of films to be made here.

As the Dust Settles

Without underestimating the importance of financial stability in what is always a high-risk industry, one would like to see the journals and newspapers able to stop talking so much about money and to begin discussing the films again. To date, the new Australian cinema has been dominated stylistically and thematically by the concern for social realism. More *consciously* than in countries with a more established industry, Australian films have addressed themselves to exploring aspects of the national life: its myths, its past, its landscape, its urban problems. A film such as Richard Franklin's *Roadgames* which so successfully exploited genre conventions rather than 'the way we are' (or, often, 'the way we *were*') did not find favour in the manner of, say, Peter Weir's *Gallipoli* (1981) which is more obviously concerned with explaining us to ourselves. On the other hand, the financial failure of *Strikebound* compared with the huge popularity of the myth-espousing *The Man from Snowy River* suggests that as a film-going nation we prefer blandly flattering self-images to grittier truths. However, apart from *Snowy River* and the 'Mad Max' series, the preferred Australian films, here and abroad, have tended to be modestly budgeted and small-scale, decently humanist in their orientation, often rather literary, and often exhibiting a strongly nostalgic element. Given the protected nature of the Australian industry to date, it seems to an outsider that it could afford to be more risk-taking than it is. Perhaps its protected nature has been one reason for a certain inhibited decorousness, a safely middle-brow Australian-ness in those well-received films which Susan Dermody described as belonging to the 'AFC genre'[30] (*Picnic at Hanging Rock, My Brilliant Career*, etc.), the very films on which the idea of a renaissance has been built. These, in fact, are the kinds of films many people, Australians and others, equate with the notion of the new Australian cinema at large.

As I write, the films on the horizon seem in some cases to be following well-worn trails. Graeme Clifford's *Burke and Wills* is an expensive epic which dramatized a famous national failure, recalling the interest of *Gallipoli* and *Breaker Morant* in other moments of failure or defeat in our history. Stephen Wallace's *For Love Alone*, based on Christina Stead's novel of a young girl's search for fulfilment, sounds like a descendant of *The Getting of Wisdom* and *My Brilliant Career*, both also based on 'classic' Australian novels. Tim Burstall's long delayed version of D. H. Lawrence's *Kangaroo* appears at last to be underway and the combined abrasiveness of Burstall and Lawrence may unsettle the Australian reputation for 'tasteful adaptations'. There are, as well, several other productions which suggest, at least tentatively, new directions: Neil Armfield is filming *Twelfth Night*, Australia's first Shakespearean film: Scott Murray has all but finished *Devil in the Flesh* which is boldly described and conceived as 'a love story'; Ray Lawrence's *Bliss*, from Peter Carey's novel, is a black social comedy which was played at Cannes, has been much cut since then, and is currently nominated in every category of the Australian Film Institute Awards; Bill Bennett's *A Street to Die*, also much nominated, draws on Australia's Vietnam experience, as it affects an Agent Orange victim; and actress Robyn Nevin is directing *The More Things Change ...* which *Cinema Papers* describes as a

A farewell scene between Marthe (Katia Caballero) and Paul (Keith Smith) in Scott Murray's *Devil in the Flesh* (1985).

'contemporary story about role reversal and relationships'. The latter is produced by Jill Robb and, like her *Careful, He Might Hear You,* based on a novel by Sumner Locke Elliot: one hopes that its allusive title is not prophetic about the future of the Australian cinema.

As one looks back over the years since 1970, it is clear that a great deal has been achieved. There is, however precariously, an industry that certainly was not here before 1970, and there is a body of films which have deservedly found favour around the world. They are not, as a rule, the most exciting films being made anywhere but at their upper levels they are wholly respectable, in the best sense of the word. That is to say, they are made with a care, affection and craftsmanship that have commanded wide respect. They are, it needs to be added, in other ways *too* respectable: too unwilling to take major artistic risks; too tastefully anti-'ocker'; too ready to use the past (historical and literary) as an occasion for triumphs of *mise-en-scène* rather than as a means of exploring the indocile present.

[1]   Colleen Ryan, 'Your financial affairs', *The National Times,* 14 to 20 June, 1985, p.55.

[2]   Phillip Adams, 'Two Views', *Cinema Papers,* No.44–45, April 1984, p.71.

[3]   In interview with the author.

[4]   In interview with the author.

[5]   In interview with the author.

[6]   Sylvia Lawson, 'Not for the Likes of Us', *Quadrant,* 1965, Vol.IX, No.3, p.29.

[7]   Sue Mathews, 'Flavor of the Week: Australian Films in the U.S.', in Peter Beilby and Ross Lansell (eds.), *Australian Motion Picture Year Book, 1983,* 4 Seasons and Cinema Papers, 1982, p.50.

[8]   Tim Pulleine, 'Their brilliant careers', *Radio Times,* 18–24 February, 1984, pp.14–15.

[9]   'Pauline Kael and the Australian Cinema'. Interview by Sue Mathews, *Cinema Papers,* No.40, October 1982, p.421.

[10]   Mathews, *op. cit.,* p.48.

[11]   Peter Ellingsen interviews Paul Cox, 'Man of Films', *The Age,* Melbourne, 3 May 1985, p.11.

[12]   'Angela Punch McGregor'. Interview by Jim Schembri, *Cinema Papers,* No.49, December 1984, p.471.

[13]   Cf. producer Jim McElroy, who blames it for the failure of many Australian films, in Kristin Williamson, 'A Triumph of Mediocrity: What's gone wrong with Australian films?', *The National Times,* Sydney, 17 to 23 May, 1985, p.28.

[14]   Lawson, *op. cit.,* p.31.

[15]   Scott Murray, 'The Australian Film Industry: A Brief History', in Al Clark (ed.), *The Film Year Book, Vol. 2,* Melbourne: Currey O'Neil Ross, 1984, Australian Supplement, p.14.

[16] Kristin Williamson, 'Co-productions: the New American Threat', *The National Times*, Sydney, 16 to 22 August, 1985, p.28.

[17] Quoted by Caroline Baum, 'Films: Melbourne on the Riviera', *The Herald*, Melbourne, 17 January, 1985, p.21.

[18] Rowena Stretton, 'You too can be in the movie business', *The Herald*, Melbourne, 27 February, 1985, p.21.

[19] Rosslyn Beeby, 'Big budgets can distort a picture, says director', *The Age*, Melbourne, March 1985, p.14.

[20] Ryan, op. cit., p.55.

[21] Barbara Hooks, 'Tele Scope', *The Age*, Melbourne, 30 July 1985, p.2.

[22] John Dingwall, 'Film villain a threat to a national dream', *The Age*, Melbourne, 5 August 1985, p.11.

[23] Ryan, *op. cit.*

[24] Dingwall, *op. cit.*

[25] Producer Jill Robb, quoted in Michael Gill, 'Success with an eye above the bottom line', *The Age*, Melbourne, 12 January 1985, 'Saturday Extra', p.9.

[26] In interview with the author.

[27] In interview with the author.

[28] Adams, *op. cit.*, p.71.

[29] *Ibid.*, p.72.

[30] In a lecture during the Melbourne Film Festival, at the State Film Centre, Melbourne, 30 June 1985.

Postscript

The two issues referred to at the start of Chapter II — the announcement of annual Australian Film Institute's Awards and the Government's decision on Section 10BA of the Income Tax Assessment Act — have since been settled. As to the Awards, Ray Lawrence's bizarre black comedy, *Bliss*, was chosen as Best Film and has since been distributed by its producers and exhibited by the Greater Union chain. None of the other three nominees has yet secured major release. On the tax front, the 10BA concessions have been reduced as follows: from 133 to 120 per cent deduction for investment in Australian film, and from 33 to 20 per cent exemption for income on such investment. The Government has not, that is, deserted the industry, but there has been a predictable outcry from the industry that the cuts will deter investors. Time will tell; so will the films that get made.

Bibliography

Adamson, Judith: *Australian Posters 1906-1960*, Sydney: Currency Press, 1978

Baxter, John: *The Australian Cinema*, Sydney: Angus & Robertson, 1970

Beilby, Peter (ed.): *Australian Motion Picture Year Book 1980*, Melbourne: Cinema Papers in association with the New South Wales Film Corporation, 1981

——: *Australian Motion Picture Year Book 1981/82*, Melbourne: Cinema Papers in association with the New South Wales Film Corporation, 1981

Beilby, Peter and Lansell, Ross (eds): *Australian Motion Picture Yearbook 1983*, Melbourne: Four Seasons in association with Cinema Papers, 1982

Bertrand, Ina and Collins, Diane: *Government and Film in Australia*, Sydney: Currency Press and the Australian Film Institute, 1981

Clark, Al (ed.): *The Film Yearbook, Volume Two*, (Australian section edited by Tom Ryan), Melbourne: Currey O'Neil Ross, 1984

——: *The Film Yearbook 1985*, (Australian section edited by Tom Ryan), Melbourne: Currey O'Neil Ross, 1984

Hall, Ken G.: *Australian Film: The Inside Story*, Sydney: Summit Books, 1980

Hall, Sandra: *Critical Business: The New Australian Cinema in Review*, Adelaide: Rigby Publishers, 1985

Hutton, Anne (ed.): *The First Australian History and Film Conference Papers*, Sydney: The History and Film Conference and the Australian Film & Television School, 1982

Lansell, Ross and Beilby, Peter (eds): *The Documentary Film in Australia*, Melbourne: Cinema Papers in association with Film Victoria, 1982

Levy, Wayne, Cutts, Graeme and Stockbridge, Sally: *The Second Australian History and Film Conference Papers*, Sydney: The History and Film Conference and the Australian Film and Television School, 1984

Long, Joan and Long, Martin: *The Pictures that Moved: A Picture History of the Australian Cinema 1896-1929*, Melbourne: Hutchinson Group, 1982

Mathews, Sue: *35mm Dreams: Conversations with Five Australian Directors*, Melbourne: Penguin, 1984

McFarlane, Brian: *Words and Images: Australian Novels into Film*, Melbourne: Heinemann Publishers in association with Cinema Papers, 1980

Murray, Scott (ed.): *The New Australian Cinema*, Melbourne: Thomas Nelson Australia in association with Cinema Papers, 1980

Pike, Andrew and Cooper, Ross: *Australian Film 1900-1977*, Melbourne: Oxford University Press in association with the Australian Film Institute, 1980

Reade, Eric: *The Australian Screen: A Pictorial History of Australian Film Making*, Melbourne: Lansdowne Press, 1975

——: *History and Heartburn: The Saga of Australian Film, 1896-1978*, Sydney: Harper & Row, 1979

Shirley, Graham and Adams, Brian: *Australian Cinema: The First 80 Years*, Sydney: Angus & Robertson Publishers and Currency Press, 1984

Stewart, John: *An Encyclopaedia of Australian Film*, Sydney: Reed Books, 1984

Stratton, David: *The Last New Wave: The Australian Film Revival*, Sydney: Angus & Robertson, 1980

Tulloch, John: *Australian Cinema: Industry, Narrative and Meaning*, Sydney: George Allen & Unwin, 1982

——: *Legends on the Screen: The Australian Narrative Cinema 1919-1929*, Sydney: Currency Press and the Australian Film Institute, 1981

White, David: *Australian Movies to the World*, Melbourne: Fontana Australia and Cinema Papers, 1984

Index

P

Q

R